From Your Friends at **The MAILBOX®**

The BIG BOOK
MONTHLY IDEAS

GRADES 4-6

Project Manager:
Karen A. Brudnak

Editors:
Becky S. Andrews
Cayce Guiliano

Art Coordinator:
Teresa R. Davidson

Cover Artists:
Nick Greenwood
Clevell Harris
Kimberly Richard

www.themailbox.com

©2000 by THE EDUCATION CENTER, INC.
All rights reserved.
ISBN #1-56234-428-5

Manufactured in the United States

10 9 8 7 6 5 4 3 2

ABOUT THIS BOOK

Get a year's worth of seasonal and holiday ideas in this handy resource! We've compiled outstanding curriculum-related activities, ready-to-go reproducibles, and timely themes from our best-selling Monthly Idea Books for grades 4–6. You'll find

- Super starters for the first days of school
- High-flying activities for Thanksgiving
- Dozens of December holiday delights
- Warm ways to welcome the new calendar year
- Outstanding ideas for commemorating Black History Month
- Legendary activities for St. Patrick's Day
- Unforgettable ideas for a year-end Reading Carnival
- And much more!

TABLE OF CONTENTS

SEPTEMBER

YAHOO IT'S A NEW YEAR!

It's back-to-school time, and you're ready to take the bull by the horns and plan a ripsnortin' successful year! How do you get started on the right foot? A great place to begin is this collection of back-to-school bulletin boards, activities, tips, and reproducibles. With these teaching tools in your saddlebags, you can bet your bottom dollar it'll be a rootin'-tootin' terrific year!

A Rootin'-Tootin' Welcome!

Say howdy to your new class with a bulletin-board display that doubles as a back-to-school discussion starter. Enlarge and color the cowpoke pattern on page 11; then mount it on a bulletin board. Add the speech bubble as shown. Duplicate the sheriff's badge pattern (one per student) on page 16 on yellow paper. After cutting out the badges, label them with student names and mount them with pushpins on the board. On the first day, give each child a copy of the reproducible on page 12. Have each student answer the questions; then have her attach her paper to the board, pinning her badge to a corner of the paper. During the first week, discuss the suggestions on the sheets with the class. Use this discussion to lead into a session during which you and your new students establish classroom rules and goals for the year.

First-Day Tickets

Here's an idea that guarantees a ripsnortin' successful first day! A week before school begins, send each student a short, personal note welcoming her to your class. Inside the note, insert a copy of the first-day ticket on page 11. Instruct the student that she will need to bring the ticket to school on the first day to gain admittance into your class.

On the first day, have students deposit their tickets in a cowboy hat or other container as they enter the room. (Be sure to have extra tickets on hand for students who forget theirs.) As you progress through the day, periodically stop and draw a ticket from the hat. Reward the student whose name is on the ticket with a small treat, such as a new pencil, an inexpensive set of markers, or another school supply. Continue drawing names throughout the day until every student has won a prize.

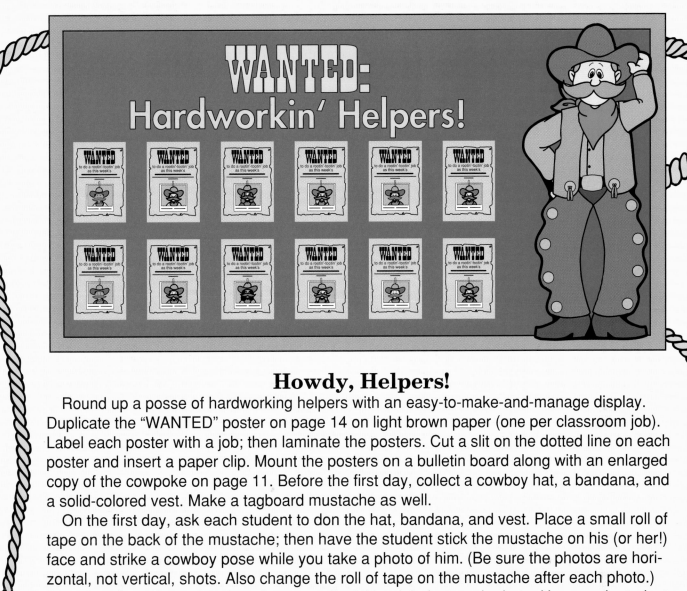

Howdy, Helpers!

Round up a posse of hardworking helpers with an easy-to-make-and-manage display. Duplicate the "WANTED" poster on page 14 on light brown paper (one per classroom job). Label each poster with a job; then laminate the posters. Cut a slit on the dotted line on each poster and insert a paper clip. Mount the posters on a bulletin board along with an enlarged copy of the cowpoke on page 11. Before the first day, collect a cowboy hat, a bandana, and a solid-colored vest. Make a tagboard mustache as well.

On the first day, ask each student to don the hat, bandana, and vest. Place a small roll of tape on the back of the mustache; then have the student stick the mustache on his (or her!) face and strike a cowboy pose while you take a photo of him. (Be sure the photos are horizontal, not vertical, shots. Also change the roll of tape on the mustache after each photo.) After the pictures are developed, put a self-sticking label on each photo. Have each student write a cowboy name for himself or herself, such as Deadeye Davey or Quickdraw Quincy, on the label. Collect the photos and store them in an envelope attached to the board. Assign jobs each week by clipping the students' photos to the posters.

Bulletin Boards Without The Bother

The start of a new school year is busy enough without having to labor over bulletin boards. Use these quick tips to create dazzling displays without the bother:

- Add pizzazz to a plain bulletin board by placing self-sticking metallic stars on the background paper.
- For an eye-catching way to display students' work, mount artwork or favorite papers on solid-colored paper placemats.
- Need more display space? Make a mini bulletin board by laminating a large piece of colorful poster board. Transparent or masking tape will adhere any object—from student papers to seasonal cutouts—to the poster.
- Make a stunning border in a jiffy by mounting two-inch-wide ribbon—solid colored, striped, or any design—around the edges of your board.

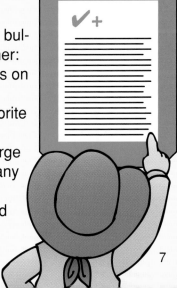

Lookin' Ahead!

Give your new students a sneak peek at the year ahead with this fun display! Enlarge the steer pattern on page 14; then make three copies to color, cut out, and staple to the bottom of a board as shown. Add the title "Have You 'Herd' About ___ Grade?" Directly on the background paper, use brightly colored markers to list items that students can look forward to in the coming year—new skills they will acquire, units they'll study, field trips, etc. After seeing this display, your students will be thrilled they've "mooooved" up a grade!

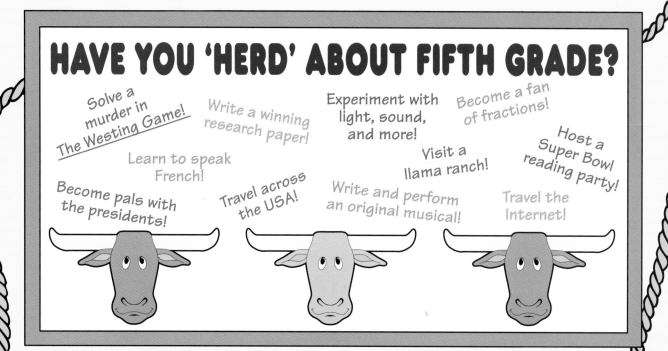

Birthday Bonanza

There's no doubt about it—intermediate kids still get a kick out of celebrating their birthdays! To make a birthday display that is maintained by students (instead of you), duplicate the small boot patterns on page 16 (one per child). Instruct each student to write his name and birthdate on his boot, color it with crayons or markers, and then cut it out. Have two students glue the boots around the edges of a large piece of poster board as shown. Label the poster with the title "Kick Up Your Heels—It's Your Birthday!"; then laminate it.

Each month assign a cooperative group to be in charge of updating the birthday poster. On a child's birthday, the group in charge writes the honored student's name and birthdate on the poster with a wipe-off marker. After a rousing rendition of "Happy Birthday," ask one student from the group to pass around a construction-paper copy of the boot pattern on page 13. Have each student write a compliment about the birthday child on the boot before passing it to the next classmate. Clip a copy of the no-homework coupon on page 11 to the boot before giving it to the child to take home.

8

Sit A Spell And Read

Try these ideas to create a reading center that invites book lovers to sit a spell and read:

- To extend a western theme, sew four bandanas together as shown. Make several of these large squares. Stitch two of the squares together, leaving a small opening for stuffing with fiberfill. Hand-stitch the opening closed, and you've got a soft, colorful pillow for your reading center.

- Have each student bring an old, clean T-shirt to class. Let students decorate their shirts with fabric paint; then have a parent volunteer sew up the neck opening, one sleeve opening, and the bottom of each shirt. Show each student how to stuff her shirt with fiberfill through the unsewn sleeve opening. Then show students how to hand-stitch the opening shut. There you have it—comfortable pillows that will suit your students to a "tee"!

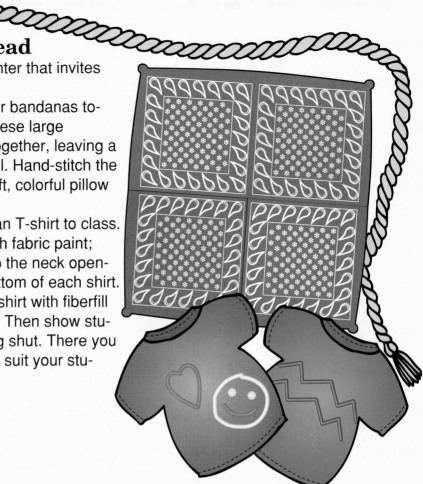

Say Howdy To The Head Honcho

Introduce yourself to your new cowpokes with an eye-catching teacher feature. Use a small bulletin board or other display area in the classroom. In the display, include the following items that focus on you, the "new teacher": family photos, diplomas, awards that you've earned, an elementary-grade report card, a picture of yourself when you were in the same grade that you're currently teaching, plus items that represent some of your favorite sports, hobbies, and pastimes. During the first week of school, take time to share these items with your students. It's one way of letting your students know that you're a person outside the classroom too!

Say Howdy To Each Other

More than likely, you'll have students in your class who are new to the community and school. A scavenger-hunt activity is the perfect icebreaker for students on the first day back to school. Duplicate page 15 for each student. Instruct students to circulate about the classroom seeking their classmates' signatures to fill the boxes. (A student should not sign his or her name more than twice in any vertical, horizontal, or diagonal row.) Challenge students to completely fill their grids with signatures. After a predetermined amount of time, have students return to their seats. Follow up this activity with the graphing lessons on page 10.

Say, pardner— how many brothers and sisters do you have?

First-Day Graphs

Use the information that your students gathered in the "Say Howdy To Each Other" scavenger hunt on page 9 to complete each of the following graphing activities:

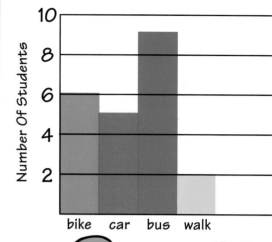

How Students Get To School

- Ask each student whose first and last names begin with the same letter to raise her hand. Then ask how many students are in the class. Finally ask students how they would show such information in a circle graph. Determine the two criteria for the graph: students whose first and last names begin with the same letter and students whose names begin with different letters. After counting how many students fit in each category, have each student make a circle graph to show that information. When everyone is finished, draw a large circle on the chalkboard and invite a volunteer to illustrate his graph in the circle.

- Use the information about students' hobbies gathered in the scavenger hunt to create a class pictograph. List all of the students' hobbies on the chalkboard, including ones not listed on the reproducible scavenger hunt. Then use tally marks to show the number of students who enjoy each hobby. Ask students to suggest symbols to represent the different hobbies. Then have each student create a pictograph. When everyone is finished, ask a volunteer to draw his pictograph on the chalkboard.

- Expand the information about students who ride their bikes to school. List the different ways that students get to school: by car, school bus, bicycle, walking, and any other categories. Poll students one at a time and make a tally mark beside one of the categories for each student. Then instruct students to make bar graphs that show the information.

Dear Mrs. Gonzalez, Luis has made wonderful progress with his multiplication facts. He passed the last timed test with flying colors!
Mrs. Krieg

Parent Photo Notes

Give your new students' parents an up-close and personal look at your class every time you send a note home. During the first weeks of school, take a roll or two of photographs showing students engaged in a variety of classroom activities. After having the film developed, ask a photo shop to transform the pictures into photo cards similar to those sent by many families at Christmas. Jot notes home to parents on the blank portion of the cards. When you want to send a note home, you'll not only be keeping the lines of communication open, but you'll also be treating the parent to a photo of your class in action. Take new photos as the year progresses and order new cards periodically.

Use the cowpoke pattern with "A Rootin'-Tootin' Welcome!" on page 6 and "Howdy, Helpers!" on page 7.

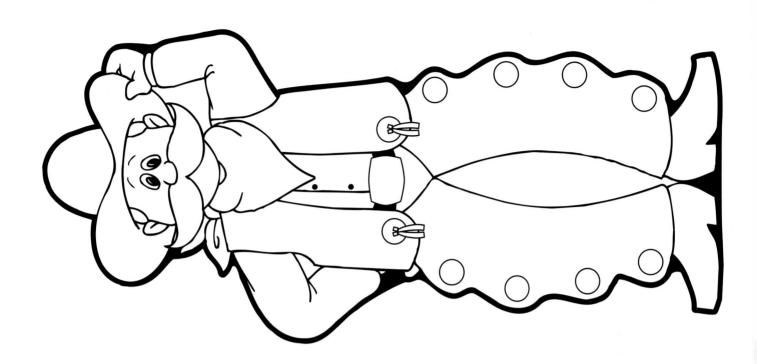

Use the no-homework coupons with "Birthday Bonanza" on page 8. Use the tickets with "First-Day Tickets" on page 6.

ADMIT ONE

Back-To-School Buckaroo
to
_____'s _____-Grade Class
on the first day of school.

Write your name here; then bring this ticket with you
to school on the first day of class.

_____

ADMIT ONE

Back-To-School Buckaroo
to
_____'s _____-Grade Class
on the first day of school.

Write your name here; then bring this ticket with you
to school on the first day of class.

_____

GIVE HOMEWORK THE BOOT TONIGHT!

In honor of your birthday, take a night off from
homework by skipping the following
assignment: _____

Happy Birthday, Buckaroo!
To: _____
From: _____
Date: _____

GIVE HOMEWORK THE BOOT TONIGHT!

In honor of your birthday, take a night off from
homework by skipping the following
assignment: _____

Happy Birthday, Buckaroo!
To: _____
From: _____
Date: _____

Together We Can Make It
A ROOTIN'-TOOTIN' TERRIFIC YEAR!

Name _____

Howdy, pardner! Welcome to your new class and the beginning of a ripsnortin' successful year! To get things off to a sensational start, sit a spell and answer the following questions. Your answers will be used to help our class plan a rootin'-tootin' terrific year!

What are two things that your teacher can do to make this a rootin'-tootin' terrific year? (Sorry, pardner, but homework can't be eliminated!)

1. _____

2. _____

What are two things that your classmates can do to make this a rootin'-tootin' terrific year?

1. _____

2. _____

What are two things that you can do to make this a rootin'-tootin' terrific year?

1. _____

2. _____

What are two rootin'-tootin' topics you would like to learn about this year?

1. _____

2. _____

Together We Can Make It
A ROOTIN'-TOOTIN' TERRIFIC YEAR!

Name _____

Howdy, pardner! Welcome to your new class and the beginning of a ripsnortin' successful year! To get things off to a sensational start, sit a spell and answer the following questions. Your answers will be used to help our class plan a rootin'-tootin' terrific year!

What are two things that your teacher can do to make this a rootin'-tootin' terrific year? (Sorry, pardner, but homework can't be eliminated!)

1. _____

2. _____

What are two things that your classmates can do to make this a rootin'-tootin' terrific year?

1. _____

2. _____

What are two things that you can do to make this a rootin'-tootin' terrific year?

1. _____

2. _____

What are two rootin'-tootin' topics you would like to learn about this year?

1. _____

2. _____

©The Education Center, Inc. • Big Book of Monthly Ideas • TEC1488

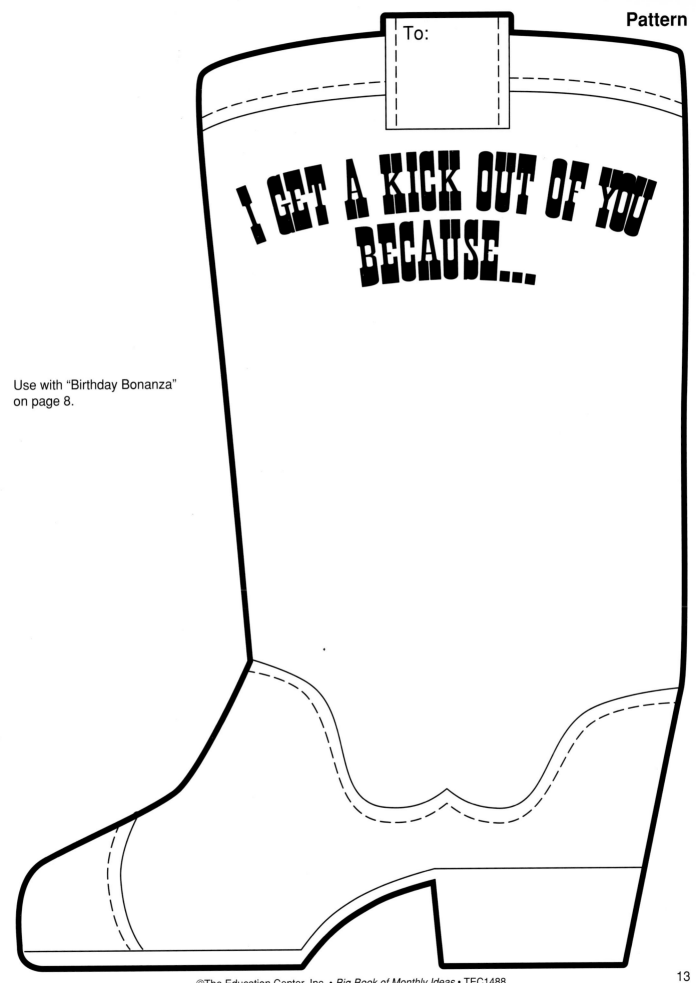

To:

I GET A KICK OUT OF YOU BECAUSE...

Use with "Birthday Bonanza" on page 8.

Patterns

Use the steer pattern with "Lookin' Ahead!" on page 8. Use the "WANTED" poster with "Howdy, Helpers!" on page 7.

WANTED

to do a rootin'-tootin' job as this week's

_____
(job)

- - -

HOWDY, PARDNER!

Say, "Howdy, Pardner," to each of your classmates with this scavenger-hunt activity. Walk around the classroom and visit with the other students. Try to get a signature in each box of the grid. A student should not sign his or her name more than two times in any vertical, horizontal, or diagonal row.

_____'s first and last names begin with the same letter. *Suzie Smith*	_____ was born in another state.	_____ has visited a foreign country.	_____ is the youngest child in a family of three children.	_____ walks to school.
_____'s favorite food is pizza.	_____'s first name has more vowels than consonants. **Aimee**	_____ loves science fiction movies and books. *A Wrinkle In Time*	_____ has read ten books by the same author. *Goose Bumps*	_____ has ridden a camel or an elephant (a real one!).
_____ has an autograph of a famous person. *Cal Ripken, Jr.*	_____ has both an older brother and a younger brother.	_____ traveled somewhere by train this summer.	_____ loves to fish.	_____'s hobby is collecting coins (or stamps, baseball cards, etc.).
_____ visited at least five states during the summer.	_____ loves to skate.	_____ attended a professional ball game during the past six months. *Astros*	_____ visited an amusement park during the summer.	_____ can water-ski.
_____ earned all *A*'s during at least one grading term last year. *Report Card*	_____ knows how to cross-stitch. *LOVE*	_____ learned how to swim over the summer.	_____ rides his or her bike to school.	_____ has at least five pets.

Bonus Box: Count all of the squares in the grid above. How many do you see?

Note To The Teacher: Use with "Say Howdy To Each Other" on page 9.

Patterns

Use the boot patterns with "Birthday Bonanza" on page 8. Use the badge patterns with "A Rootin'-Tootin' Welcome!" on page 6.

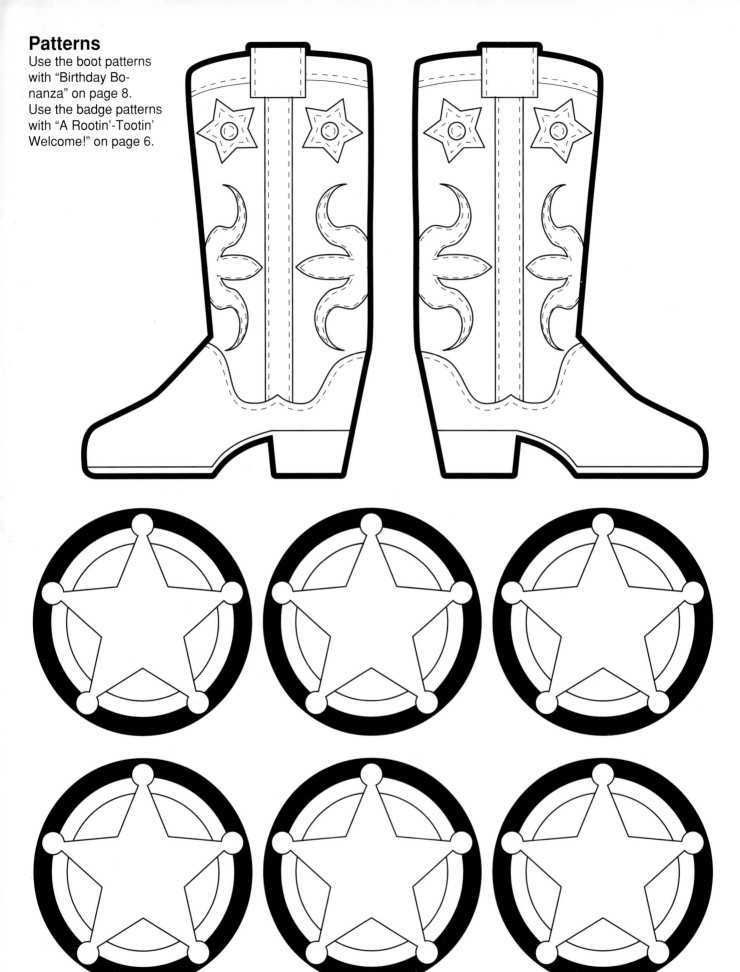

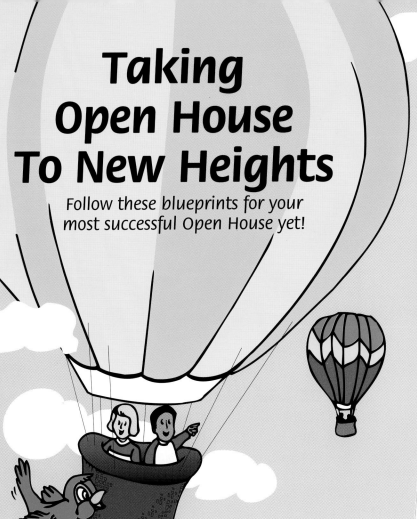

Taking Open House To New Heights

Follow these blueprints for your most successful Open House yet!

Pop-Up Invitations

Grab parents' attention with both the wording and the design of a pop-up-style invitation. Provide students with 9" x 11" sheets of white construction paper. Instruct them to fold and cut the paper according to the reproducible directions on page 20. Have students copy the specific information you want included on the invitation from the board. Supply colored pencils to use for coloring. Send the invitations home.

WANTED: Your Attendance At Open House!

When: Sept. 9th at 7:30

Where: Greenfield Elementary

- Watch your child star in a video!
- Take a trip around the classroom!
- Participate in activities with your child!
- Ask questions, get answers!
- Meet teachers, parents!
- Win door prizes!

We Want To See You There!

Josh Callie Johnny Rico Peter Sarah Tad

Jenny Cathy Allie Michael Grant Allen Rich

Handprinted Welcome Banner

Personalize your classroom's welcome banner by having students make and decorate it. Provide markers to color in the letters of a handmade or computer-generated banner. Set out aluminum pie pans that contain fall-colored paint. Have students give the banner individual stamps of approval by making fall-colored handprints around the wording. Be sure to have the students autograph their imprints after the imprints have dried.

Courtney is a friend to all.

The Apples Of My Eye

Teachers are the usual recipients of apples, right? Give this custom an unexpected twist by providing apples for the parents! Prior to Open House, cut a paper leaf for each child; then write a complimentary statement on it. After laminating the leaves, tape each leaf to the stem of an apple. Place the apples on the children's desks. Parents will enjoy reading comments like "Adam is the apple of my eye because he always leaves his desk in order," or "Courtney is a friend to all."

No-Mistake-About-It Nametags

End forever those embarrassing introductions sometimes encountered when a remarried parent has a different last name from her child. Use nametags that include lines for both the child's name and the parent's name (see the handy patterns on page 20). Then, when meeting the parent for the first time, you've reduced the chance of getting off on the wrong foot.

Not The Usual Form

Capitalize on the Open House format to gather helpful information that can be used later during parent conferences or throughout the year. Duplicate copies of the reproducible on page 23 and place it on each student's desk for Open House. Ask that the parent sit down and answer (with the child's help) questions on this very different form—questions like "What are your child's strongest academic subjects?" and "What should be your child's three main academic goals for the first nine weeks?" You'll receive data that identifies a student's learning style from questions like "When your child receives a gift that needs to be assembled, does he read the directions first, or does he dive right in and try to figure it out as he goes?" Use the information gained to help you focus on individual student needs, to make lesson plans, and to conduct conferences.

Team Spirit

Capture the rampant spirit of teamwork at Open House with an instant picture! Ahead of time prepare a bulletin board titled "We Make A Strong Team." Also make simple, paper miniframes for the photos you will take by slightly folding inward the four sides of five-inch squares of paper. Staple the miniframes to the board so that the photos can be added right after they're taken. Enlist a volunteer for Open House (hubbies or beaus are great at this!) to snap a photo of you posing between each parent and his child. When the bulletin board is taken down, send the framed photos home to the parents as keepsakes.

Rising Stars

Bring out the ham in students and surely increase parents' attendance at Open House with this impromptu-styled activity. Videotape each student completing the following statement(s):

- "What I like best about school is…."
- "If I were principal for a day, I would…."
- "Someday I would like to be a…because…."

At Open House simply start the video, relax, and let the kids shine!

"Guess Who?" Hanging Mobiles

Have some fun by challenging parents to find their own child's desk. Earlier in the week have each student make his own three-paneled mobile. Give each student three sheets of 8 1/2" x 11" white paper. Ask the student to attach a silhouette or baby picture of himself to one sheet and then make his handprints (using paint) on the second sheet. Instruct the student to write a four- to five-line riddle about himself on a third sheet. Have each white sheet stapled to a 9" x 12" sheet of colored paper. Then have a long edge of one panel stapled to a long edge of the second panel. Continue until all three panels have been stapled side-to-side in a triangular shape. Punch one hole at the top of each colored sheet; then tie a length of yarn through each of the holes. Join the yarn lengths and attach them to a jumbo-sized, bent paper clip. Suspend each student's three-dimensional mobile over his desk. At Open House ask each parent to walk around the room, study the clues she finds on the mobiles, and sit at her child's desk when she has identified it.

- She has blue eyes.
- She has blonde hair.
- She plays the piano.
- She has a brother named Allen.

Who is she?

"Purr-sonal" Puzzles

Find out how well parents *really* know their children when you ask them to work these puzzles! Provide each student with an enlarged copy of one of the reproducibles from page 21 or page 22. When the puzzle forms have been completed, laminate them and then return them to the students. Ask each student to cut the pieces apart, place them inside an envelope, and write "_____'s 'Purr-sonal' Puzzle" on the outside of the envelope. Also have students use an ink pad to stamp several of their thumbprints on the envelopes. Then provide markers and allow the students to create cats and other animals from their thumbprints.

At Open House have fun observing the looks on parents' faces as they work to assemble the puzzles AND learn more about their child at the same time. Allow parents to take the keepsake home with them.

Peter's "Purr-sonal" Puzzle

Patterns

Use with "No-Mistake-About-It Nametags" on page 18.

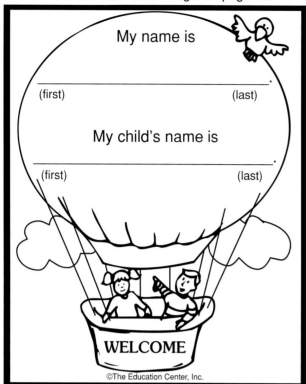

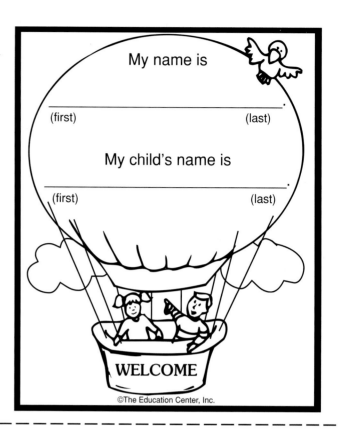

My name is

_____
(first)   (last)

My child's name is

_____
(first)   (last)

©The Education Center, Inc.

Name _____   *Open House: invitation*

You're Invited!

Get ready for Open House by making this high-flyin', fun invitation!

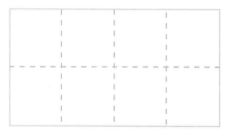

1. Fold your paper into eight sections; then unfold the paper.

2. Draw a hot-air balloon shape so that it extends above the horizontal fold as shown.

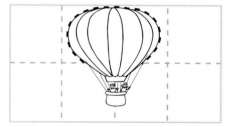

3. Using sharp scissors or an art knife, cut along the dark dotted line as shown.

4. Fold the top half of the paper back along the horizontal fold. Pull up the cut-out portion as shown.

5. Copy the information about your Open House from the chalkboard onto the invitation. Color the invitation.

Note To The Teacher: Use with "Pop-Up Invitations" on page 17. Provide each student with a copy of these directions, a sheet of white construction paper, sharp scissors or an art knife (used with supervision), and markers or crayons.

Pattern

Use with " 'Purr-sonal' Puzzles" on page 19. See pattern for girls on page 22.

1. My favorite school subject is

_____

because _____

_____

_____.

2. The subject I have the most trouble with is

_____

because_____

_____.

3. The easiest subject for me is _____

because _____

_____.

4. My favorite activities at school are _____

_____

_____.

5. I need to work on

_____

because _____

_____

_____.

6. If I could change one thing about school, I'd change

_____

because _____

_____.

7. I would like to learn more about _____

this year because _____

_____

_____.

8. A goal I have for this school year is _____

_____

_____

because _____

_____

_____.

9. My behavior in school is _____

because _____

_____

_____.

10. I hope someday to be a

_____ because

_____

_____.

Pattern

Use with " 'Purr-sonal' Puzzles" on page 19. See pattern for boys on page 21.

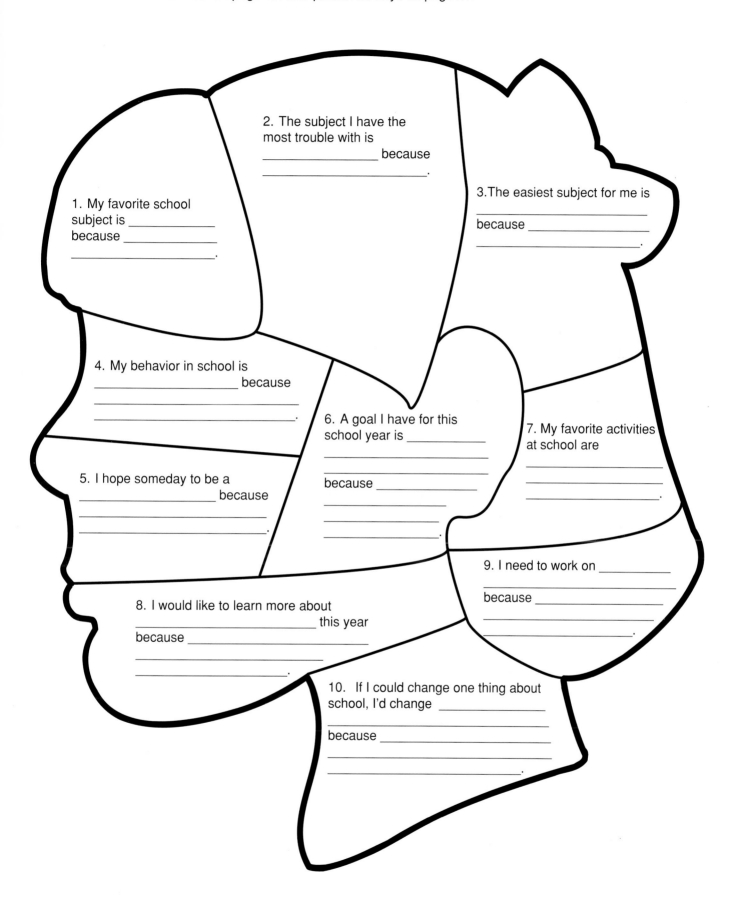

1. My favorite school subject is _____ because _____ _____.

2. The subject I have the most trouble with is _____ because _____.

3. The easiest subject for me is _____ because _____ _____.

4. My behavior in school is _____ because _____ _____.

5. I hope someday to be a _____ because _____ _____.

6. A goal I have for this school year is _____ _____ because _____ _____ _____.

7. My favorite activities at school are _____ _____ _____.

8. I would like to learn more about _____ this year because _____ _____ _____.

9. I need to work on _____ because _____ _____ _____.

10. If I could change one thing about school, I'd change _____ _____ because _____ _____ _____.

Name _____

Parent-Child Questionnaire

Please take a moment to answer each of the following questions as carefully and thoughtfully as you can. Then return the form to your child's teacher. Use the back if you need more space.

1. What are your child's major interests? _____
_____

2. What are your child's strongest academic subjects? _____
_____

3. What are your child's weakest academic subjects? _____
_____

4. Which reading skill(s) would you like to see strengthened? _____
_____

5. Which math skill(s) would you like to see strengthened? _____
_____

6. Which writing skill(s) would you like to see strengthened? _____
_____

7. Which study skill(s) would you like to see strengthened? _____
_____

8. What should be your child's three main academic goals for the first nine weeks? _____
_____

9. When your child receives a gift that needs to be assembled, does he read the directions first, or does he dive right in and try to figure it out as he goes? _____

10. Is your child more apt to complete a three-step direction if you simply give him oral instructions, or do you need to write the instructions for your child? _____
_____

11. Would your child rather watch television or play outside? _____

12. Does your child prefer listening to music or reading a book? _____

13. If your child could choose the subjects he studied in school, what would he choose? _____
_____

14. Which would your child prefer to do: write a story, read a story, or act out a story? _____

15. Would your child rather make a craft after hearing the directions, reading the directions, or watching someone make a sample? _____

16. Do you read to your child? _____ If so, how often? _____

17. If you do read to your child, is it done on a school night, during the weekend, or both? _____
_____

Note To The Teacher: Use with "Not The Usual Form" on page 18.

NATIVE AMERICANS: HONORING THEIR HERITAGE

Native American Day is celebrated on the last Friday of September. This special day honors the contributions of North America's Native Americans. Investigate the diverse cultures and heritage of Native Americans with the following learning-packed activities.

A TIME TO CELEBRATE?

To people of European descent, Christopher Columbus's historic voyage was a magnificent event that led to the discovery of North America. But to many Native Americans, Columbus represents the beginning of an era that altered the Indian way of life forever. Whose perspective is correct? Could both be correct? After discussing the two perspectives, divide the class into groups. Have each group divide a piece of chart paper in half. On the top half of the paper, have students list reasons why many people celebrate Columbus Day. On the other half, have students list reasons why others—including many Native Americans—don't celebrate this day. Point out the two sides of this issue; then ask each student to reflect on a disagreement she has had and to write about the conflict from her perspective. Then have her write about the problem from the point of view of the other person(s) involved. Discuss how trying to see things through someone else's eyes can help to resolve a conflict.

HOME SWEET HOME

Homes are a direct result of the type of environment that surrounds a people. In the case of Native Americans, homes also reflected their belief systems and social structure. Use the reproducible on page 28 to introduce students to the variety of Native American homes. After students have played the Concentration-style game, discuss why different regional tribes built certain types of homes (the climate, natural resources, etc.). Then include this information in a variation of the game. On each nonpicture card, direct students to list the materials used to make that particular home. Have students play the game again, adding a new rule that a player can keep a match only if he can state a reason why the tribe built that style of shelter.

*The terms *Native American* and *Indian* are both used in this unit. Explain to students that Christopher Columbus —upon reaching the New World—mistakenly thought that he had reached the Indies and so named its inhabitants *Indians*. The word *Indian* was not in the vocabulary of Native Americans since almost every tribe had its own name. Today many Indians refer to themselves as Native Americans.

MYTHS AND LEGENDS

Native American literature is rich in colorful legends that explain the world and nature. Read aloud some Native American tales that explain natural phenomena such as how the moon was created (see the resource list below). Explain that even though these phenomena can be explained scientifically, the myths help us learn about Native American beliefs and cultures.

After reading several stories, give each pair of students one of these topics:

volcanoes	earthquakes	constellations
mountains	rain	tornadoes
hail	sunrise/sunset	snow
rainbows	moon	comets

Have each pair research and write a one-page report about the scientific facts behind its topic. Then have the students write a brief myth or legend that explains the phenomenon in a manner similar to the Native American tales they have read. Have each pair mount its writings back-to-back on a piece of construction paper. Then hang the projects from your ceiling at eye level so students can flip them back and forth.

Resource list:
Thirteen Moons On Turtle's Back: A Native American Year Of Moons retold by Joseph Bruchac & Jonathan London
The Woman Who Fell From The Sky: The Iroquois Story Of Creation retold by John Bierhorst
The First Strawberries: A Cherokee Story retold by Joseph Bruchac
How The Stars Fell Into The Sky: A Navajo Legend by Jerrie Oughton

DISEASE: THE SILENT KILLER

It is estimated that between 7 and 15 million Native Americans lived on North America when Columbus touched its shores in 1492. By 1900 there were only 250,000 Indians left. What happened? Though many Native American lives were lost fighting for their land, many more millions died from diseases brought by the white man from Europe. Help students visualize these staggering and sad statistics with the reproducible math activity on page 29. After students complete the sheet, discuss with them the effect this drastic change in population would have on the Native American culture.

DIG THIS!

Buried under the earth is a storehouse of knowledge about the lifestyle, beliefs, and customs of Native Americans. Discuss with students how archaeologists read history by digging up and examining *artifacts* (items made by humans long ago). Show students a rock and ask, "Is this an artifact?" Students should conclude that since the stone was not made by a human, it's not an artifact. Next tie the rock to a stick and ask the same question. Students should conclude that since the stone has been fashioned into a tool by human hands, it could now be considered an artifact. Follow up this discussion by having students complete the "Dig This!" reproducible on page 32.

BUFFALO AND THE PLAINS INDIANS

Native Americans who lived on the Great Plains used the limited natural resources of their environment efficiently and effectively. For example, almost every part of the buffalo had at least one use. As buffalo herds were massacred by the white man, the damage done to the Plains Indians and their culture was staggering.

Help students grasp the importance of the buffalo to the Plains Indians' culture with the reproducible on page 31. Before distributing the sheet, explain that the buffalo was like a general store to the Plains Indians because they could use its parts to meet many basic needs. Let students complete the activity individually, in pairs, or in groups. After revealing the answers (page 229), invite students to write summaries in which they explain how losing the buffalo harmed the Plains Indians' culture and lifestyle.

RESEARCH STORY STICKS

The diversity of Native Americans is tied to the varied regions in which they lived. To help students understand this diversity, give each child a copy of page 30. (Or make a transparency to display on an overhead projector.) Have students note the different tribes listed for each region on the map. Point out that the stereotypical Native American symbols—tepee, war bonnet, buffalo, etc.—represent only a small group of Indians who lived in the Plains region. Have each cooperative group research one of the tribes listed on the map. Post these questions for groups to answer as they research:

- Where did the tribe live?
- How was the tribe organized and governed?
- What type of clothing did the people wear?
- What types of food did they eat?
- What types of shelter did they use?
- What made the tribe different from other Native American groups?
- Where is the tribe today?

After students have completed their research, have each group complete the following steps to create a giant story stick detailing its research.

Making The Research Story Stick:

1. Divide a large piece of poster board into eight horizontal, equal-sized sections.
2. Write the name of your tribe in the top section.
3. In each remaining section, answer one of the research questions posted. Include an illustration or symbol in each section.
4. Bend the poster board into a cylindrical shape; then tape the edges together with clear tape.
5. Cut out a circular cap for each end of your cylinder from construction paper. Tape each cap to an end of the cylinder, using clear tape.
6. Staple several real or paper feathers to a long strip of thick yarn or fabric. Tie the strip around one end of your research stick.

NATIVE AMERICAN SHELTER GAME

Native Americans living in different regions of North America had their own ways of building shelters. How they designed their homes depended on the climate of their region, the building materials that were available, how often the tribe moved, and their religious beliefs. Below are nine types of Native American homes. After examining them, pair up with a partner and play the Native American Shelter Game!

To make the game:
1. Get nine index cards. On each card, copy the caption listed under one home.
2. Get nine more index cards. Cut out the pictures of the homes (without the captions) from one copy of this page. Glue each to an index card.
3. Write "Answer Key" at the top of the other copy of this page.

To play the game:
1. Shuffle the 18 cards; then place them facedown in a 3 x 6 grid.
2. Player One turns over two cards. If the cards match (picture and caption), he keeps both cards and takes another turn. If they don't match, he turns the cards back over, and Player Two takes a turn. Check matches by looking at your Answer Key page.
3. The player with the most cards at the end of the game is the winner.

Longhouse Northeastern Woodlands	Chickee Southeast	Plank House Northwest Coast
Tepee Great Plains	Igloo Arctic	Earth Lodge Great Plains
Log Hogan Southwest	Wigwam Northeastern Woodlands	Pueblo Southwest

Note To The Teacher: Use with "Home Sweet Home" on page 24. Provide each student with a copy of this page.
Provide each pair of students with scissors, glue, and 18 small index cards.

Name_____ *Making graphs*

NUMBERS PAINT THE PICTURE

Christopher Columbus first touched North America's shores in 1492. Historians think that as many as 15 million Native Americans lived in North America at that time. By the end of 1900, there were only 250,000 Native Americans in North America. What happened? Many Native Americans died from diseases brought to the New World by Europeans. By 1990, the Native American population had risen to about two million.

Directions: Use the information below to complete each graph.

1492:	15,000,000	Native Americans
1900:	250,000	Native Americans
1990:	2,000,000	Native Americans

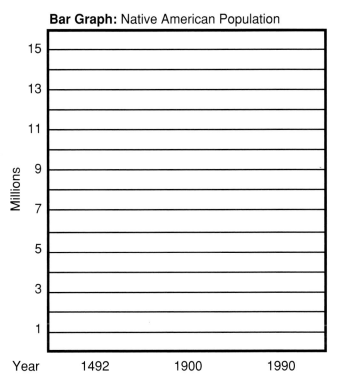

Bar Graph: Native American Population

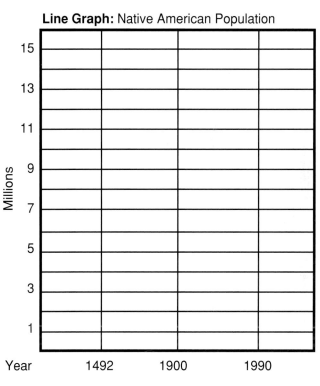

Line Graph: Native American Population

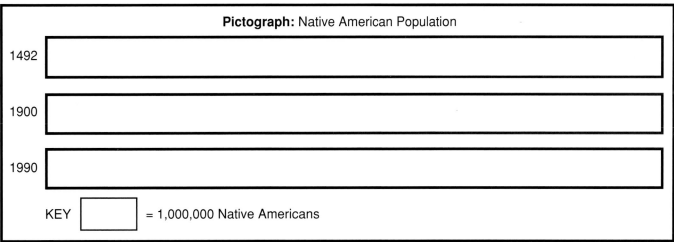

Pictograph: Native American Population

1492

1900

1990

KEY [   ] = 1,000,000 Native Americans

Answer on the back of this page: Why do graphs make it easier to understand statistics like the ones in the box above?

©The Education Center, Inc. • *Big Book of Monthly Ideas* • TEC1488 • Key p. 229

Note To The Teacher: Use with "Disease: The Silent Killer" on page 25.

29

NATIVE AMERICAN CULTURE AREAS

Below is a map that shows some of the major regions, or *culture areas,* in which Native Americans lived long ago. Tribes living in the same region were alike in some ways; but in other ways they were different.

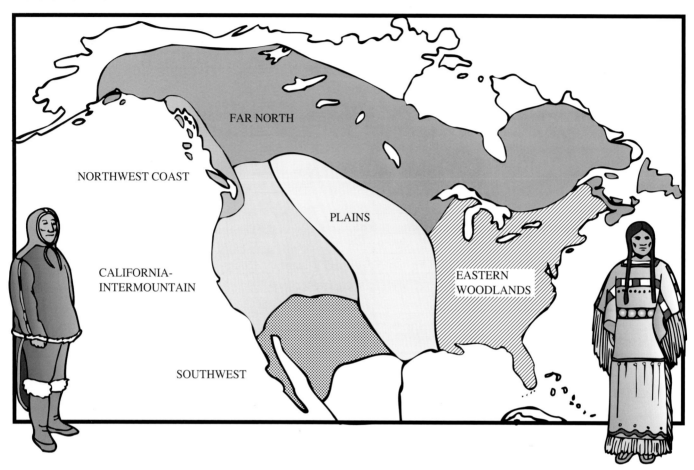

Northwest Coast
Tlingit
Haida
Klikitat

California-Intermountain
Pomo
Maidu
Paiute
Shoshone
Ute
Nez Percé

Southwest
Apache
Navajo
Pueblo
Hopi

Plains
Arapaho
Cheyenne
Pawnee
Sioux
Comanche
Mandan
Crow

Eastern Woodlands
Iroquois
Huron
Seneca
Shawnee
Cherokee
Chickasaw
Seminole

Far North
Chippewa
Cree
Algonquin

Note To The Teacher: Use with "Research Story Sticks" on page 27.

THE BUFFALO MALL

Native Americans who lived on the Great Plains depended on the buffalo for most of their needs. They had at least one use—and sometimes more—for almost every part of the animal.

Directions: Welcome to "Buffalo Mall"! Look at the list of buffalo parts below. Decide which part was used to make each necessity listed in the stores below; then write the letter of the part in the blank. Some necessities may have more than one letter in the blank. Happy shopping!

A. soft hide*
B. rawhide*
C. tail
D. dung
E. gall bladder

F. stomach contents
G. bones
H. tendons
I. hooves
J. brains

K. teeth
L. blood
M. horns
N. ribs
O. tongue

P. fat
Q. hair/fur
R. liver
S. backbone

*Rawhide was hairless, tough, waterproof buffalo hide that hadn't been tanned. It was used to make tougher and heavier things like cooking pots. Soft hide was tanned with the hair on and was used for clothing or blankets.

Clothes R Here
____ mittens
____ coat/robe
____ dress
____ belt
____ leggings
____ necklace

Feet First Shoe Store
____ moccasins
____ laces
____ shoe soles

Feel Better Pharmacy
____ medicine
____ diapers
____ flyswatter

Arts & Crafts Shack
____ paints
____ brushes
____ tanning oil

Groceries Galore
____ pudding
____ soup
____ cold cuts

Beauty-Mart
____ hair gloss
____ hairbrush
____ soap
____ makeup

Sporting Spot
____ arrows
____ bow
____ shield
____ club
____ knife

Toys & More
____ doll
____ ball
____ dice
____ top
____ rattle

The Transportation Depot
____ dogsled
____ toboggan
____ boat
____ saddle

Kitchen Corner
____ water container
____ spoons
____ bowl
____ food storage bin
____ fuel for fires

Note To The Teacher: Use with "Buffalo And The Plains Indians" on page 26.

DIG THIS!

Archaeologists are people who study early cultures by looking at things they left behind. An archaeologist chooses a small area that she thinks might contain buried *artifacts*. (An *artifact* is something made by a human being.) Then she covers the area with a grid made of string. The grid is numbered and labeled like the one below. When an archaeologist finds an artifact, she labels it with a number and letter according to where she found it. Later she uses a picture of the grid to identify where the artifact was found.

Directions: Here is a picture of a Native American archaeology site. Draw conclusions about the Native American artifacts found here by answering the questions below. Use the back of this page if you need more space.

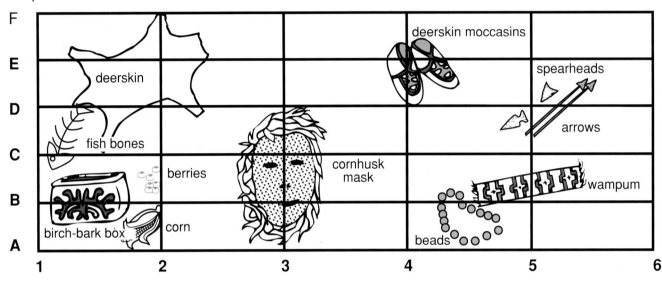

1. What artifact did you find at E-2? _____ What can you conclude about this tribe from the artifact? _____.

2. What coordinates tell you where to find the cornhusk mask? _____
   What does the mask tell you about the culture of these Native Americans? _____
   _____.

3. What part of the site was where the people probably prepared their food? _____
   _____.
   What types of food did these people eat? _____
   _____.

4. What material might these people have used to make clothing? _____
   _____ What helped you come to this
   conclusion? _____
   _____.

5. Did these Native Americans trade with each other or other people? _____
   How do you know? _____.

Bonus Box: Create your own archaeological site! Research a Native American group. Then draw a grid like the one above. Draw artifacts belonging to your tribe in the grid. On another piece of paper, describe each artifact, its location on the grid, and what it tells about your Native American group.

©The Education Center, Inc. • *Big Book of Monthly Ideas* • TEC1488 • Key p. 230

32   **Note To The Teacher:** Use with "Dig This!" on page 26.

"Howl-oween" Hoedown

"Phan-tastic" Halloween Activities, Projects, And Fun

by Peggy W. Hambright
and Ann Fisher

Bewitching Tales

Turn narrative writing into a spirited event by having students rewrite well-known fairy tales with Halloween themes. Suggest titles like "Snow White And The Seven Ghosts," "The Three Little Monsters," or "The Town Witch And The Country Witch." Have each student fold a 12" x 18" sheet of white paper accordion-style, with one-inch folds; then have him copy his story on the folds (one line per fold). Next have him staple a cut-out head, a pair of arms, and a pair of feet to the resulting body as shown. Plan a time for the tales to be shared with a younger class.

Gordon, a groovy green monster, grinned as he greedily gobbled gobs of gooey, green gum.

Ghost Writers

Excite students with some ghostly science that's disguised as magic! Have each student use Q-tips® dampened with lemon juice to write a Halloween tongue twister on white paper. After the papers have dried, have each student hold his paper up to a light to read his message, which has magically turned brown. Explain to students that the lemon juice turned brown because of a chemical change that takes place when the paper is warmed by the light. Lemon juice contains carbon. When it is heated, the heat causes a chemical change that breaks apart the juice and frees the carbon to show its true dark color.

Rib Ticklers

You'll tickle a few funny bones with this writing activity! Assign each student to write an original Halloween riddle or joke on a large bone cutout as shown. Encourage students to use homonyms and/or plays on words. Have students write the answers to their riddles on the backs of their bones; then staple the bones together to make a class book titled " 'Phan-tastically' Funny Bones." Share the book during a class Halloween party. Or have a student read one riddle/joke a day over your school public-address system during the last two weeks of October.

Monster Motel is near which lake?

Lake Eerie.

Look Whoooo's In My Group!

Create a magical moment when you form groups for cooperative activities during the Halloween season. Stamp the backs of index cards (one card per student) with four or five different Halloween stamps (one stamp per card). Distribute the cards to students; then form groups based on the pictures stamped on the cards.

Halloween Mad Lib

During the Halloween season, have fun reviewing nouns, verbs, and adjectives with a Mad Lib activity. Explain to students that a Mad Lib is a sentence into which certain parts of speech have been randomly placed. The results of the random placement can be quite humorous. Give each student a copy of the reproducible on the bottom half of page 39. After students have followed the instructions and filled the blanks in Part One, read Part Two aloud. At each numbered blank, ask a volunteer to insert the matching word that he wrote in Part One. Listen for laughter as students realize how silly words sound when they do not fit the context. As a final step, direct each student to number the back of his reproducible 1–12; then have him write a list of words that *would* make sense within the context of the paragraph. Let students compare their lists.

She woke up in her dishwasher?

Halloween Page Peekers

As Halloween draws near, imagine a mischievous ghost peeking over the page of a student's favorite book as he reads! Give each student a 2 1/2" x 8" rectangle of tagboard, markers, a pair of wiggle eyes, glue, and scissors. Have the student draw and color the face of a Halloween character on the top one-third of his rectangle, adding a pair of wiggle eyes. Then direct the student to cut out around his character's face and then make a cut on the top half of the bookmark as shown. The resulting tab can be slipped over a page to mark the student's place.

35

Hobgoblin Safety Tips

Involve your class in a campaign to remind younger students of trick-or-treat safety rules—and ingrain the rules in your *own* pupils at the same time. Brainstorm a list of safety reminders with your class. Then have each student devise a creative way to share these tips with or teach these tips to kindergartners or first graders at your school—a skit, a rap or rhyme, a trick-or-treat license, a letter, a puppet show, a recipe for safety, etc. Schedule a time for small groups of students to make their presentations to classes of younger students.

Wear a costume that makes it easy for you to be seen.

Haunted-House Writing Center

Ghostly ghouls will gradually inhabit a haunted house when students use this free-time writing center! Ask a group of students to draw and cut out a haunted house from a large piece of brown bulletin board paper. Make sure students draw six to eight windows on the house. Mount the house on a bulletin board or wall. Then write the following story starters on small ghost cutouts:

- Scary Halloween movies are...
- The best trick I ever played on Halloween was...
- Halloween should/should not be banned because...
- If I could make a magic brew, it would...
- Halloween has been canceled this year because...
- In the year 2025, Halloween will be...
- If I could trick-or-treat on the Internet, I would go to...
- If I could travel back in time to trick-or-treat, I'd go to...

Glue each ghost cutout to a window so that it appears to peek out at students. Duplicate a class supply of the ghost form on page 39 to place at the center. After each student writes on his form, have him cut out the ghost shape and post it near the haunted house. The more students use this haunted center, the spookier the house will become!

Ghost Money

Students can readily tell you how they spend their money. But how might *ghosts* spend their cold hard cash? For a creative-writing activity, challenge each student to think of five ways that a ghost might use money (to pay for howling lessons, to buy an abandoned house to haunt, etc.). Then direct the student to use his ideas to write and illustrate a story about a ghost who wins a sweepstakes. Compile the students' stories into a book titled "I Just Won The 'Boo-blishers' Clearinghouse Sweepstakes!" Place the book in your reading center. Or plan to read aloud several stories a day as time fillers.

This time, try using a veeeery scaaaaary voice.

Like this? oooo-- aaaaa-- eeeee-- iiiiiii-- uuuu--

Abracadabra Patterns

Create fun, magical patterns with this math activity! Have a group of students help you fill individual Ziploc® bags—one per student—with a pipe cleaner, 24 black tri-beads, and 12 orange tri-beads (tri-beads are available from a craft store). Give each student one of the bags. Challenge the student to determine a repeating pattern that can be made by threading all of the beads onto the pipe cleaner. Be sure to inform students that there is more than one solution to this challenge; then set them loose to start threadin'! *(The following repeating patterns are possible with this set of beads: two black and one orange bead, six black and three orange beads, and 12 black and six orange beads.)*

Scary Words

Challenge students to expand their vocabularies with this Halloween activity. First have students brainstorm a list of "scary" words—words they encounter in spooky stories or scary movies. After you've listed about 15 words on the chalkboard, divide your students into pairs and instruct each pair to write a Halloween story—*without* using any of the words on the board. Challenge students to use dictionaries and thesauruses to find synonyms for the words on the board. After each pair has shared its story with the class, add the new words these students used to a chart. Encourage students to use these new words in other Halloween projects.

Candy-Corn Close-Up

Weave a science-processing skill lesson into the holiday season with this sweet activity. Purchase a large bag of candy corn and give each student a piece. Ask the student to study his piece of candy carefully. What is its shape? Its dimensions? How would you describe its size? What are its colors and how are they arranged? Set a timer for 15 minutes and ask the students to list on paper the candy's characteristics. When time is up, have a volunteer read his list of attributes aloud, one characteristic at a time. As each attribute is read, have students discuss its accuracy. Write each attribute that is accurately supported on a piece of poster board. Have a group of students decorate the chart by gluing leftover candies side by side to make one or more large 3-D pieces of candy corn!

Candy Corn Attributes

shaped like a triangle
3 colors: white, yellow, orange
3 vertices

CANDY CORN

A Math Trick

Stump your students with a math trick that may just drive them batty! Draw four ghost shapes on the chalkboard. Number the ghosts one through four with colored chalk; then use white chalk to add the other numbers to the ghosts as shown. Ask a student to choose a white number written on one of the ghosts. Tell him not to tell you the number he chose but to tell you which ghosts have that number. (For example, if the student chooses the number nine, he would tell his teacher that his number is on ghosts number two, three, and four.) Tell the student that you know the number he chose—even though he hasn't told you. (To figure out the number, add the numbers of the ghosts in which the number appears: 2 + 3 + 4 = 9, which is the number the student chose.) Challenge the class to determine how you did it!

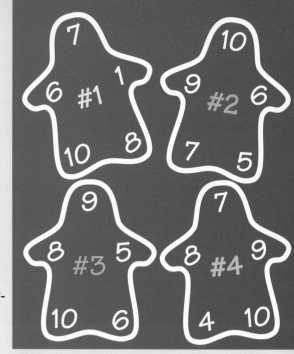

Pumpkin Pals

Use a hands-on art activity as a springboard to a narrative and descriptive writing exercise. Obtain a small or mini-sized pumpkin for each student. Supply each student with markers or acrylic paints, yarn, glue, and other art materials. Give each student time to paint or draw a face on his pumpkin and let it dry. Then have the student glue on yarn hair and a hat. Don't forget to ask the student to name his new pumpkin pal!

To extend the activity, instruct each student to describe his pumpkin pal's personality in a story that tells how he and his orange buddy became such good friends. After the stories have been shared, let each student take his pumpkin pal home to use as a table centerpiece.

Hee-haw Susie

Ghostly Graphics

Here's an easy way to relate the math curriculum to your class's Halloween party. Request that each student bring in a bag of individually wrapped candies. (Ask parents to provide extra bags for students who are unable to make such a donation.) Have each student set a Halloween treat bag labeled with his name on his desk. Allow each student to pass out the candies he brought from home by dropping one piece (or more) into each classmate's bag. Then tell each student to empty the contents of his treat bag onto his desk and sort the candies into groups. Direct each student to construct a bar graph that shows the different classifications of candy in his bag. After the graph is complete, have each student rebag his candy to enjoy during the class Halloween party!

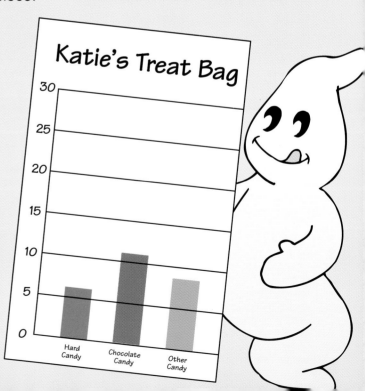

Katie's Treat Bag

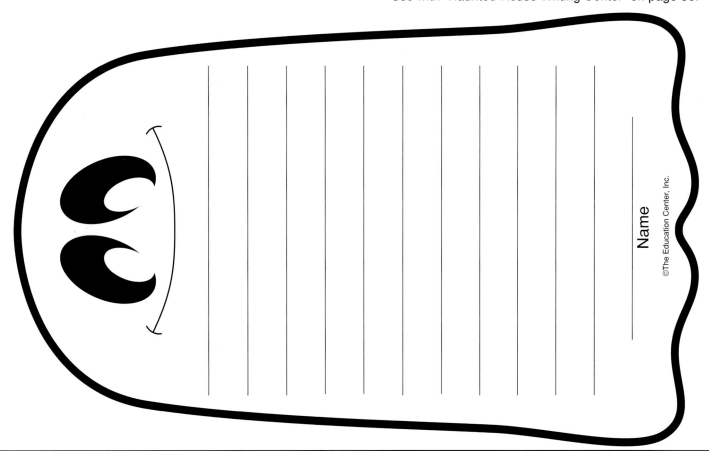

Name

©The Education Center, Inc.

Name_____ *Parts of speech; context*

A Parts-Of-Speech Nightmare

To complete this parts-of-speech challenge, cover Part Two with paper. Write a word to fill each blank in Part One. Then uncover Part Two. Read the paragraph, filling in the blanks with the words you wrote in Part One. Sounds pretty silly, right? Now number 1–12 on the back of this page. Write a word that does make sense in each blank.

Part One:

1. _____
   proper noun (place)
2. _____
   plural noun
3. _____
   noun
4. _____
   adjective
5. _____
   adjective
6. _____
   adjective

7. _____
   present-tense action verb
8. _____
   present-tense action verb
9. _____
   present-tense action verb
10. _____
    noun
11. _____
    noun
12. _____
    adjective

Part Two:

Mrs. Frank N. Stein had a nightmare. She dreamed she was in (1)_____. She had brought three (2)_____ with her, but to her dismay she forgot to bring her (3)_____. Two (4)_____ jack-o'-lanterns, (5)_____ cats, and (6)_____ ghosts were also there. The jack-o'-lanterns, cats, and ghosts liked to (7)_____ and (8)_____ all the time. Mrs. Stein got weary, so she decided it was time to (9)_____ home. She woke up in her (10)_____ and discovered her (11)_____ right where she had left it. It was still (12)_____.

Costume Combinations

Cosby's Costume Closet has just received a new supply of Halloween costumes. Here are a few of the items for sale:

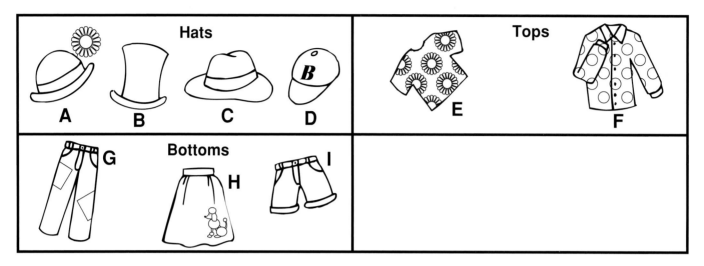

1. Using the letter of each item, list all the different possible combinations of tops and bottoms:

   _____

   How many combinations are there in all? _____

2. Using letters, list all the different possible combinations of hats, tops, and bottoms:

   _____

   _____

   _____

   How many combinations are there in all? _____

3. If two masks were added to the collection above, the number of combinations of hats, tops, bottoms, and masks would (circle one):
   • stay the same
   • double
   • triple

4. A. Look back at number 1. There were _____ choices of tops, _____ choices of bottoms, and _____ combinations in all.
   B. In number 2, there were ___ choices of hats, ___ choices of tops, ___ choices of bottoms, and ___ combinations in all.
   C. In number 3, there were ___ choices of hats, ___ choices of tops, ___ choices of bottoms, ___ choices of masks, and ___ combinations in all.

5. What is the trick or shortcut in finding the number of possible combinations? _____
   _____

6. Add your own drawings of three different pairs of shoes in the empty box above. Now how many different combinations of hats, tops, bottoms, and shoes will there be? _____
   _____

Bonus Box: How many different combinations of two letters are possible using the entire alphabet?

Trick-Or-Treat Trail

Jan and Stan will be trick-or-treating on Halloween night at the eight houses shown below. They live in a very friendly neighborhood, and all the neighbors want to be sure they don't miss the trick-or-treaters. The neighbors have given different bits of information to Jan and Stan to help them plan their route. The neighbors are all very generous and talkative, so Jan and Stan need to allow ten minutes for each stop.

Help Jan and Stan plan their path. Number the houses in the diagram from one to eight in the order they should be visited. Also, write in the name of the person who lives in each house and the time that Jan and Stan will visit.

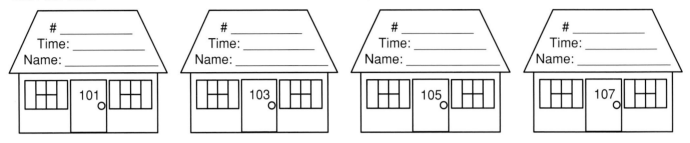

Shady Lane

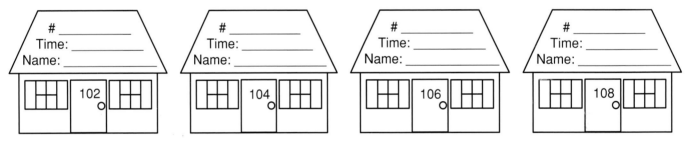

1. Mr. Green at #107 has to leave for the evening at 5:30 P.M.

2. Mr. Black at #102 won't be home until 6:00 P.M.

3. Mrs. Smith wants to be the first to hand out treats when the trick-or-treating begins at 5:00 P.M. She lives two houses west of Mrs. Jones.

4. Ms. Rose, who lives at #103, wants to be visited after Ms. Daisy and before Mr. Brown.

5. The children have been told to go immediately to Mr. White's at #101 after visiting #104.

6. When Jan and Stan are finished at Mr. Green's, they are to go next door to Ms. Daisy's house.

7. Mrs. Jones, who lives across the street from Mr. Green, wants to be visited immediately after Mr. Brown, who lives at #106.

Bonus Box: A man and a woman in the neighborhood above are brother and sister. Both live on the same side of the street, and both have neighbors on each side of them. Who are they?

Word Webs

A few Halloween spiders have been busy spinning unusual webs. Can you complete each web? Place the letters below each web into the blank spaces to spell six common words of five letters each. Each word begins in the center of the web and reads outward. Cross out each letter below the web as you use it. The word PURSE has been completed in the first web as an example.

1.

A I C D E I K L C $\cancel{S}$ T $\cancel{U}$

2.

A H R I M N O N Q R S O

3.

A A C E H I L L O P T U

4.

D E G G I L L L N N P S

Bonus Box: How many five-letter words beginning with the letter *H* can you list within a two-minute time limit? Have a classmate keep time for you.

DIVING INTO THE DICTIONARY

Noah Webster spent 50 years writing his *American Dictionary Of The English Language.* But it doesn't have to take your students that long to discover its treasures! Celebrate Dictionary Day on October 16 (also Noah Webster's birthday) by submerging your class into the following dictionary activities.

by Christine A. Thuman

Rx: One New Word A Day

Increase your students' vocabularies—and their use of the dictionary—by creating a Word-Of-The-Day bulletin board. Decorate a small bulletin board with a cutout submarine as shown. Have students add paper fish to the display. Each week select a word from a sentence, comic strip, or cartoon; then display a card labeled with the word and a copy of the source on the board. Have each student write a guess about the word's meaning on a slip of paper. Read the guesses aloud; then have students compare them with the actual definition. Challenge each student to use the word correctly during the day. Remove the word card and source at the end of the day; then mount the word along the bulletin board's border to build a visual dictionary of newly learned words.

Final Four

Increase the speed at which your students use the dictionary by playing a fast-paced game of Final Four. Provide each student or student pair with a dictionary. Write a word of seven or more letters on the board; then underline the last four letters of the word. On your mark, have each student look in the dictionary for a new word beginning with those final four letters. When a student has found a word, have one of his classmates verify that it begins with the correct four letters. Award one point to the student who found the new word; then write the new word on the board, underline its last four letters, and continue play. If no word beginning with the final four letters exists, select a new word and begin the game again.

Sporty Respellings

How well do your students use respellings to pronounce new words? Give them plenty of practice by playing Touchdown. Make a supply of football cutouts. On each cutout write the respelling of one dictionary entry word. Number each cutout and make a key on a separate sheet of paper. Place the cutouts in a football helmet or a basket. Label two additional football cutouts "Team A" and "Team B."

Sketch a football field on the chalkboard as shown. Assign each of two teams an end zone; then flip a coin to determine which team goes first. To play, one team member from Team A picks a football from the helmet. If he pronounces the word correctly, he tapes the "Team A" football to the ten-yard line nearest his team's end zone; then another member of Team A takes a turn. If the pronunciation is incorrect, the team fumbles the ball and the opposing team takes a turn, also starting at its end zone. With each correct answer, a team advances its ball ten yards. Each time a team scores a touchdown, it earns six points and play goes to the opposing team. The team scoring the most points wins.

large hairpiece	=	big wig
azure church seat	=	blue pew
angry employer	=	cross boss
sneaky insect	=	sly fly
happier dog	=	merrier terrier

Time To Rhyme

These days you can find a dictionary on just about any subject. One very useful dictionary is a rhyming dictionary. Use it to help your students create *hinky pinkys*—clever synonymic expressions formed by putting two rhyming words together. The first word should be an adjective and the second word should be a noun (for example, *fat cat*). After each child has created a hinky pinky, have him think of a synonym for each word (in this case, *overweight feline*). Direct him to give a partner this second set of words and challenge her to figure out the corresponding hinky pinky.

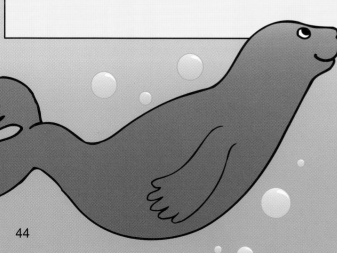

44

Terminology Tricksters

How convincing are your students when it comes to defining unfamiliar words? Find out by selecting 12 or more unknown words to share with your students. (See the list on page 49 for examples.) Give one word to each pair of students. Instruct each pair to write down the correct definition of its word after checking a dictionary; then have the pair create and write an alternate—but believable—definition. In turn have each pair stand and read its word and both definitions. Challenge the remaining pairs to guess the correct definition. Award a point to each pair that guesses correctly.

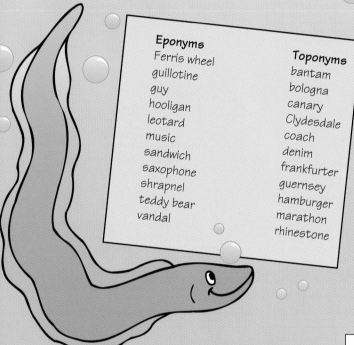

Eponyms
Ferris wheel
guillotine
guy
hooligan
leotard
music
sandwich
saxophone
shrapnel
teddy bear
vandal

Toponyms
bantam
bologna
canary
Clydesdale
coach
denim
frankfurter
guernsey
hamburger
marathon
rhinestone

Don't Take Your Teddy Bear On The Ferris Wheel!

Scholars agree that there are more than 600,000 words in the English language. Where did this many words come from? Some come from things that were named after people. These are known as *eponyms* (from *epi*, meaning "after," and *onyma*, meaning "name"). Others come from things that are named after places, or *toponyms* (from *topos*, meaning "place," and *onyma*, meaning "name"). Challenge students to find the origins of the words on the left using their dictionaries. How many more eponyms and toponyms can they find?

Go To The Head Of The Class!

Many words in our language have multiple meanings. We need to look no further than our own bodies to see examples of this truth. You have a head, but so does a bed. You may think your feet are big, but a mountain has a much bigger foot than you do. Help students explore these varied meanings by drawing a sketch of a human body on the board. Label the body parts as shown in the illustration. Challenge students to find each label in the dictionary and read its definitions. Then have them identify other objects that have the same names as the body's parts. Add their findings to the sketch as shown.

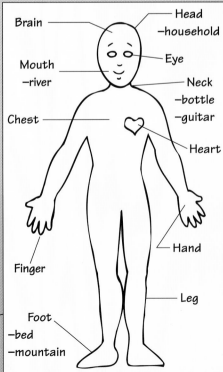

Brain
Head
—household
Mouth
—river
Eye
Neck
—bottle
—guitar
Chest
Heart
Hand
Finger
Leg
Foot
—bed
—mountain

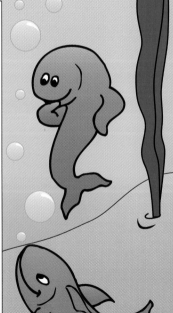

45

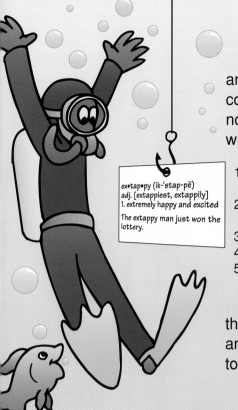

That's Nonsense!

When Lewis Carroll wanted to describe that unique blend of a chuckle and a snort, he created the nonsense word *chortle*. Help students become familiar with the format of a dictionary entry by having them create nonsense words. Give each student a large index card. Instruct her to write the following information on separate lines on the card:

ex•tap•py (ik-'stap-pē)
adj. [extappiest, extappily]
1. extremely happy and excited

The extappy man just won the lottery.

1. The entry word; the phonetic respelling in parentheses, including stresses and syllabication
2. An abbreviation of the word's part of speech; alternate spellings of the word with different endings
3. Definition(s) of the word (which may take more than one line)
4. A sentence using the word
5. An illustration of the word, if possible

Collect the invented words, read them to the class, and then display them on a bulletin board. Appoint a committee to alphabetize the entries and bind them together to create a class dictionary. Challenge students to use their invented words in conversations and in their writing pieces.

Fun With Big Words

What can you do with a *really* big word? Challenge your students with the words listed on page 49 and these activities:

- Say one word aloud. Instruct each student to write the word—guessing at the correct spelling. Have several volunteers write their guesses on the board. Then have each student look up the word to check his guess with the actual spelling.
- Write a big word on the board. Have each student guess the pronunciation and then write a possible definition of the word. Have students share their guesses. Then have them look up the actual pronunciation and definition.
- Give each student a card on which to write a big word, its definition, an illustration, and a sentence using the word. Tape a different card to each student's desk. Each day, rotate the cards to familiarize students with all the new words.

Little Words Mean A Lot!

Anyone who's played a word game or completed a crossword puzzle knows that little words go a long way. Place students in pairs. Have each pair comb the dictionary to discover new three- and four-letter words. Direct the students to keep a record of each word and its definition. Then have each pair use its words to create an original mini crossword puzzle to swap with another pair.

Name(s) _____

What Is It?

Use a dictionary to find the meanings of these words. Write each word under the proper heading to show if it is a plant ("Grow It"), an animal ("Feed It"), or an article of clothing ("Wear It").

What would you do with each of the following?

acacia	echidna	liana
addax	fichu	monkshood
banyan	forsythia	oryx
bolero	gambadoes	snood
buskins	gaur	ulster
capote	hyssop	urial
chinquapin	ibex	wapiti
citron	jerboa	whin
cloche	jodhpurs	wimple
durra	kudu	zebu

Grow It	Feed It	Wear It
_____	_____	_____
_____	_____	_____
_____	_____	_____
_____	_____	_____
_____	_____	_____
_____	_____	_____
_____	_____	_____
_____	_____	_____
_____	_____	_____
_____	_____	_____

Bonus Box: Define each of the following words on the back of this page: *aphid, auk, azurite, carpal, cicada, curculio, egret, fibula, heron, incus, mica, quartz.* Then classify them into groups according to their common characteristics. Label each group.

Using a dictionary; vocabulary

mania

phobia

confidante

confident

lay

lie

Muddled No More

Some words are so similar that they're easy to confuse. Below is a calendar of 20 confounding word pairs. Look up the definitions of each square's words; then fill in the blanks correctly.

1
stationary
stationery

Bob's _____ position in front of the television lasted for hours. Therefore, he no longer had time to write a thank-you note on his _____.

2
lay
lie

Stephanie will _____ the book on the table, and then she'll _____ down until she feels better.

3
counsel
consul

The foreign _____ was not eager to give _____ on political matters.

4
adapt
adopt

If that family decides to _____ a baby, they will have to _____ to a very different lifestyle.

5
all ready
already

We had _____ gone shopping for food when Mom came back to say that dinner was _____.

6
complement
compliment

I want to _____ you on a fine meal. The meat and vegetables _____ each other nicely.

7
confidante
confident

José is _____ that Marcia can be trusted as a _____.

8
fatal
fateful

On that _____ day, the race-car driver almost had a _____ accident.

9
set
sit

_____ that pot on the stove before you _____ on the chair.

10
principal
principle

Leave it to our school's _____ to make us _____ aware of that important _____.

11
accept
except

The new store will _____ all coupons _____ those that belong to other stores.

12
raise
raze

In order to _____ money for a new building, the city must first _____ the old building.

13
quiet
quite

Harold is such a _____ guy that most people don't realize that he's _____ funny.

14
affect
effect

The new law will go into _____ immediately. Who knows how it will _____ most people?

15
respectfully
respectively

Brutus behaved _____ in front of the officers, shaking the hands of Mr. Smith, Mrs. Bentley, and Ms. Cannon _____.

16
graceful
gracious

The dance instructor made a _____ comment about the _____ movements of the dancers.

17
capital
capitol

When we visit Raleigh—the _____ of North Carolina— let's be sure to go inside the _____ building.

18
between
among

During the football game, Mark sat _____ Sara and Tyler as all three sat _____ the huge crowd of people.

19
advice
advise

When asked for his _____, the minister was happy to _____ the couple who wanted to get married.

20
mania
phobia

Clara would not take part in the shopping mall _____ be- cause she had a _____ about being in crowded places.

©The Education Center, Inc. • *Big Book of Monthly Ideas* • TEC1488 • Key p. 231

Note To The Teacher: Duplicate this page for each student or student pair to complete. Or write one word pair and sentence(s) on the board each day for students to complete during their free time.

Don't Let These BIG WORDS Get Away!

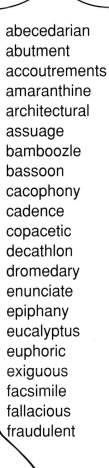

abecedarian
abutment
accoutrements
amaranthine
architectural
assuage
bamboozle
bassoon
cacophony
cadence
copacetic
decathlon
dromedary
enunciate
epiphany
eucalyptus
euphoric
exiguous
facsimile
fallacious
fraudulent

garrulous
gyrate
heinous
hyperbole
hypocrite
imbroglio
impervious
impudent
insinuate
jaborandi
jeopardy
kindred
labyrinth
lachrymose
lackadaisical
lethargy
loquacious
luminous
maelstrom
melancholy
menagerie
mesmerize

metropolis
nebulous
noxious
obstinate
obstreperous
orifice
palindrome
pandemonium
perpendicular
phenomenon
polyglot
predicament
quadruped
quandary
recurrence
repudiate
repugnant
resplendent
saponaceous
schism
serpentine
smithereens

soothsayer
spontaneous
spurious
tatterdemalion
termagant
timorous
tintinnabulation
tourniquet
transient
ultimate
universal
vacuous
vagabond
variegated
venomous
vestibule
virtuoso
voracious
woebegone
ziggurat
zucchini

obstreperous

Note To The Teacher: Use this reproducible with "Terminology Tricksters" on page 45 and "Fun With Big Words" on page 46.

"PURR-FECTLY" POETIC

Celebrate National Poetry Day on October 15 by introducing your students to poetry and their own "purr-fect" potential as poets. Get started with the following creative and easy-to-do ideas. You'll agree that they're the pick of the litter!

by Mary Lou Schosser

danger → dog → bark → run → tree → bird → DINNER!

FREE ASSOCIATION WARM-UP

Flex those creative brain waves with a free-association activity. Call out a word to the class. Instruct each student to write down the first thing that comes to his mind as he hears that word. The response may be another word, a phrase, or a more detailed description. Have students share some of their responses and explain how their thoughts were triggered. Point out that these unique thought patterns are what make us individual thinkers.

Extend this activity by calling out another word. Have each student write the first word that he associates with it, and then use that word to think of a third word, continuing this process to create a unique chain of associations. Have several students share their chains with the class.

THE COLORS OF LIFE

Artists aren't the only ones who know how to express ideas through color. For another free-association activity, have each student write down all of the thoughts that come to her mind when you call out the name of a particular color. Encourage the student to use all five senses—describing what that color looks like, smells like, sounds like, tastes like, and feels like. Next have the student refine her phrases or sentences so that each one describes a different aspect of the color. After the student has organized her phrases into a poem that begins with the name of the color, have her write the poem on a copy of the crayon pattern on page 55. (Duplicate student copies of this pattern on manila or white paper.) Direct the student to complete the pattern by coloring around the poem with the matching color of crayon or marker. Post the cutout crayons on a bulletin board titled "Color Us Poetic!"

Blue.
Berries hanging ripe on the bushes,
A lonely trumpet playing taps,
Sugary frosting flowers that melt in your mouth,
Dad's favorite checkered shirt, smelling of cologne.

A POET TREE

Add a splash of autumn to your classroom by creating this poetry bulletin board. Cover the bottom of your board with green paper for grass and the top with light blue paper for the sky. Add a large branching tree cut from brown bulletin board paper. Duplicate the leaf pattern on page 55 onto yellow, red, and orange paper. Give each student a leaf pattern to use for completing one or more of the activities listed below. Display the completed leaves on the tree's branches, falling from the tree, and lying on the grass next to the tree. Add the title "We're Falling For Poetry!"

- Undoubtedly your study of poetry will include a look at the lives and works of famous poets. Keep track of those poets on your bulletin board. Instruct each student to select a different poet to research; then have the student write the poet's name, some brief biographical information, and the title of at least one of the poet's poems on a leaf pattern. Mount the leaves on the display.
- Have each student write an autobiographical poem on a leaf pattern.
- Honor favorite poets by having each student select a favorite poem (or a stanza from the poem) to write on his leaf. Be sure the student includes the poet's name.

We're Falling For Poetry!

A THREE-DIMENSIONAL ALTERNATIVE

As an alternative to the bulletin board shown above, have students display the projects completed in the activities above on a three-dimensional tree. Use a small live or silk tree, or create your own tree. To make a tree, mix plaster of paris in a two-gallon bucket. Before the plaster hardens, prop the base of a large tree branch upright in the bucket. Secure the branch until the plaster hardens (about two days). Place the tree in an attractive planter and cover the base with moss or bark. Have students hang their completed leaf patterns from the branches using string or yarn.

YOU'RE PROBABLY...

Invite students to honor some of their favorite people with this poetry-writing activity. Instruct each student to think of someone he knows well. As the student pictures that person, have him write sentences describing what he thinks his person is doing, saying, wearing, or thinking at that moment. Then direct him to format his sentences into poetry using the sample shown as a guide. Mount each poem on construction paper along with a photo or illustration of the person in the poem.

You're probably...
    watching the baseball game
    tonight on TV,
    holding on to your lucky baseball
    as you yell at the ump.
You're probably...
    wondering why balls are strikes
    and whether or not our team will win.
And I'm thinking of you.

PARTICIPATION POETRY

Everyone contributes to this class poem idea! Cut a three-foot length of bulletin board paper and draw a five-inch border around all four edges. Write an unfinished phrase at the top of the inside section. Keep the phrase simple, such as "Fall is…," "Love is…," "Science is…," or "Halloween is…." At his desk, have each student write several endings to the phrase. Let students share their endings; then have each student select his favorite to write under the title on the large paper. Next have your students decorate the border around the poem with artwork that illustrates the topic. For example, if the poem starts with "Fall is…," then have each student make a leaf rubbing, cut it out, and glue it to the border. Display the completed class poem in the hall for others to enjoy.

Fall is...

leaf dust in your nose.
raking, raking, raking, and
    raking!
shorter days and longer nights.
hot chocolate burning your
    tongue.
kicking leaves as you walk down
    the sidewalk.
tumbling into a pile of leaves
    with Spot.
football games on Monday
    nights.
time for a new jacket!
relief from summer's heat!

ALPHABET POEMS

Enhance dictionary skills and improve students' vocabulary by creating alphabet poems. Instruct each student to pick a letter of the alphabet; then have him use a dictionary to make a list of nouns, verbs, and adjectives beginning with that letter. Next have him use these words to create sentences that personify the letter by describing it and the things that it does or says (see the sample). Once the student has organized his edited sentences into a poem, have him write a final copy on a sheet of paper. To embellish the poem, have the student glue a spray-painted pasta letter at the beginning of each word that starts with that letter. Mount each poem—along with a large cutout of its letter—on a bulletin board as shown.

COOKING UP A POT OF POETRY

A was Angry. She Argued.
She Annoyed Another letter.
She even set her Adobe Ablaze.
A Announced,
"This is Absurd, Abysmal!"
An Acrobatic Attorney Accompanied
Her to court as she Admitted,
"I Always Act Abominably in Autumn!"

TWO-VOICE POEMS

Instruct each student to select two characters—animate or inanimate—that have something to say to each other. Suggest real-life or make-believe partners such as the sun and the moon, a student and a teacher, a predator and its prey, or an addition and a subtraction problem. As the student writes her poem, have her add emphasis by writing each voice in a different color of pen or with different print on different lines. Finally instruct the student to read her poem with a partner so that the audience will hear the two separate voices.

HEY, CAT!

what?

I'VE WATCHED YOU CLAW THE
FURNITURE AND HISS AT THE
MAILMAN AND SLEEP AWAY
YOUR DAY. WHY?

why not?

I read "The Owl And The Pussycat" and...

How can your students get to know poetry? By reading lots of it, of course. Post a new and different poem on the board or overhead each day during your unit. Instruct each student to consider each poem by responding to one of the following incomplete sentences. Have students write their responses in their journals. At the end of the unit, have students share their responses. Remind students that their responses will be as varied as the poems you present and that differences of opinion are okay.

Possible journal starters
The first thing I thought of when I heard this poem was…
This poem made me wonder…
I didn't understand…
I liked how the poet…
This poem made me feel…
My favorite phrase was…
This poem reminded me of…
I wish this poem…

CLOUDS...

giant ships in the sky

as white and fluffy as cotton balls

swimming their way through a sea of blue

by Jamison

HANGING OUT WITH POETRY

If your students hang out with poetry, it won't be long till they become familiar with *figures of speech.* Provide students with practice in recognizing similes, metaphors, and personification by completing the reproducible on page 56. Then have each student put these figures of speech to use by creating a mobile poem.

To create the mobile, instruct each student to think of an inanimate object. Direct the student to cut out five shapes that represent that object from light-colored paper. On each shape have him write one of the following: the name of the object, a metaphor describing the object, a simile describing the object, a phrase personifying the object, and his name. Have the student use string and tape to connect the cutouts (see the sample). Hang the mobiles from your classroom ceiling.

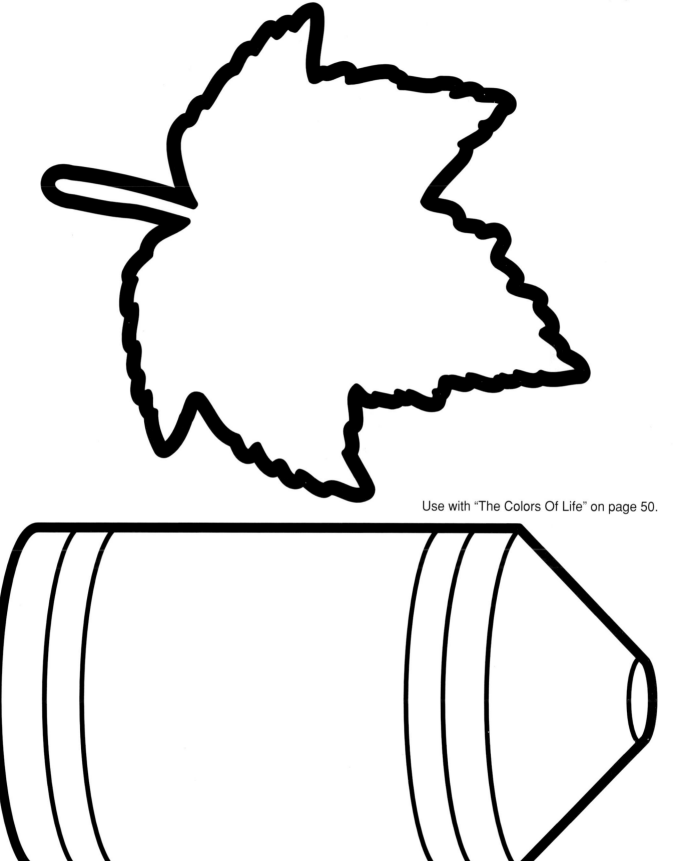

Use with "The Colors Of Life" on page 50.

Name_____ *Figures of speech*

She Was An Ice Cube

Many poets use figures of speech to enrich their poetry. Three common figures of speech are *similes, metaphors,* and *personification.*

A **simile** describes something by saying that it is like another thing. It often uses *like* or *as.* For example: *My face was as red as an apple.*
A **metaphor** describes something by saying that it is another thing (figuratively speaking). For example: *The road is a twisting snake.*
Personification describes a nonhuman object as if it had human characteristics. For example: *The flowers danced in the breeze.*

Directions: Using the definitions above, label each of these sentences with an **S** if it contains a simile, an **M** if it contains a metaphor, or a **P** if it is an example of personification. Underline the figure of speech in each sentence.

_____ 1. The tree branches tapped the windows, asking to be let in.

_____ 2. She was an ice cube after being outside too long.

_____ 3. The car became a bullet as it shot out of the garage.

_____ 4. The small child charged around the store like a bull in a china shop.

_____ 5. The table groaned under the weight of all the food upon it.

_____ 6. When he came in from raking leaves, Sam's nose was like a red cherry.

_____ 7. The spider was a weaver working on his silken web.

_____ 8. The trees looked as tall as New York City skyscrapers.

_____ 9. The waves licked the sandy shores of the beach.

_____10. The stone skipped playfully along the water.

_____11. Janet was as busy as a bee while doing her homework.

_____12. When he became hungry, the baby sounded like a wailing siren.

_____13. The moon was a spotlight shining on the deer in the field.

_____14. Leaves played ring-around-a-rosy in the whirling wind.

_____15. The desert is an oven during the afternoon hours.

Bonus Box: Think of something you saw on the way to school this morning. On the back of this page, write a description of that object using one or more of the figures of speech described above. Then use your description to write a short poem about the object.

©The Education Center, Inc. • *Big Book of Monthly Ideas* • TEC1488 • Key p. 231

56   **Note To The Teacher:** Use with "Hanging Out With Poetry" on page 54.

Thumbs Up For Thanksgiving!

Creative Classroom Activities For Celebrating "Turkey Day"

Sitting down to enjoy a Thanksgiving meal with family and friends—it's one of the oldest customs on Earth. Celebrate the spirit and simplicity of Thanksgiving with the following creative teaching activities.

by Irving P. Crump and Lynn Tutterow

Before The Pilgrims

Ask any intermediate student to describe the first Thanksgiving and he or she will probably relate the story of the Pilgrims' harsh first year in the New World—and the feast we call the "first" Thanksgiving. But Thanksgiving's roots extend to biblical times. Moses, the leader of the Hebrews, told his people how to celebrate the Feast of the Tabernacles, a celebration much like our Thanksgiving. The ancient Greeks also held thanksgiving celebrations every year after a good harvest.

But for Americans, Thanksgiving commemorates a small group of colonists who journeyed across the Atlantic so they could worship as they pleased. It is a time to give thanks not only for nature's bounty, but also for freedom. Read aloud the First Amendment to the Constitution. Ask students what these basic freedoms mean and why they were so important to our founding fathers. Have students share their thoughts about this amendment in essays titled "The First Amendment: What It Means To Me."

Thank-You Board

Watch this appealing display fill up quickly with tons of thank-yous! Cover a classroom or hallway bulletin board with white paper. Add the title "Thank You!" near the top of the display. Provide a supply of colorful markers and crayons nearby. Get the ball rolling by writing (directly on the paper) the name of someone you wish to thank for a kind deed. Add a comma after the person's name; then express your thankfulness in a brief sentence. Invite other faculty members and students to add to this gigantic thank-you card.

Mrs. Wilson,
Thanks for helping me with my multiplication facts.

Danny

An Easy Bulletin Board? Thanks!

Need a simple bulletin board for the Thanksgiving season? Also need some good writing topics for November? Look no more! Duplicate a copy of the writing activities on page 62 for each student. While students are working on their writings, cut letters to spell "THANKS!" out of large pieces of yellow bulletin board paper or poster board. After each child has written his final copy for each topic he chose and mounted it on a piece of construction paper, divide the class into six groups. Give each group one of the letter cutouts (including the exclamation mark). Have the group color the letter with designs using colorful markers. Post the letters in the middle of a bulletin board; then arrange the students' written work around the letters. Now, thankfully, wasn't that simple? *(For another simple November bulletin board, see "Thank-You Board" on page 58.)*

'Twas The Night Before Thanksgiving...

...And all through your classroom, you'll hear giggles of creative glee with this fun project! Share with students Clement Clarke Moore's famous poem, " 'Twas The Night Before Christmas." Then divide the class into groups and provide each group with a copy of the ballad. Instruct each group to write a new (and shorter) version of the poem titled " 'Twas The Night Before Thanksgiving." Have the groups write their ballads from a turkey's point of view.

Tabletop Turkeys

Create colorful turkey napkin rings to add a festive touch to students' Thanksgiving mealtimes. Begin by collecting enough empty toilet-tissue tubes so that each student has one. Then provide each student with a copy of page 61 (duplicated on tagboard or other sturdy paper if possible), plus a half-sheet (9" x 6") each of red, yellow, orange, and brown construction paper and the other materials listed on page 61. The reproducible gives directions for making one napkin ring. Suggest that each student make at least two to four napkin rings for her Thanksgiving table. Since four turkey bodies can be cut from each toilet-tissue tube, one tube per student will be sufficient.

Share The Spirit

Looking over a delicious, bountiful Thanksgiving spread reminds us not only of how thankful we are, but also that there are many people who are not as fortunate. Use this theme of sharing to motivate your class or grade level to sponsor a schoolwide canned food drive. Plan to begin the drive about two or three weeks before Thanksgiving to allow plenty of time to divvy up responsibilities to students. Be sure to let students make as many decisions as possible about the drive, with you acting as a facilitator. As canned foods come into your classroom, provide students with copies of page 63. Have students use colorful construction paper strips and the graphics on that page to create bands of Thanksgiving greetings to wrap around the tops of the cans.

Bird, Beast, Or Fish?

What was it like being on board the *Mayflower* for 66 long (and probably very boring!) days? Share with students that the children on the ship were not allowed on deck, so there was no room for playing games or running around. To pass the time, they studied their lessons and played quiet games. In one such game, a leader pointed to a player and said, "Bird," "Beast," or "Fish." That player then had to respond with an animal name that matched the category before the leader counted to ten. An animal name could not be repeated. If a player couldn't think of one within ten seconds, he lost and was out of the game. The game grew more difficult as the more common animal names were used.

Play a similar game as a five-minute filler during the Thanksgiving season. Use categories related to topics you're currently studying (for example: "State, state capital, or Canadian province"; "Multiple of 2, multiple of 5, or multiple of 7"; etc.).

Tabletop Turkey

Add a festive touch to your family's Thanksgiving meal with this colorful turkey napkin ring!

Materials: red, yellow, orange, and brown construction paper; ruler; pencil; scissors; glue; toilet-tissue tube; black, felt-tipped marker

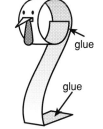

Make the tail:
1. Carefully cut out the eight patterns on the left side of this page.
2. Following the directions on each one, trace the patterns on construction paper. You will make 14 strips in all.
3. Cut out each colored strip.
4. Loop each feather strip over without creasing it. Glue the ends together as shown. Set it aside to dry.
5. Lightly draw a line on the brown body strip, 1/4 inch from the top (as shown on the pattern). Also make a light mark in the middle of this strip where indicated on the pattern. Place the body strip in front of you with the pencil lines showing.
6. Glue the two long orange loops onto the body strip—one on either side of the midpoint pencil mark. The bottom edges of the orange loops should touch the horizontal pencil line. Hold each loop in place a little while to dry.
7. Next glue two long yellow loops, two red loops, two brown loops, two short orange loops, and two short yellow loops—in the order shown.

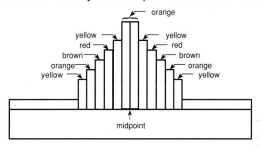

Make the head:
1. Curl one end of the head strip around your finger to make a loop. Glue the loop in place as shown.
2. Add details by cutting pieces of construction paper and gluing them on the head. Use the marker to draw eyes.
3. Measure about 1/2 inch from the other end of the head strip and make a pencil mark. Fold back this end to make a tab.

Complete the project:
1. Measure about 1 inch from one end of the toilet-tissue tube, make a mark, and cut off this section. This is the turkey's body.
2. With its penciled side up, apply a thin layer of glue along the feather strip. Wrap it around the tube, overlapping a little. Hold it in place until the glue dries.
3. Bend the feathers up to look like a turkey's tail.
4. Apply glue to the tab at the bottom of the head as shown. Attach it to the body. Hold it in place until the glue dries.

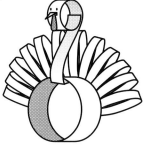

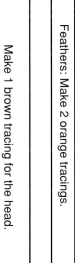

Feathers: Make 2 brown tracings.

Feathers: Make 2 orange tracings.

Feathers: Make 2 yellow tracings.

Feathers: Make 2 yellow tracings.

Feathers: Make 2 red tracings.

Feathers: Make 2 orange tracings.

Make 1 brown tracing for the head.

Make 1 brown tracing for the body.

1/4 inch

midpoint

©The Education Center, Inc. • *Big Book of Monthly Ideas* • TEC1488

Note To The Teacher: See "Tabletop Turkeys" on page 60 for helpful information on preparing for this art activity.   61

62

Thank You! Thank You! Thank You!

Thank you very much! I appreciate what you did! I'm very grateful! Thanks a lot! No matter how you say it, telling someone "thank you"—for whatever reason—is simply good manners and takes little time or effort.

Read the topics below. Choose three to write about. When you're finished, have a friend proofread each completed writing for you. Then rewrite all three in your very best cursive handwriting, each on a separate sheet of paper.

And...thank you!

- Did Grandma send you a crisp $10 bill on your last birthday? Or perhaps Uncle Pete gave you the latest book by your favorite author. Did you, by chance, forget to write a thank-you note? (It happens!) But it's never too late to express thanks to someone. Write a thank-you note to someone who's given you a gift in the recent past, and whom you've forgotten to thank properly. Begin with an apology for taking so long to write.

- Is there a special coach, Sunday school teacher, Scout leader, or other adult in your life whom you really look up to? Write that person a thank-you letter, describing why you appreciate him or her.

- What famous person would you like to say "thank you" to? An inventor? An entertainer? A sports hero? Write a letter to that person that includes several reasons why you are thanking him or her.

- When accepting special awards, entertainers are sometimes completely surprised and have a difficult time expressing their thanks. Others prepare their acceptance speeches ahead of time—just in case they win! What special award would you like to win? Write a brief acceptance speech that expresses your gratitude.

- Have you ever been thankful for something...but then later changed your mind? Write about this experience.

- Have you ever seen a "Thank You For Not Smoking" sign? In what places would you like to see similar signs? Perhaps a "Thank You For Not Littering" sign on your street? Make a list (or draw pictures) of five "Thank You For Not..." signs you would love to see.

©The Education Center, Inc. • *Big Book of Monthly Ideas* • TEC1488

Note To The Teacher: Use with "An Easy Bulletin Board? Thanks!" on page 59.

ABCDEFGHIJKLM
NOPQRSTUVWXYZ

We Give Thanks

Note To The Teacher: See "Share The Spirit" on page 60 for suggestions on using this page of graphics.

Booking A Trip
Reading Activities For Celebrating National Children's Book Week

Make plans now to cruise through National Children's Book Week in November with the help of the following creative activities. Use these terrific ideas—each designed to give students an unsinkable desire to enjoy reading—together as a thematic unit that helps you sail through Book Week. Or pull individual ideas anytime you want to keep students' interest in reading afloat!

by Simone Lepine and Christine Thuman

Ship's Manifest

Booking A Trip

Around The World!

Step Aside, Samsonite®!

Create this colorful bulletin board that serves as the centerpiece of your reading activities! Center a world map on a large board. Enlarge, color, and cut out the cruise ship pattern on page 69 to add to the board as shown. Punch out paper circles with a hole puncher. Then write each student's initials on a punched-out circle and glue it to the top of a pushpin. Store the pins on the board by pushing them in along the border of the map. Instruct each student to cut out a large suitcase shape from a 9" x 12" sheet of colored paper and to add details such as handles and pockets. Post the suitcases around the map.

Duplicate a supply of the Book Week Travel Tags on page 70 and cut them out. Store them in a basket near the bulletin board. Each time a student completes a Book Week activity, instruct her to fill out one tag with her name, the name of the activity, and her destination (a city and country somewhere in the world). To ensure that she travels the world, instruct her to select a different city and continent for each activity. After pasting her tag onto her suitcase, have her move her pushpin to that city on the map. By the end of the unit, she will have collected a tag for each activity and "booked" a trip around the world!

Around The World

Sean's Scrapbook

Mementos

Like anyone traveling on a trip, it is fun for students to keep mementos of each place visited. Have your students create scrapbooks in which to keep each activity they complete during your Book Week celebration. Have each student staple 10–15 sheets of paper together between two construction paper covers. Duplicate the cruise ship pattern on page 69 for each student. Have the student cut out the ship, color it, and paste it to the cover of his scrapbook. Instruct each student to glue any mementos or patterns from his Book Week activities to the inside pages of his scrapbook. At the end of the unit, each student will have a keepsake to help him recall the many things he learned on his cruise through Book Week!

The Best Christmas Pageant Ever
Roll Of Thunder, Hear My Cry
Summer Of The Monkeys
The Lion, The Witch, And The Wardrobe
Little House On The Prairie
Maniac Magee
Number The Stars
Charlotte's Web
Dear Mr. Henshaw
Sounder

The Test Of Time

Some books are so good that they become favorites to several generations of readers. Find out if this is true by having your students create a Best-Sellers List. Instruct your students to survey the adults in their lives to discover their top three favorite children's books. Complete the survey by having students question school faculty and staff and adding their votes to the count. Tally the results and rank them to create a list of these adults' top ten favorite children's books. Next have your pupils survey each student in the other intermediate classes to discover his top three favorite children's books. Again rank the results to reveal the top ten books. Compare these two lists. Are any book titles listed on both top ten lists?

Take this activity one step further by having students create a bar graph of one of the top ten lists. Post this graph in the school lobby for everyone to see. Have students copy the completed graph in their scrapbooks.

Top Ten

Ticket To The Future

Do you often hear students complain that they can't find a good book to read? Here's a motivating activity to help them make better reading choices. Duplicate page 71 for each child. Explain that the survey will help each student recognize his interests. Have each student complete the survey; then discuss each of the survey items and ask students to explain their choices. List the books that students noted as their favorites on the board.

Next group students according to the types of books they like to read (mystery, humor, etc.). Have students in each group share the names of books from the group's category that they would recommend to each other. Designate one child from each group to add these titles to the list on the board. Have each student look at this list—and the one generated in "The Test Of Time" activity on page 65—to select three titles he'd like to read. Instruct each student to write these three titles on his "Ticket To The Future" pattern (bottom half of page 71). Have the student cut out his ticket and glue it inside his scrapbook. Each time the student reads one of these books, have him bring his scrapbook to you so that you can stamp the space under the book's title.

Reading Survey		
Mystery	Humor	Historic Fiction
Adventure	Fantasy	Biograph

Book Title Alphabet

Sometimes all it takes to spark interest in new books is to give students a chance to browse the shelves. Add some purpose to your browsing by informing students that they will be creating a Book Title Alphabet. Schedule a visit to the media center. Have each student bring a pencil and a notebook with the letters of the alphabet listed down the side of one sheet of paper. Instruct each student to search the shelves to locate a book title starting with each letter of the alphabet. Remind students that the words *the, a,* and *an* do not count as the beginning of a title, and that the card catalog and the browser are off-limits in this activity! Have each student attach his list of titles, along with authors, to a page in his scrapbook. Then have him draw a star by any book that looks like it might be interesting to read in the future. Reward each student who completes this list with a bookmark.

Snowball Fight

Introduce your students to a variety of authors while releasing some pent-up energy! Gather a supply of intermediate-level books that each have a short biography about the author (one for every two students). For each book, write the author's name on one piece of paper and the book's title on another piece. Wad up each piece of paper and place it in a bag. Have each student pick one of the wadded pieces out of the bag. Then let your class have a 30-second "snowball" fight by throwing the wads of paper at one another in the room. At the end of the fight, make sure each student has one piece of paper. Instruct each student to open her paper to discover if she has an author or a book title; then direct each student to locate the person who holds the matching book title or author.

Once two students think they have found the correct author/title match, instruct them to come to you. If they do not have the correct match, have them go back and look for their rightful partners. Give each correct pair a copy of its book along with instructions to read about the author. Have each student in the pair write down five facts about her author in her scrapbook. Invite each pair to share facts about its author with the class.

Pass the mysteries, please.

I sure would like a second helping of historical fiction!

Books Are Good For You

Evaluating books was never so delicious! Duplicate a supply of the book nutrition label on page 72. Cut out each label and paste it to a large index card. Each time a student reads a new book from your classroom library, have him fill out one of the labels. Instruct him to write a short summary of the story on the back of the index card and then place the completed card inside the book. The next time another student wants to know if a book is interesting, he has only to read his peer's review along with the book jacket's description. Instruct each student to fill out a duplicate label and staple the top edge of it into his scrapbook.

Novel Nutrition Facts

Title: *Charlotte's Web*
Author: *E. B. White*

Rating (1–10: 1 = "poor," 10 = "fantastic"): 10
Reasons For Rating: *A real page-turner!*

Amount Per Book	% Value
Fantasy	
Historical Fiction	50
Humor	
Mystery	50
Realistic Fiction	
Science Fiction	
Other:	

INGREDIENTS: Write a story summary on the back.
Main Character(s):
Charlotte the spider, Wilbur the pig, Fern the little girl
Setting: *a farm*

To Be Or Not To Be...
A Student Reader

Harness the dramatic energies of your pupils by having them create story tapes for younger students. Select several outstanding picture books to tape-record. Divide your class into groups of two to four, depending on the number of speaking parts required by the story. Give each group one of the books to read aloud. Encourage students to use dramatic voices and sound effects while reading the book. Then have each group, in turn, record its story on tape. Place each tape with a copy of the book in a large plastic bag; then rotate these book/tape sets among the primary classes for their listening enjoyment. Younger students will be thrilled to hear the big kids speaking, and the primary teachers will appreciate having new selections to use in their listening libraries.

Open Up Your World With Books

Chances are that many of your students have not yet traveled to faraway countries. However, with the growing number of multicultural books, they can learn about different cultures without leaving their desks! Divide your class into six groups. Assign one of the following continents to each group: Europe, North America, South America, Africa, Australia, Asia. Instruct each group to browse in the library to find trade books, folktales, or informational books about countries located within its continent. Next have each group member select a different country from his group's continent and a library book based or set in it. Instruct the student to read his book and complete the postcard pattern on page 72. Then have him flip the card to the blank side and draw a picture that represents something about his book's country.

To display these postcards, enlarge the pattern on page 73 onto poster board. Color and cut it out. Cut the completed world in half; then arrange it on a board as shown. Attach the postcards to the board with pushpins. Invite students to browse through the worldly display of informational book evaluations.

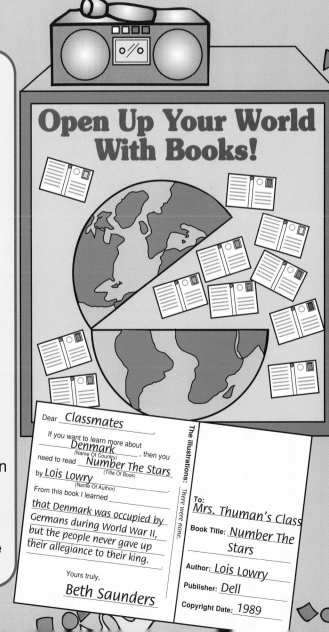

Open Up Your World With Books!

Dear __Classmates__

If you want to learn more about __Denmark__ (Name Of Country), then you need to read __Number The stars__ (Title Of Book) by __Lois Lowry__ (Name Of Author)

From this book I learned __that Denmark was occupied by Germans during World War II, but the people never gave up their allegiance to their king.__

Yours truly,
__Beth Saunders__

The illustrations: There were none.

To: __Mrs. Thuman's Class__

Book Title: __Number The stars__

Author: __Lois Lowry__

Publisher: __Dell__

Copyright Date: __1989__

Pattern

Use this pattern with "Step Aside, Samsonite®!" on page 64 and "Mementos" on page 65.

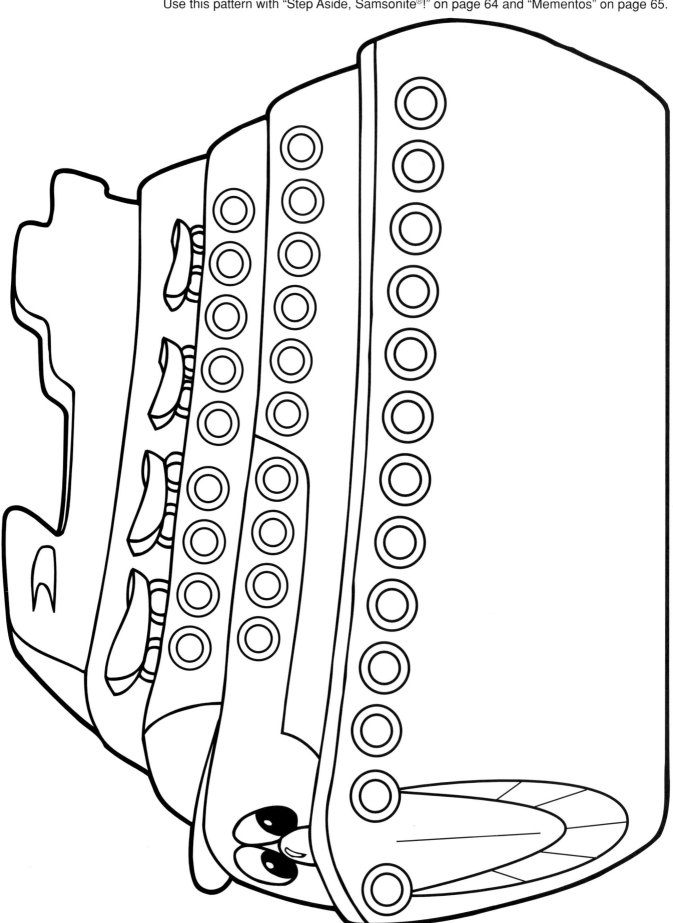

Patterns

Use with "Step Aside, Samsonite®!" on page 64.

Destination

Activity

Student

Destination

Activity

Student

Destination

Activity

Student

Destination

Activity

Student

Destination

Activity

Student

Destination

Activity

Student

Destination

Activity

Student

Name_____ *Reading survey*

Ticket To The Future

Reading definitely takes you to places you have never been! Complete the survey below to discover the types of books that interest you. Then fill out your "Ticket To The Future" with the titles of three interesting books you would like to read. After reading each book, have your teacher stamp the space below the book's title. Bon voyage!

Reading Survey
Complete the statements below. You may check more than one answer.

1. I like to read books that belong to the following group(s):
   _____ Mystery   _____ Biographical
   _____ Science Fiction   _____ Poetry
   _____ Humor   _____ Fantasy
   _____ Historical Fiction   _____ Other: _____
   _____ Informational

2. I like books in which the main characters are:
   _____ Girls
   _____ Boys
   _____ Animals
   _____ Adults
   _____ Other: _____

3. I like to read books that are:
   _____ Really long
   _____ Short
   _____ Collections of short stories

4. Hobbies and/or interests of mine are _____
   _____

5. My favorite book is _____
   I like this book because _____
   _____

Ticket To The Future Admit One _____ Student Name	TITLE STAMP	TITLE STAMP	TITLE STAMP

©The Education Center, Inc. • *Big Book of Monthly Ideas* • TEC1488

Note To The Teacher: Use this page with "Ticket To The Future" on page 66.

71

Patterns

Use the book nutrition label with "Books Are Good For You" on page 67. Use the postcard pattern with "Open Up Your World With Books" on page 68.

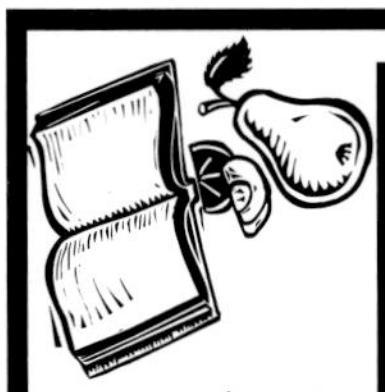

Novel Nutrition Facts

Title: _____

Author: _____

Rating (1–10: 1 = "poor," 10 = "fantastic"): _____

Reasons For Rating: _____

Amount Per Book   % Value

Fantasy _____

Historical Fiction _____

Humor _____

Mystery _____

Realistic Fiction _____

Science Fiction _____

Other: _____

INGREDIENTS: Write a story summary on the back.

Main Character(s): _____

Setting: _____

Dear _____,

   If you want to learn more about

_____, then you

(Name Of Country)

need to read _____

(Title Of Book)

by _____.

(Name Of Author)

From this book I learned _____

_____

_____

_____

_____.

      Yours truly,

_____

The illustrations:

_____

To: _____

Book Title: _____

_____

Author: _____

Publisher: _____

Copyright Date: _____

Geography Gems

Creative Activities To Improve Geography Skills

Tired of digging in your files for a fresh, new way to sharpen geography skills? Then take a closer look at this treasure trove of geography activities—perfect for National Geography Awareness Week (usually the third full week in November) or anytime you want to improve students' geographical know-how.

by Patricia Twohey

> Travel six steps north. Take four steps northeast. Turn to the east.
>
> Take two steps toward the pencil sharpener. Go straight past the third desk. Stop near the math center.

X Marks The Spot!

Keep your students on their directional toes with this fun location game. Mount posters labeled with the *cardinal directions* (north, south, east, and west) on appropriate walls in your classroom or gym. Review *absolute directions* (north, southeast, west, etc.) and *relative directions* (near, next to, etc.) with students.

Begin by choosing one student to be the *Locator*. Instruct the Locator to turn around and hide her eyes while the rest of the class scatters around the playing area. Call out, "Freeze location!" Each student should stop moving and remain in one spot. Silently select a student to be *Student X* and another student to be the *Navigator*. Direct the Navigator to give directions to the Locator as to the identity/location of Student X, without using student names or giving feedback about the correctness of the Locator's movements. Instruct the Locator to follow the Navigator's directions until she thinks she has located Student X. If the student she points out is Student X, the round ends and another begins with different students in the key roles. If the Locator cannot correctly identify Student X after three guesses, her turn ends; then the Navigator reveals the identity of Student X and a new round begins.

World Geography Datelines

For a world geography activity that also familiarizes students with current events, post a large world map at a center. Also place a supply of old newspapers, an atlas, glue, construction paper, pushpins, and a pair of scissors at the center. During free time, a student clips a dateline from a newspaper; then he glues it to a small strip of construction paper. Finally he uses an atlas to find the location of the dateline on the world map. When he locates the city/country, he pins the dateline to its location on the map. Challenge your class to search for datelines that aren't yet pinned on the map.

Mental Maps

Do your students know that they always carry a set of maps in their heads wherever they go? These mental maps help them to get around the school grounds as well as find their sock drawers each morning. Have students brainstorm a list of the mental maps that help them daily. For example, they each have mental maps that help them find the bathroom from the classroom and navigate their own bedrooms in the dark. Instruct each student to select a different mental map to illustrate on a cloud-shaped cutout. Arrange these illustrations on a bulletin board around a large head cutout as shown.

Aarg! I know Africa goes here somewhere!

Mapmaker, Mapmaker, Make Me A Map

Test the accuracy of your students' global mental maps with this activity. Give each student a large sheet of construction paper. Instruct the student to make a map of the world by tearing the paper into shapes to form the seven continents. Have the student glue his continents in their correct positions on another sheet of paper; then have him label the continents and oceans on the map. After assessing your students' knowledge of the position and location of the continents and oceans, save the maps. Then repeat this exercise later in the year to see if your students' mental maps have improved.

Geography Hide-'N'-Seek

Employ a little mystery to reinforce the use of latitude and longitude. Duplicate the map on page 80 for each student. Using a hole puncher, punch circles from heavy paper; then give about 20 to each student. Have one student, the *Hider,* come to the front of the class with his map and place a marker on a latitude/longitude intersection on his map, hiding the location from the class's view. Instruct the other students—the *Seekers*—to take turns guessing the location by calling out latitude/longitude coordinates. Help students keep track of coordinates that have been guessed by writing them on the board and having students mark them on their maps. Instruct the Hider to reveal any parts of the guess that are correct. For example, if the hidden location is 45°N/60°E and a Seeker guesses, "15°S/30°E," the Hider can reply, "One of the directions you named [E] is correct." The next Seeker takes note of that hint and guesses, "45°N/45°E." Since both directions and the latitude degree are correct, the Hider replies, "Both of the directions and the latitude are correct." Play continues until the hidden location is identified. The first Seeker to identify the location becomes the Hider for the next round.

What If I Lived There?

Take students on a spin around the world to test their critical-thinking skills. Set your class globe on a table and gently spin it. In turn, have each student stop the spinning globe with one finger. If the student's finger doesn't land on water or his own home region, have him make the following predictions about the spot on the globe he has pinpointed:

- What kinds of land, climate, and seasons does this region have?
- What kinds of people inhabit this region of the world?
- What kinds of clothes do the people wear? What kinds of food do they eat?
- What kinds of animals inhabit this region?
- How do people use the land and water in this region?
- How have people adapted to or changed the environment so that they can live comfortably in this region?

Invite students to share and discuss their predictions. Then have each student research his location and compare his findings with his predictions. Finally ask students to draw some conclusions about regions and people based on their research and discussions.

Land Regions

A geographic region is defined by its physical and human characteristics. Five distinctive land regions are the *desert, polar, plains, mountain,* and *rain forest* regions. By adapting to the climate, humans can live in all five regions. Divide your class into five teams and assign each team one of the regions. Give each team a three-foot-long sheet of bulletin board paper. Instruct each team to cut the paper into a giant shape that symbolizes its region. Possible shapes include: a giant saguaro cactus for *desert,* an igloo for *polar,* a tornado for *plains,* a craggy mountain for *mountain,* and a tall, canopied tree for *rain forest.* Instruct each group to record facts about its region on the top half of its cutout. In the center of the cutout, have the group list places around the world that are examples of that region. At the bottom of the cutout, have the group list ways that humans adapt to or change the environment in order to live in that region. Invite each group to share its completed project while showing the locations of the sample regions on a world map.

source→stream→silt→tributaries→river→riverbed→
riverbanks→river basin→current→sandbars→canyon→
course→flood→delta→mouth

To Be, Or Not To Be...A River

Which landform has played a key role in transportation, trade, travel, agriculture, and energy? The *river,* of course. And for these reasons people have often settled along rivers. Small or great, rivers change the land as they wind their way along. Introduce your students to rivers by role-playing the life of a river. Duplicate "The River Runs" on page 79 for each student. This skit is designed for 20 to 30 students. Establish the teacher or a student as the narrator. Assign the remaining parts based on your class size and the number of students suggested. To prompt students as they act, write the sequence shown above on the board.

How Far Is It?

Students can't go the distance in using maps until they know how to use a map scale. Duplicate "How Far Is It?" on page 82 for each student to complete as practice on this important skill. After students complete the reproducible, collect maps that use different scales. Divide the class into cooperative groups and give each group one map. Instruct each group to label a sheet of paper with the title of the map and then write five word problems using the map and its scale. Have the group record its solutions on a separate sheet of paper labeled with the title of the map. Collect the maps, problems, and solutions. Give each group a different map and set of matching word problems to solve. Rotate the maps and problems until each group has seen every map. Check the answers as a class.

Geography Bee

Test your students' geographic know-how by conducting a Geography Bee. Begin by compiling a list of questions and answers, using resource books such as *Everything Is Somewhere: The Geography Quiz Book* by Jack McClintock and David Helgren, Ph.D. (William Morrow & Co., Inc.). Or have students use almanacs and other books to devise their own questions. For a class of 25 students, collect about 150 questions. Add nine questions for every extra student after that. Type the questions and answers on paper. Set two tables with two chairs each at the front of the class.

Conduct the bee in three rounds.

Round 1: Invite the first four students to come to the tables with papers and pencils. Ask the first question, marking it off your list as you do. Allow two minutes for the contestants to write their answers. Call time and ask each contestant to give his answer; then give the correct answer. Award one point to each contestant who gave the correct response. After asking three questions, have four different students come to the tables. Continue play until all students have answered three questions. Any child who gave at least two correct answers during Round 1 moves on to Round 2.
Round 2: Ask three questions of each contestant group as before. Students with at least two correct answers move on to Round 3.
Round 3: Play continues as before. If you need to eliminate contestants at a faster rate, require them to answer all three questions correctly.

Call an end to the bee when there are only three contestants left. Reward all students for their participation, with special honors to the three finalists.

The River Runs

Follow your teacher's directions to conduct this river skit.

Narrator: *(Reading slowly and pausing to allow the students time to act out the boldfaced words)*

The **source,** or beginning, of many rivers is in the mountains, where collected rain, melting snow, or springwaters form a **stream.** This stream flows downhill—carrying soil, or **silt,** and rock along with it while it carves out a path. Other rivers and streams, called **tributaries** or branches, join it and make it larger. It is now called a **river.**

The bottom of the river is called the **bed**. The sides are called the **banks**. The land area from which all of this water comes is called the **river basin.**

At times—when the land is flat—the river **current** slows down and drops some of the sand and rocks it has been carrying. These deposits can form **sandbars,** or small islands, in the river. Over long periods of time, swift river currents can erode the soil and rock of the riverbed. This erosion forms a **canyon.**

The river's path, or **course,** can sometimes shift and change directions, wandering across the land. Where riverbanks are low or when there is a lot of rain, the river will **flood** the land that surrounds it.

As a river approaches the sea, it drops its silt and forms a wide area of fertile, built-up land called a **delta.** This is the river's **mouth,** where it reaches its final destination, the sea.

Key Word	Actions By Student(s)
Source	One student stands on a table or counter as a mountain.
Stream	A new student climbs up next to the source and slowly climbs down. This student will lead the river all the way to the mouth. She waves a blue streamer in each hand.
Silt	Two students join the stream, tumbling behind it.
Tributaries	Two students come from different directions and join up behind the original stream. They each hold streamers in their hands.
River	The stream and tributary students now make up the river and continue moving in a line together.
Riverbed	Two new students lie on the floor as the stream passes by.
Riverbanks	Two new students on each side of the riverbed (four students in all) kneel on the floor, arms out to their sides.
River Basin	Four new students fan out in a semicircle from the sides of the river to form the riverbed.
Current	The river students continue to walk slowly.
Sandbars	One of the silt students deposits himself on the floor and no longer follows the river.
Canyon	Two new students on each side of the river (four new students in all) stand on chairs with arms outstretched.
Course	The river students slowly zigzag along between the canyon walls.
Flood	Two of the river students walk off to the sides waving arms in all directions, then rejoin the main river student(s).
Delta	Three new students form a triangle, arms outstretched. The remaining silt student sits down and no longer follows the river.
Mouth	Two students stand with hands on hips to indicate the sea. The river students walk past the delta and sea students.

Note To The Teacher: Use this page with "To Be, Or Not To Be…A River" on page 77. You will need one sturdy table or counter; four chairs; and a pair of three-foot-long, light blue crepe paper streamers for each *river* student (optional).

Map

Use with "Geography Hide-'N'-Seek" on page 76. Have each student color the equator red and the prime meridian green.

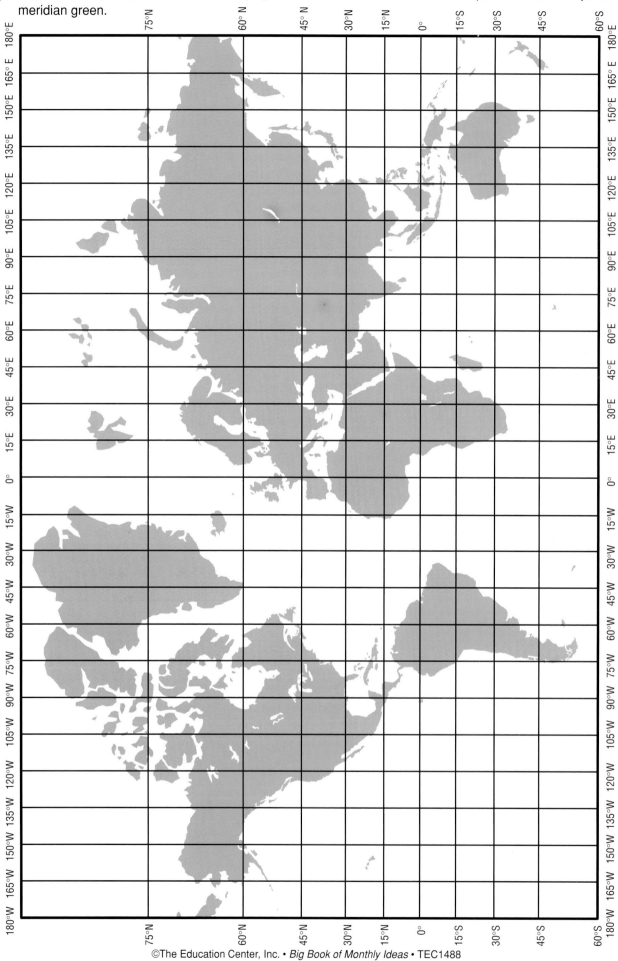

Name _____

U.S. regions

Piecing It Together

Our great nation is huge and is made up of several different regions. Pieced together these regions make up one whole country! Color the key to assign a different color to each region. Then use a resource book or your textbook to help you color each state according to the region in which it's located.

When you've finished coloring the map, number a sheet of paper 1–50. Write the name of each state and its capital on the paper, using the map as your guide.

Key

Color	Region
☐	New England States
☐	Middle Atlantic States
☐	Southeast States
☐	Great Lakes States
☐	Southwest States
☐	Plains States
☐	Mountain States
☐	Pacific States

Not to Scale

Bonus Box: Add each state's postal abbreviation to the list of state names and capitals.

©The Education Center, Inc. • *Big Book of Monthly Ideas* • TEC1488 • Key p. 231

Note To The Teacher: Students will need an atlas or a U.S. map and colored pencils or crayons.

81

How Far Is It?

Calculating the distance between places on a map is easy if you know how to use the scale. The steps below explain how.

1. Mark a piece of paper to show the distance between the two points (Step 1).
2. Place the paper along the map's scale. Line up the left mark with the zero on the scale (Step 2).
3. If the map scale is shorter than the distance, mark on the paper the endpoint of the scale and the distance it represents. Then line up that endpoint with the zero on the scale (Step 3). Estimate the additional distance according to the scale. Add the two distances to find the total.

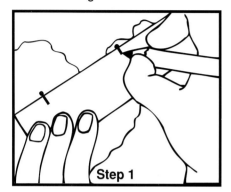
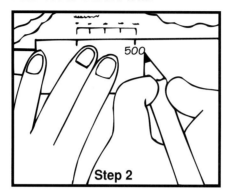
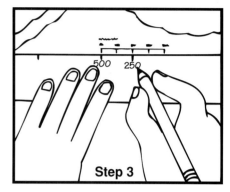

Directions: Use a ruler to draw straight lines connecting the points on the map in ABC order. Use the map scale to find the distance between each two cities (the distance between city A and city B, between city B and city C, between city C and city D, etc.). You may use either miles or kilometers. Write the distance between two points on the line that connects them. The first one is done for you.

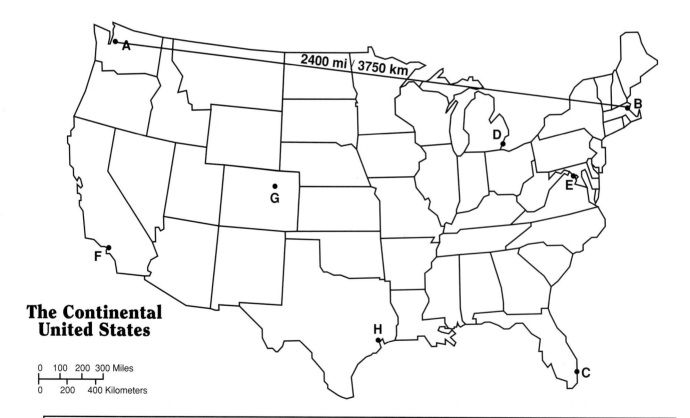

Bonus Box: Each of the points on this map stands for an important city. Compare the map to an atlas. Identify each city by its location on the map. Write your guesses on the back of this page.

©The Education Center, Inc. • *Big Book of Monthly Ideas* • TEC1488 • Key p. 231

Note To The Teacher: Use this page with "How Far Is It?" on page 78. Each student will need a ruler and an atlas or a U.S. map to complete the activity.

DECEMBER

The Most Wonderful Time!

Teaching Ideas For Celebrating The Christmas Season

Like the song says, "It's the most wonderful time of the year!" So celebrate with a host of cross-curricular activities—all designed to keep your excited elves busy and motivated during those long, preholiday school days.

by Chris Christensen

The 12 Days *Before* Christmas

Generate anticipation for the upcoming holiday season with this fun countdown-calendar activity. About 15 school days before the first day of your holiday vacation, make a master copy of the tree pattern on page 89; then copy it on green construction paper for each child. Have each student carefully cut around the dashed line of each ornament on his tree (leaving the solid line at the top intact) and then cut out the tree. Invite students to decorate their trees with glitter, yarn, buttons, or other materials. In addition, provide each student with 12 gummed stars to close the ornament flaps.

Next program your master copy of the pattern with 12 activities for students to complete during the 12 days preceding the holiday. Activities can include writing topics, math problems/puzzles, vocabulary exercises, research questions—anything that will keep students motivated and on-task during these hectic days.

On the 12th day before your holiday vacation begins, have each student align a copy of the programmed tree under his green tree; then have him staple the two together. Direct students to open the flap for ornament 12 and complete its activity. Continue with an ornament per day, counting down to the final school day before the holidays.

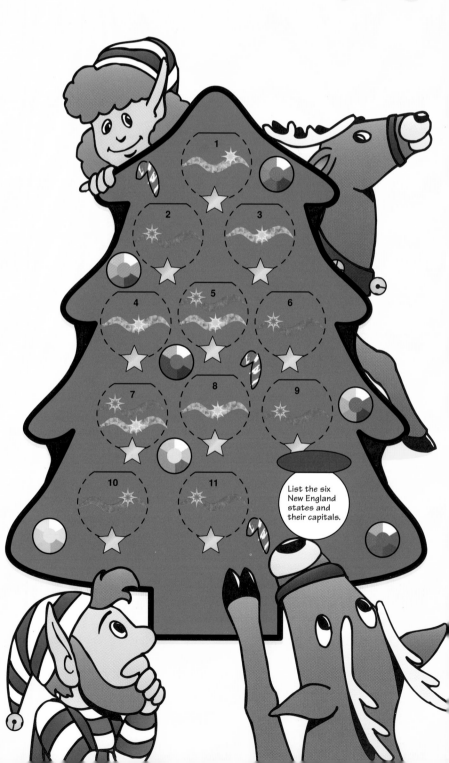

List the six New England states and their capitals.

84

Reindeer Treats

During this time of giving and sharing, have your little dears make these treats for Santa's reindeer—then present the snack to a class of younger children. Divide students into groups of five. Have each group be responsible for obtaining its ingredients and other materials needed.

Reindeer Treats

Ingredients needed (for each group of five):
2 cups unflavored oatmeal
2 cups bran cereal
2 cups shredded coconut
2 cups raisins
2 cups Grape-Nuts®

Other materials needed:
large bowl for mixing
large mixing spoon
5 plastic, zippered bags (sandwich size)
5 copies of poem on page 90
5 lengths of ribbon

Directions:
1. Pour all of the ingredients in a large bowl and mix.
2. Fill each zippered bag with the mixture (about 2 cups).
3. Color and cut out a poem for each bag.
4. Punch a hole in the top middle of each bag and at the dot at the top of the poem.
5. Tie a poem to each bag with ribbon.

While each group completes the first two steps in the directions, distribute copies of the poem on page 90, one per bag. When all of the treat bags are ready, have your students present them to a kindergarten or first-grade class.

Home For The Holidays

Discuss with students the many sights, sounds, tastes, and smells that they experience during the holiday season. Then have them work independently to make these creative-writing shape booklets. First provide each student with a white, construction-paper copy of the house pattern on page 91. Instruct each student to personalize the house with her family name, then add her favorite decorations: candles in windows, strings of colorful lights, wreaths, etc. Next have each student cut around the bold outline of the house, creating the cover of her "At My Home" holiday booklet.

Every day for several days provide each student with a blank sheet of duplicating paper. First have the student trace her cover on top of the sheet; then have her illustrate a holiday favorite (see the samples) on the top half of the shape. On the bottom half, have the student write a paragraph telling why that particular item is so special. After completing six or seven pages, have each student cut out the house tracings and combine them with her cover to create a take-home booklet of holiday favorites.

Decorate-The-Tree Game

This simple game is sure to keep the holiday spirit alive in your classroom. Provide each student with a copy of the reproducible game on page 92 and a regular paper clip. Next divide students into groups of two, three, or four to play the game. Each group will need colored pencils, crayons, or colored markers. Direct students to use a paper clip under a pencil tip as a spinner for the game.

Turn this game into a skill game by requiring that a student spell a word, answer a question, or give the answer for a multiplication fact before he spins the spinner. Or use the game as a party-time activity.

Pasta Trees

This pasta tree is an easy-to-make, fun centerpiece to decorate the family dinner table over the holidays. First provide each student with a 9" x 12" sheet of tagboard. Have each student roll his sheet into a cone shape, then staple and tape it so that it retains its shape. Next have each student trim the bottom of the cone so that it will stand level, creating a Christmas-tree shape.

Have each student paint a small section of his tree with glue, then cover it with a variety of pasta shapes. Each section should dry completely before work begins in another area. After the tree shape has been completely covered with pasta and has dried sufficiently, spray-paint it with silver or gold paint. After allowing a day for drying, spray each tree with a clear, polyurethane finish.

Suggest that students display their trees in inexpensive plastic goblets, with bows tied around the bottom as shown.

Get Cracking!

Another holiday season tradition is the presentation of *The Nutcracker,* the world's most popular ballet. Students often hear the wonderful music of Tchaikovsky without realizing that it is from *The Nutcracker* ballet. Why not develop a center based on this holiday story that dates back over a hundred years ago? Below are suggestions for creating a Nutcracker minicenter for your students. To prepare, ask your students and their parents to help you collect the following items for the center:

- an assortment of nutcracker figures, ornaments, and pictures
- a basketful of various kinds of unshelled nuts
- three to five books that tell the story of the Nutcracker (see the suggestions below)
- 2" x 9" white construction paper strips
- graphing paper
- construction paper scraps

Next reproduce a supply of activity cards (see the bottom half of page 90). Label the cards with the following activities; then display them on a bulletin board near your center.

Activity Card Tasks:

- Nutcracker figures come in a variety of sizes and can look quite different from one another. Select any two nutcrackers or illustrations of nutcrackers at the center. Compare and contrast them in a Venn diagram.
- Sort the nuts in the basket. Make a graph showing the number of each type.
- Make a pattern using the nuts in the basket. Draw your pattern on a paper strip.
- There are different versions of *The Nutcracker.* Choose one of the books in the center and read it with a partner. Then write a review of the book together.
- The ballet version of *The Nutcracker* was based on a story called *The Nutcracker And The King Of Mice.* Using construction paper, create your own version of the Mouse King and display it at the center.
- Write one more chapter for the book describing what you think happened after Marie woke up.
- Write about and illustrate your favorite part of the story.

Write one more chapter for the book describing what you think happened after Marie woke up.

Children's Books Based On *The Nutcracker:*
The Nutcracker Ballet by Vladimir Vagin (Scholastic Inc.)
Stories From The Classical Ballet by Belinda Hollyer (Viking)
Of Sugarplums And Satin Slippers by Violet Verdy (Scholastic Inc.)

Decorative Nests For The Tree

Tradition says that a spiderweb or bird's nest in the Christmas tree is a symbol of good luck for the upcoming year. Help your students have a good new year by making these nest ornaments.

Materials:

a spring-type clothespin, spray-painted red or green
half of a walnut shell
a bit of dried moss
small dried white beans
glue
yarn
red or green construction paper
rubber cement
pencil
two-inch square of white paper
three-inch square of colored paper
hole puncher

Directions:

1. Glue some moss inside the walnut shell half to resemble a nest.
2. Glue three or four beans in the nest. Let dry.
3. Glue the walnut shell to the clip end of the clothespin and let it dry.
4. Copy the poem shown on the white paper square. Add decorations if desired.
5. Rubber-cement the white paper square onto the colored paper square. Punch a hole in the top right corner.
6. Thread the yarn through the wire coil of the clothespin, then through the hole on the card.

This tiny Christmas nest
Brings more than holiday cheer.
It's sure to bring good luck to you
Throughout the coming year!

Half-Moon Ornaments

These easy-to-make ornaments will become lasting mementos of your students' school year. Ask each student to bring to school a current school picture or any recent snapshot—as long as the photo is a close-up facial shot. Provide each student with one-half of a Styrofoam® ball (3-inch diameter), glue, and glitter. Instruct each student to glue the photo, trimming it if necessary, to fit in the middle of the flat side of the Styrofoam® hemisphere. Next have each student brush water-thinned glue on the remainder of the flat side and sprinkle on glitter. After this section has dried, instruct each student to add glue and glitter to the rounded side of the ornament. To complete the project, have each student pin a small bow at the top of her photo.

To make a hanger, have each student tie together the ends of a 10-inch length of ribbon, then pin the knotted end to the back of the ornament. It's then ready to take home and display on the tree!

Reproducible Poem

Use with "Reindeer Treats" on page 85.

Reindeer Treats

Why is it, oh dear Santa Claus,
It always is just you
Who gets the treats on
    Christmas Eve,
And never just a few?

Your faithful reindeer guide the way;
    They're always filled
        With joy!
They also must get hungry
As they visit girls and boys!

So here's a little reindeer treat.
Please feed it to your crew,
And give a kiss to Rudolph,
        Dear Santa,
        I love you!

©The Education Center, Inc.

Reproducible Activity Card

Use with "Get Cracking!" on page 87.

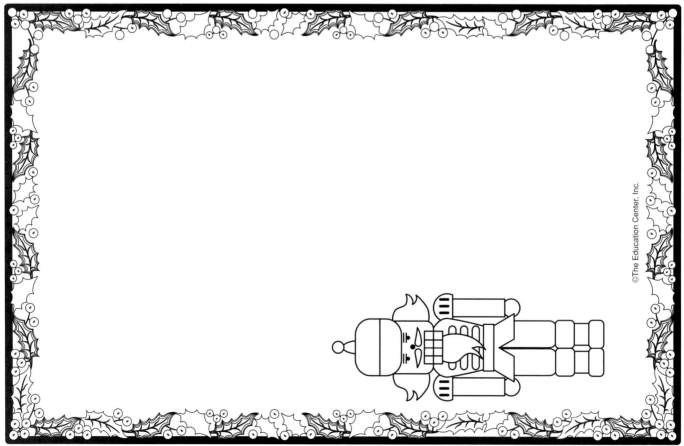

©The Education Center, Inc.

Decorate-The-Tree Game

How fast can *you* decorate a tree? Play this game with one to three friends. The winner is the first person to completely decorate his tree. When it's your turn, use the spinner to find out what to do.

To use the spinner, place the end of a paper clip at its center. Place your pencil inside the paper clip with its point on the center. Flick the paper clip so that it spins around.

Spinner sections:
- Lose a turn.
- Color the tree skirt red.
- Color two ornaments.
- Outline the tree in green.
- Color one garland strip.
- Color one gift.
- Color one ornament.
- Color an opponent's ornament.

Spinner

Name _____ *Spelling, word play*

Christmas Connections

In order for the entire set of lights to come on, each bulb must contain a correct answer! Look at each set of letters below. Each set is really a compound word or pair of words about Christmas. But the two parts of the word pair have been woven together. To solve each one, just separate the two words—without changing the order of any letters. Write each answer in its matching bulb.

Example: **CM**HER**RIST**M**RAYS** = Merry Christmas

1. NISACHOILNATS
2. DREEIERN
3. CACANNEDY
4. SCLANATUAS
5. WGIRAFPT
6. SLRIEDIGEH
7. FRCUAIKTE
8. BGIRENGEARD
9. GEREVEERN
10. BEJILNGLLSE
11. SNILIEGNHTT
12. MITSOTLEE
13. CLAINDGLHET
14. WHOLRELATYH
15. FAREMUINLIYON
16. COCUTOKITEER
17. FSLANOKEW
18. MUCHOSIRIC

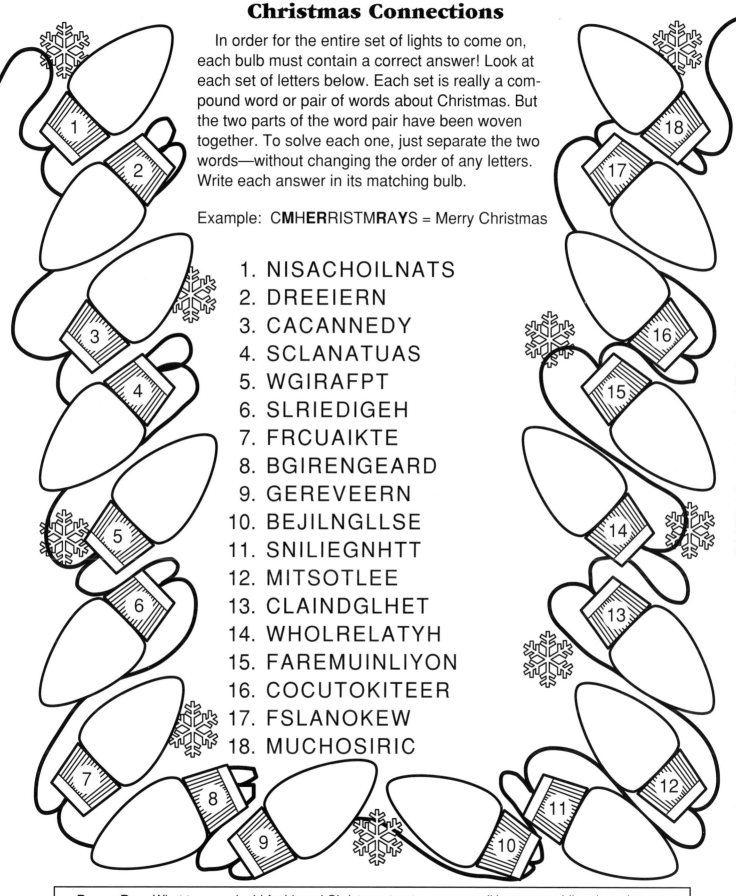

Bonus Box: What two-word, old-fashioned Christmas treat can you spell by unscrambling these letters: D I P G U L P M U N D ?

©The Education Center, Inc. • *Big Book of Monthly Ideas* • TEC1488 • Key p. 231   93

Eight Nights, Eight Lights
Sharing The Rich Tradition Of Hanukkah

Hanukkah is one of the happiest of times for Jewish families. This eight-day holiday—also called the Festival Of Lights—includes games, songs, stories, gifts, and the lighting of a special candelabra called the *menorah*. Bring this 2,400-year-old tradition into your classroom with the following creative teaching suggestions.

by Paula Holdren

A Brief History Of Hanukkah

When Jewish families gather to celebrate Hanukkah, they commemorate a time more than 2,000 years ago when their ancestors were forbidden to observe the Sabbath. The city of Jerusalem and the Jews' beloved temple were taken over by the Syrians, and many holy items were broken or destroyed. Judah Maccabee and a small group of Jewish farmers rebelled against the Syrians and reclaimed the city and temple. The temple was reconsecrated in a celebration that lasted eight days. Judah decreed that the anniversary of the reconsecration should be celebrated for eight days every year. After cleaning the temple, Judah's companions searched for oil to relight the Eternal Light. There was barely enough oil to last one day. It was lit anyway and miraculously the oil lasted for eight days until new oil arrived. Hanukkah lasts for eight days and reminds Jewish people of this miracle and their ancestors' successful fight for religious freedom.

A Window On Hanukkah

Happiness—with generous doses of fun and games mixed in—best describes Hanukkah. To highlight this special time, decorate a bulletin board to resemble a large, eight-paned window. Use blue paper (representing justice), white borders and windowpane dividers (representing truth), and gold lettering (representing the lamp of Eternal Light). Divide students into eight groups. Assign each group one windowpane of the board. Instruct each group to fill its pane with an item, symbol, or picture that represents the spirit of Hanukkah.

A Window On Hanukkah

Latkes

In Our Own Words

More than likely, many of your students may not know the whos, whats, and whys of Hanukkah. Provide them with an even better understanding by inviting a rabbi or other Jewish citizen of your community to your classroom to share the story of Hanukkah. Ask the visitor(s) to bring personal items, such as menorahs and dreidels, and to recall family traditions that he or she treasures most. Make sure that students have the opportunity to ask lots of questions.

Out Of The Darkness

A menorah is a special type of candelabra with eight candleholders—one for each night of the festival that commemorates the miracle of the sacred oil. A central *shammesh,* or helper candle, is used to light the others. After darkness falls, families gather to light the candles—one the first night, two the second night, and so on until all of the candles are lit.

Times have changed and so have menorahs. In addition to the popular traditional shape, menorahs in various interesting and unique designs are now available. A menorah simply must have eight candleholders plus space for a shammesh, which should be elevated above the others. After viewing traditional menorahs (or pictures), review the two requirements mentioned above. Challenge your students' creativity by having them draw and/or build "new" menorahs. Then brainstorm interesting themes and media to use. Menorahs can take any shape and can be made of any materials. They can be large or small. But most all, they're fun to create!

Easy Menorahs: These paper-plate menorahs will stand tall during the Hanukkah season, or you can attach them to a bulletin board to complement seasonal creative writings.
1. Fold a paper plate in half to serve as the base.
2. Cut four straws in half for candles. Glue or tape four on either side of the plate.
3. Cut one straw a little longer than the rest and secure it in the center as a shammesh.
4. Crumple orange tissue paper into small tufts to represent flames. Stuff the tissue into the top of each straw.

Oil Lamp Menorahs: These bright menorahs make great table centerpieces.
1. Pour olive oil into eight small glass containers, such as baby-food jars.
2. Cut eight 2 1/2-inch lengths of wick.
3. Submerge a wick in each container of oil, leaving about 1/4 inch of wick above the surface.
4. Arrange four containers on either side of a candle (shammesh).

Delightful Dreidels

Jewish people were not allowed to pray or study under Syrian rule. When they secretly gathered to study and pray, they brought along small tops called *dreidels* and began to play with them when soldiers were around. In doing so, they could escape potential punishment.

A dreidel is a four-sided object with a Hebrew letter on each side. The letters are the first letters of the Hebrew words that mean "a great miracle happened there." Have your students follow the directions below to make their own dreidels. Provide each student with a copy of the dreidel game rules on page 98, which also includes the letters needed to complete the dreidel.

Egg-Carton Dreidels: Cut off two sections of a cardboard egg carton. Paint both sections. When the paint has dried, tape the open ends together. Cut out the Hebrew letters on page 98 and glue one to each side of the dreidel. Stick a sharpened pencil through the dreidel.

Paper Dreidels: Mark and cut a 3-inch square from an index card. Draw diagonals on the square. Cut out the Hebrew letters on page 98 and glue one in each section of the square. Push a sharp-pointed toothpick through the center of the card at the intersection of the two diagonals.

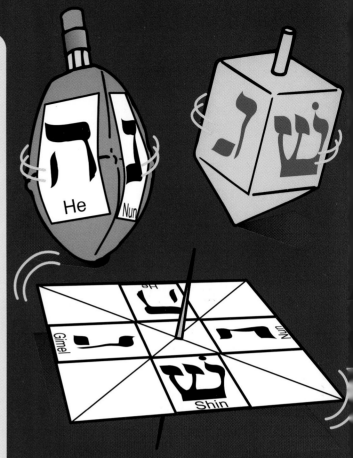

The Best Gift

Friendship, kindness, love, and loyalty are gifts that reflect the true spirit of Hanukkah gift giving. These priceless gifts are available to anyone at no cost! Yet their value is immeasurable. Brainstorm with your class to determine a "student-to-student" gift wish list—gifts that don't cost money. Items might include eating lunch together, helping with a particular subject area, sharing a good book, helping clean a desk, or completing a classroom job together. Next have students write their names on slips of paper and place them in a hat. Have each student then draw a name for a class gift exchange.

Instruct each student to determine the gift he will give his classmate. Provide each student with a brightly colored piece of paper and a length of ribbon. Have the student describe his gift on the piece of paper, roll it up like a scroll, then tie it with the ribbon. Invite students to exchange gifts, filling the eight days of Hanukkah with goodwill and caring for one another.

Tell Me The Story Of Hanukkah

Hanukkah may be a holiday that is unfamiliar to many students. To spread the news about this special holiday, check to see if your class can be responsible for leading oral-reading storytimes for several primary classes during their library periods. With assistance from your media specialist, select several Hanukkah books and assign them to individuals or small groups in your class (see the list of books on page 98). Have each student (or group) familiarize himself with the book so that he will feel comfortable reading it aloud to younger students. Vary the participants, stories, and schedule so that everyone has the opportunity to share a story of Hanukkah with the younger children. Or team up with one primary-grades teacher and plan story-sharing sessions during the eight days of Hanukkah.

Love Those Latkes!

What would Hanukkah be without latkes? These yummy potato pancakes are a holiday food tradition that Jewish families enjoy as a much-anticipated part of their celebrations. Latkes are eaten because they are prepared in oil, a symbol of Hanukkah.

Invite parent volunteers to come to class with their electric skillets and spatulas. Organize the necessary supplies so that small groups of students divide up the responsibilities—and fun!—of cooking and eating these tasty treats.

Potato Latkes

Ingredients:
4 potatoes
2 eggs (beaten)
1 teaspoon salt
3 tablespoons flour
1/2 teaspoon grated onion
oil for frying

Directions:
1. Peel the potatoes and grate them finely. Squeeze them dry.
2. Add the onion, beaten eggs, flour, and salt.
3. Stir until well blended.
4. Drop the batter by tablespoonfuls into hot oil.
5. Fry until both sides are crisp and brown.
6. Drain on paper towels and serve hot with applesauce or sour cream.

Linking Up With Literature

Be sure to share some of the following outstanding literature with your students during the Hanukkah season:

- *The Hanukkah Ghosts* by Malka Penn (Holiday House, Inc.; 1995)
- *The Gift* by Aliana Brodmann (Simon & Schuster, 1993)
- *Spotted Pony: A Collection Of Hanukkah Stories* retold by Eric A. Kimmel (Holiday House, Inc; 1992)
- *Hanukkah Lights, Hanukkah Nights* by Leslie Kimmelman (HarperCollins Children's Books, 1992)
- *The Story Of Hanukkah* by Bobbi Katz (Random House Books For Young Readers, 1995)

Let's Play The Dreidel Game!

Nun
(Do nothing.)

Gimel
(Take all of the pot.)

He
(Take half of the pot.)

Shin
(Put two items in the pot.)

Directions:

1. Divide the playing pieces (beans, hard candies, buttons, peanuts, etc.) equally among all players.
2. Each player places one item in the center of the playing area—the "pot."
3. The first player spins the dreidel and follows the direction that matches his spin.
4. Play then continues to the left.
5. Play continues until each player has had a certain number of spins or the game has been played for a predetermined length of time.
6. When there are no items in the pot, repeat step 2.
7. The winner is the player with the most items at the end of the game.

Math Hint: When you take half of the pot—and the pot has an odd number of items—round up the number. For example: 1/2 of 7 = 3 1/2 = **4**; 1/2 of 11 = 5 1/2 = **6**; etc.

Cut out and use these letters on your dreidel:

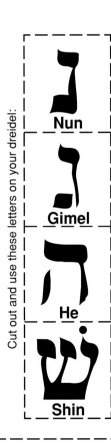

Nun

Gimel

He

Shin

Note To The Teacher: Use this reproducible with "Delightful Dreidels" on page 96. Provide each group of students with a supply of items such as those listed in Step 1 to use as playing pieces.

Name_____ *Geometry*

The Star Of David

The six-pointed Star of David is also called *Magen David,* which means "Shield of David." It was believed to have been a decoration on King David's shield. For hundreds of years it was used by Jews as well as non-Jews. In the 19th century, the Star of David began to appear in synagogue decorations. It became a symbol of the Jews. It now appears on the flag of the State of Israel, as well as on Jewish religious objects.

Take a closer look at this star—a truly unique geometric shape! Complete each fact below with a geometry word, one letter per blank. One letter is already included for you. Happy Hanukkah!

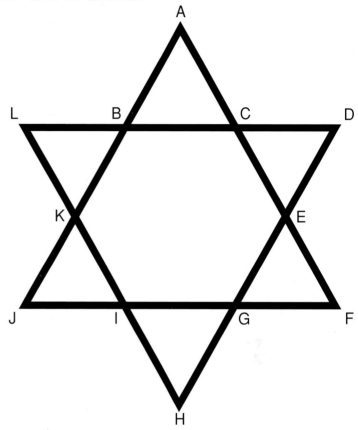

1. This six-pointed star is called a **H** _ _ _ _ _ _ _ _.

2. Its measure is less than 90°, so angle GHI is an **A** _ _ _ _ _ angle.

3. Shape BDGJ is a **P** _ _ _ _ _ _ _ _ _ _ _ _ _.

4. A hexagon is a six-sided **P** _ _ _ _ _ _ _.

5. Angles ACD and ACB are _ _ _ _ _ _ _ _ _ _ _ _ _ _ _ **Y** angles. Their measures total 180°.

6. Shape BDGJ, with its four equal sides, is also a _ _ **H** _ _ _ _ _ _.

7. Draw a segment from points K to E. Shape BCEK is a _ _ _ **A** _ _ _ _ _ _.

8. Segments LD and AF _ _ **N** _ _ _ _ _ _ _ _ at point C.

9. Triangle AFJ is _ _ _ _ _ _ **U** _ _ _ _ to triangle LDH.

10. Look at shape BCEGIK. Segment **K** _ is one of its lines of symmetry.

11. Triangle LDH is similar to triangle _ _ **K**. They have the same shape.

12. Triangle ABC is an _ _ _ _ _ _ _ **A** _ _ _ _ _ _ triangle.

13. Shape BCEGIK is a **H** _ _ _ _ _ _ _.

Bonus Box: Suppose segment AB is three inches long. What is the perimeter of the star?

KWANZAA TIME!

Help your students join the 18 million people in the United States who celebrate Kwanzaa each year. The following activities will reinforce basic principles that encourage harmony and pride in the African American community, as well as celebrate the rich history and achievements of African Americans.

by Simone Lepine

What Is Kwanzaa?

Kwanzaa is a fairly new holiday created in 1966 by Dr. Maulana Karenga. Kwanzaa is a mixture of African, African American, Afro-Caribbean, and Afro-Latin customs. Dr. Karenga based the holiday on seven principles called *Nguzo Saba.* A new principle is celebrated each day of Kwanzaa. The seven days of Kwanzaa begin on December 26 and correspond to a harvest and celebration time in Africa. It is important to note that Kwanzaa is not an alternative to or replacement for Christmas, but rather a celebration to enrich cultural harmony and pride. Families are encouraged to personalize their celebrations of Kwanzaa with their own family traditions.

Kwanzaa Symbols

The symbols used during Kwanzaa represent ideas and thoughts that cannot be seen or touched, but bring great meaning to the celebration. Listed below are seven symbols followed by activities on this page and on pages 101–102 (excluding mazao) to introduce them to your students.

- **Zawadi** .... gifts
- **Mkeka** .... a woven mat
- **Kikombe Cha Umoja** .... unity cup
- **Mishumaa Saba** .... seven candles
- **Kinara** .... candleholder
- **Muhindi** .... ears of corn
- **Mazao** .... crops (gather some locally grown foods)

Kwanzaa Gift Giving

Like other holidays, Kwanzaa includes gift giving. *Zawadi* (gifts) are given from the head, heart, and hands. Children give handmade gifts, while parents usually give educational gifts. Have students create zawadi for their parents. Set up an art center containing red, green, and black construction paper, glue, scissors, markers, glitter, yarn, etc. Instruct the students to create Kwanzaa cards using the materials in the center. Have a sample card displayed in the center showing both sides of the card decorated, a Kwanzaa greeting on the front, and a brief message inside.

Weaving History

The first symbol of Kwanzaa is the *mkeka* (a woven mat), which symbolizes African American tradition and history. Have your students create their own mkekas while learning about their family histories. Send students home with the following list of questions: From which country did my ancestors originate? Who was the first known relative to come to the United States? How long has our family been in this country? Why did our family come to the United States? Also have the students bring family photos (if available) to school. Have the students use their answers to write brief family histories. Let the students share their work; then display the family histories and photos on a bulletin board.

To create the mkekas, have each student follow these directions:

1. Fold an 8 1/2" x 11" piece of black construction paper in half lengthwise. Starting at the fold, cut strips one inch in width, stopping your cuts one inch from the end. Unfold the paper.
2. Use a ruler to measure one-inch-wide strips on a red sheet and a green sheet of construction paper. Cut them out. Weave the strips over and under the slats of the black paper, alternating red and green.
3. Use small dabs of glue to secure the strips to the black paper. Add your mkeka to the family histories display.

Step 1 **Step 2**

Unity Cup

Each day during Kwanzaa, a *libation* (water, wine, or juice) is poured into the *kikombe cha umoja,* or unity cup. Everyone sips from the cup to symbolize the unity of the family and community. After drinking from the cup, the family discusses great African Americans. Discuss the seven principles of Kwanzaa on page 108 with the students. Have each student choose a famous African American to research; then have the student write why the person is famous and what Kwanzaa principle he or she emulates on a long strip of white paper. Next have each student create a unity cup in honor of the famous African American he researched using the directions below. Finally instruct each student to roll up his strip and place it in his unity cup. Display the cups in the library for others to read.

Materials for each student: one cardboard toilet-paper tube, two large paper cups, aluminum foil, glue, scissors, and permanent markers

1. Glue the cardboard tube to the bottom of one cup.
2. Take the other cup and cut its height down to one inch.
3. Glue the bottom of the one-inch cup to the other end of the tube with the opening facing downward.
4. Cover the entire cup with aluminum foil. Write the famous African American's name on the cup with a black permanent marker. Use other colored markers to decorate the cup.

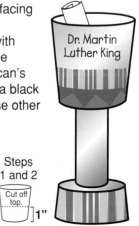

Dr. Martin Luther King

Steps 1 and 2

Cut off top.

1"

Steps 3 and 4

Muhindi

Children are an important part of the Kwanzaa celebration. They are symbolized by *muhindi,* or ears of corn. Each kernel on the corn symbolizes future generations of children. The muhindi are placed on the family's mkeka. Ask your students what is meant by the phrase "children are the hope of the future." List their ideas on the board. Next give each student a copy of page 110. Have students complete the activity; then let volunteers share their dreams in class.

As a follow-up, have students create their own muhindi using the directions below. Divide the students into small groups. Provide orange, red, yellow, and blue paint for each group. Give each student one 12" x 18" sheet of white and one sheet of brown construction paper, glue, scissors, and the following instructions:

1. Fold the white paper lengthwise; then draw an ear of corn with the top of the ear at the fold. Cut out the corn. You should have two ears of corn attached by a fold at the top.
2. Dip your index finger into different colors of paint; then press your finger on the top ear of corn to create kernels. Cover the entire ear.
3. Cut out two husks from the brown paper. Glue them to the back of the bottom ear.
4. Open up the corn and write one wish for the future of the world inside.

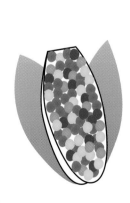

I wish that there would be no wars.

Shedding Light On Kwanzaa

The *kinara* (a wooden candleholder) and *mishumaa saba* (candles) are important symbols of Kwanzaa. The kinara holds seven candles—one for each of the seven principles of Nguzo Saba. The center and first candle to be lit on the kinara is black, representing the descendants of the African people. Three red candles to the left of the black candle symbolize the struggles ancestors of the African people faced in their fight for freedom. Three green candles to the right of the black candle symbolize the green lands of Africa and hope for the future. A new candle is lit each day (alternating red and green).

Divide the class into groups of three or four students to make classroom kinaras. Give each group a shoebox; tape; brown construction paper; scissors; black, green, and red markers; glue; one copy of page 108; and seven copies of page 109. First instruct the groups to cover their boxes with the brown paper; then have them use page 108 and the directions on page 109 to complete their kinaras. Display the kinaras throughout the room during your study of Kwanzaa.

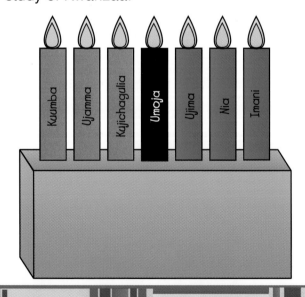

Nguzo Saba: The Seven Principles Of Kwanzaa

Kwanzaa is based upon seven principles called Nguzo Saba. *Nguzo* is Swahili for principles and *Saba* means seven. The seven principles emphasize unity and cooperation within the family, the community, the race, and the nation. A different principle is shared each day of Kwanzaa beginning December 26 and ending January 1. The Kwanzaa symbols listed on page 100 are used during the celebration of Nguzo Saba. Although Nguzo Saba is designed to help African Americans develop an understanding of their past and create a path to the future, all races can benefit from their ideals. Give each student a copy of page 108 and discuss each principle. Then use the activities on this page and pages 104–107 to celebrate Nguzo Saba.

Day 1: Umoja (Unity) No, You Can't / Yes, I Can!

This activity helps demonstrate the power of unified voices. Pick one student to start chanting, "Yes, I can." Have the rest of the class chant in unison, "No, you can't." While everyone is chanting, signal one child to switch from saying, "No, you can't," to saying, "Yes, I can." Keep signaling students to switch until there is only one child left chanting, "No, you can't." Ask the students who chanted alone at the beginning and end of the activity how they felt. Then have students share how it felt as more classmates joined them in the "Yes, I can" chant. Tell students about the Montgomery Bus Boycott of 1955–56 led by Dr. Martin Luther King, Jr., and how being unified made it successful. For over a year, the black citizens of Montgomery, Alabama, did not ride the public buses in protest of the system of segregation used on the buses. About 75 percent of the bus riders in Montgomery were black. Ask students what would happen to a business if 75 percent of its customers left. Discuss other forms of unified protests during the civil rights movement of the 1950s and '60s, such as sit-ins, freedom rides, and marches.

Day 2: Kujichagulia (Self-Determination)
I Am Free

On this day, the family reflects on their cultural heritage and their hopes and dreams for the future. Have the students get out their "Dreams For The Future" reproducibles (page 110) from the "Muhindi" activity page 102. Select students to list their dreams on the board. Next have students share what they know about slave life. Discuss how a slave's future was determined by the plantation owner. If possible, share excerpts from *To Be A Slave* by Julius Lester (Scholastic Inc.) for a realistic depiction of slave life. Have students suggest what a child slave might dream; then write their suggestions on the board beside the dreams listed previously. Let students compare the lists for any similarities.

Close this activity by having each student write a free-verse poem called "I Can Dream." Instruct students to use the dreams they listed on page 110 for ideas. Tell students that each poem should have at least five lines, with the last line stating, "I am free so my dreams are endless." Encourage students to illustrate their poems; then mount the poetry on a bulletin board.

Day 3: Ujima (Collective Work And Responsibility)
Design A Boat That Floats And A Tower That Towers

On this day the family reflects on how much can be accomplished when people work together. Divide the students into groups of two. Give each pair a sheet of aluminum foil. Have each pair use the foil to design a boat that will hold the most pennies. Place each pair's boat in a large container of water. Add one penny at a time to each boat until there is only one boat left floating. Discuss what it was like to work with a partner. Did it make the job easier? Did your partner have ideas that you hadn't thought of using?

Keeping the same groups of two, challenge students to build the highest tower out of one piece of paper. Allow only scissors to be used in making the towers. Tell students that the towers must be able to stand freely for at least ten seconds. As a class, have groups share what it was like working together a second time. Was it easier? Was your pair successful? Why?

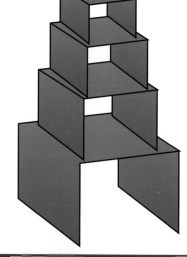

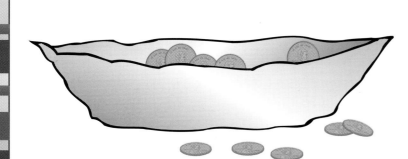

Day 4: Ujamaa (Cooperative Economics) Economic Web

The fourth day focuses on the importance of supporting local stores and starting businesses in the community. For this activity you will need a ball of yarn and a nametag for each student. Write a different name of a local business on each nametag. Have the students form a circle; then give each student a nametag. Explain that they represent business owners who are all from the same community.

Start the game by giving the ball of yarn to one student. Instruct him to grab the end of the yarn and continue holding it until the end of the game. Then have him toss the rest of the yarn to a person he wants to conduct business with. When that person gets the ball of yarn, she pulls the yarn taunt, holds on to her section, and then tosses the ball to another student. Keep tossing the ball until all the businesses have been visited. Guide the students in noticing how the yarn looks like a web. Have them jointly move the web up and down to see how it is interconnected and supported. Ask the students what would happen to the web if the yarn was thrown to a person outside the circle. Would the web be as strong? After this activity, tell each student to pick one business in your area and write a paragraph telling why the business is an important part of the community.

Day 5: Nia (Purpose) Local Biographies

The fifth day is used to discuss the achievements of ancestors and other African Americans. Contact local African American ministers, business owners, government officials, artists, and craftsmen. Make appointments for them to come and be interviewed by your students. Prior to the visits, have the students work in pairs to create lists of at least ten interview questions. Instruct the students to inquire about the individual's childhood, family life, profession, and accomplishments. Have students tape-record the interviews so they can refer to them later if needed.

After the interviews are complete, instruct the students to write short biographies of the people interviewed. Laminate the final copies and compile them into a book. Display the book in the library; then invite the people interviewed to come and see the final product.

Day 6: Kuumba (Creativity)
Karamu: The Kwanzaa Feast

This day's principle is expressed through readings, singing, dancing, and artwork. It is also the day of exchanging gifts and the big feast of Kwanzaa called *karamu*. Food is spread out on a large mkeka in the middle of the room along with the other symbols of Kwanzaa. Have the students—with the help of parent volunteers—prepare their own karamu that includes the recipes below. Other favorite foods include catfish, collard greens, black-eyed peas, and sweet potato pie. While you eat your feast, have students discuss ways they demonstrated their creativity during your Kwanzaa study.

African Sweet Potato Salad

Ingredients:
4 sweet potatoes
1/4 cup vegetable oil
2 tablespoons lemon juice
1/2 teaspoon salt
1/4 teaspoon pepper
1 chopped green pepper
1 chopped small onion
1 chopped celery stalk
parsley

Directions:
Heat 1 cup of water to boiling. Add sweet potatoes. Bring to a boil; then reduce heat and cover. Cook for about 35 minutes or until tender. Cool the potatoes and peel off skins. Cut the potatoes into cubes and put into a bowl. Combine oil, lemon juice, salt, and pepper. Pour this mixture over the potatoes. Cover and refrigerate. Before serving stir in green pepper, onion, and celery. Sprinkle with parsley. (Serves 6.)

Akwadu

(Baked Bananas And Coconuts)
A Treat From Ghana, Africa

Ingredients:
5 bananas
1 tablespoon margarine
1/3 cup orange juice
1 tablespoon lemon juice
3 tablespoons brown sugar
2/3 cup coconut

Directions:
Cut each banana into halves crosswise; then cut each half lengthwise. Put bananas in a greased 9-inch pie pan. Dab margarine on bananas; pour orange and lemon juice over them. Sprinkle bananas with brown sugar and coconut. Bake at 375° until coconut is golden brown, about 8 to 10 minutes. (Serves 5 to 6.)

Day 7: Imani (Faith)
Honor Wall

The first day of the year is the last day of Kwanzaa. This day is used to reflect on the faith an individual has in herself, her family, teachers, leaders, and race. Discuss with the students that *imani* (faith) is believing in someone or something. Have students explain what it means to be a role model. Help the students understand that a role model is a person who represents honesty, compassion, understanding, hard work, concern for others, etc. Have students create a display that honors the role models in their community, school, and families. Cover a bulletin board with bright paper and the title "Role Model Honor Wall." Duplicate a supply of the nomination forms below; then place them in a basket near the display. Let a student nominate someone for the wall by completing one of the forms, coloring its border, and stapling it to the board. If possible, post photographs of the nominees on the wall, too. Encourage other students and teachers in the school to add to your honor wall.

Pattern

Recognizing A Role Model

Nominee for the Role Model Honor Wall: _____

Nominated by: _____

I nominate this person for the Role Model Honor Wall because_____

_____

_____

_____

_____

_____

_____

Nguzo Saba

(en-GOO-zoh SAH-bah)

The Seven Principles Of Kwanzaa

Day 1: Umoja (oo-MOH-jah)
Unity
Black Candle
Helping each other in the family and community.

Day 2: Kujichagulia (koo-jee-chah-goo-LEE-ah)
Self-Determination
Red Candle
Making our own decisions.

Day 3: Ujima (oo-JEE-mah)
Collective Work And Responsibility
Green Candle
Working together to make life better for one another.

Day 4: Ujamaa (oo-jah-MAH-ah)
Cooperative Economics
Red Candle
Building and supporting our own businesses.

Day 5: Nia (NEE-ah)
Purpose
Green Candle
Being aware that our lives have meaning and purpose.

Day 6: Kuumba (koo-OOM-bah)
Creativity
Red Candle
Using our imagination and hands to create.

Day 7: Imani (ee-MAH-nee)
Faith
Green Candle
Believing in ourselves, our ancestors, and our future.

©The Education Center, Inc. • *Big Book of Monthly Ideas* • TEC1488

Note To The Teacher: Use with "Unity Cup" on page 101 and "Shedding Light On Kwanzaa" on page 102.

Pattern Use with "Shedding Light On Kwanzaa" on page 102.

Follow these steps:

1. Read page 92. Then complete and color each of your group's candles.

2. Cut out the candles; then cut on the short dotted lines at the bottom of each candle.

3. Fold on the fold lines. Fold the small flaps at the bottom outward.

4. Put glue on the tab; then fold the candle and attach the tab to the other end to make a triangular candle.

5. Glue the bottom flaps to the shoebox. Be sure to glue your candles in the correct order as shown in the illustration below.

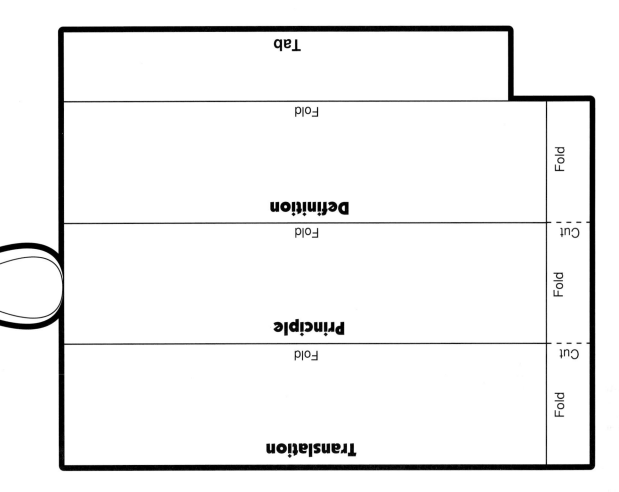

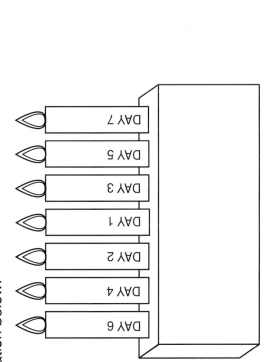

Finished Kinara

Name _____

Dreams For The Future

Directions: Complete each sentence with a dream that fits your goals for the future.

In the future, I would like to change _____

In the future, I would like to live _____

In the future, I would like to see (visit) _____

In the future, I would like to be (career) _____

In the future, I would like to make the world a better place by _____

In the future, I would like to learn how to _____

Bonus Box: List ten things you can do that will help make your dreams come true.

©The Education Center, Inc. • *Big Book of Monthly Ideas* • TEC1488

Note To The Teacher: Use with "Muhindi" on page 102 and "I Am Free" on page 104.

Ringing In The New Year

Thematic Activities For Welcoming A Brand-New Year

New Year's Day—probably the oldest holiday in the world—ushers in the beginning of a year full of new hopes and opportunities. Steer students toward making the most of the year ahead with this refreshing collection of activities.

by Peggy W. Hambright

Happy Birthday, New Year!

For thousands of years, people welcomed the New Year in the spring—as some countries still do—because that's when nature comes to life again after the winter. Some religious groups—like the Jews, Muslims, and Hindus—set their own dates for celebrating the New Year. But most people recognize New Year's Day as the first day of January in each calendar year.

Have each student create a birthday card for the New Year. Ask the student to write a verse inside that's similar to a Japanese New Year's ode—a short poem consisting of just 31 syllables—as shown. Then string the birthday cards around your classroom door.

> New Year, what will
>   you bring?
> Three hundred sixty-five
>   new opportunities?
> A chance to start over
>   again?
> That's great! I need it!

The Life And Times Of...The New Year

Ring in the New Year with a creative-writing project that chronicles the future year from infancy through retirement. Write the names of the 12 months across the chalkboard. Ask your students to brainstorm three or four major events that they predict will occur in each month of the new year. (Expect students to name catastrophes, kinds of weather, political changes, sporting events, new discoveries, inventions, etc.) As an event is named, list it under one of the months. Divide students into 12 groups; then assign each group a month. Ask each group to contribute an illustrated chapter that describes in detail the predicted events assigned to its month. When the chapters are complete, assemble them into a class book. Share a chapter each day with your class; then circulate the book for other classes to enjoy.

Feed the dog.
Be kind to everyone.
Clean my room.
Talk on the phone less.
Go to bed when asked.
Improve my grades.
Complete all homework.
Watch less television.

Toasting The New Year

Wrap up your holiday study by making special celebratory toasts. Have the children sit in a circle holding their resolution noisemakers made in "Turnin' Over A New Leaf" and warm cups of wassail from "Here We Go A-Wassailing." Have the students take turns spinning a bottle (or an extra noisemaker) to see who is the first to share any one of his resolutions. After listening to the resolution, have everyone take one sip of wassail after raising their cups in unison and saying, "Here, here!" Direct the first person who shared to spin the bottle and determine who shares next. If the bottle points to someone who's already shared, ask the person to his right to share instead. When everyone has shared, have all of the students shout, "Happy New Year!" together and shake their resolution noisemakers!

Turnin' Over A New Leaf

Make it truly seem like New Year's by making noisemakers and resolutions. Ask each class member to place a handful of popcorn kernels or dried beans inside a toilet-tissue roll. Have the student wrap his roll with a 12" x 8" piece of Radiant Wrap (shiny, colorful sheets sold in craft stores), extending it beyond the ends. Direct the student to twist both ends closed and tie them with several lengths of colorful curling ribbon or Radiant Wrap shreds as shown. Ask the student to attach a card labeled with his resolutions to one end. Be sure to see "Toasting The New Year" on this page for a great way to share these resolutions.

Here We Go A-Wassailing

Stir up a warm and spicy fruit drink that's enjoyed at New Year's by folks in Scotland and merry old England. Combine the listed ingredients in a large pot and bring them to a boil. Cover the pot and let the mixture simmer for 20 minutes. Uncover and simmer 20 more minutes. Remove the spices. Serve the warm drink in student-decorated Styrofoam® cups during the "Toasting The New Year" activity on this page.

Wassail
2 quarts apple juice
2 1/4 cups pineapple juice
2 cups orange juice
1 cup lemon juice
1/2 cup sugar
1 teaspoon whole cloves
one three-inch stick of cinnamon
(Makes three quarts.)

A Look In Both Directions

Begin the first week in January by reflecting on the old year and looking ahead to the new one. Share with students that January was named after the Roman god Janus, who was believed to have had two faces—one that faced forward and looked to the future, and another that faced backward and looked at the past. Ask each student to ponder her life during the past year and what she hopes it will be like during the next 12 months. Give the student a 9" x 12" sheet of manila paper. Have her fold the paper in half, heading the left half "Looking Back" and the right half "Looking Ahead." Have the student list positive and negative actions she took last year in the left-hand column, and improvements she hopes to make this year in the right-hand column. Challenge the student to keep her paper until December 31 for a comparison!

Looking Back
Turned in most homework assignments on time.
Could have studied more for tests.
Was late to school only once.
Ate too much junk food.
Watched too much TV.

Looking Ahead
Turn in all homework on time.
Study harder for tests.
Return library books on time.
Go to bed without complaining.
Keep my room clean.

Happy New Year Around The World

Do people in other countries make confetti of old calendar pages and throw it out office windows like they do in San Francisco? Do they throw parties and make noise? Do they attend parades with flower-covered floats—like in Pasadena, California—or ones whose participants are mum—like in Philadelphia, Pennsylvania? How different *are* our New Year's customs from those of other countries? Ask each student or group to choose one or more of the countries listed on page 115. Let the student use a variety of library resources (or surf the Internet) to research additional information; then have her briefly summarize the custom(s) on an index card. Staple the students' cards around a world map on a bulletin board. Have each student match her card and country on the board by stapling a length of black yarn between them. Also ask the student to make a small colored flag for the country she researched. Staple the flags around the perimeter of the board to make a colorful border.

New Year's Customs

Country	Custom
Bahamas	Participants—wearing strange and beautiful costumes of colorful crepe and tissue paper—march to calypso and goombay songs in the exciting Junkanoo parade.
Belgium	Farmers wish Happy New Year to their barnyard animals.
China	People enjoy a five-day festival with lion and dragon parades. They decorate pine and cypress branches with old coins and paper flowers, shoot off fireworks, and beat drums to frighten the old year away.
Denmark	People throw old pots, pans, and dishes at the doors of friends and play pranks similar to those done on Halloween in the United States.
Ecuador	Families burn a scarecrow and a will that represents the year's shortcomings.
England	People drink a hot, spicy drink called *wassail* from a bowl containing a good-luck ring. The one to drink from the cup with the ring will marry in the new year.
Former Soviet Union	Children visit the New Year Tree at the Kremlin Palace, see folk dancers perform, and get gifts from Grandfather Frost and Snow Maiden.
France	People eat pancakes to bring themselves good luck.
Germany	People sprinkle 12 onions with salt to predict whether the coming months will be wet or dry. They eat carp and save the scales to wear as good-luck charms.
Greece	Children receive cakes with a lucky coin baked inside each one; then at midnight they open gifts left in their shoes by St. Basil.
Hungary	Bells ring out across the land.
India	People cover the roofs of their houses, window ledges, and paths with small clay lamps during a five-day Festival of Lights.
Iran	Families watch to see if colored eggs sitting on mirrors move—proof that the earth shakes as the New Year begins.
Israel	Jews observe their New Year, Rosh Hashanah, at the end of summer or the beginning of autumn. They hear a ram's horn being blown, eat a bread called *challah,* and taste apple pieces dipped in honey.
Japan	People decorate their homes with pine, bamboo, and rope to bring good luck. They tie paper fortunes to trees, read cards from friends, and watch children unwrap packages of money from their parents.
Puerto Rico	Children dump pails of water out of windows at midnight to rid their homes of evil spirits.
Scotland	Families drink wassail and wait for their first visitor (or *first-footer*) to see whether he brings good or bad luck (based upon his hair color).
Spain	At midnight people eat one grape each time the clock strikes. This is supposed to bring good luck during each month of the new year.
Switzerland	People let a drop of cream fall on the floor for good luck.

A Man For His Time

A Thematic Unit About Dr. Martin Luther King, Jr.

He was a man for his time—committed to pursuing his dream of equality for all. Develop an atmosphere of cooperation and increase appreciation for the national day that remembers Dr. Martin Luther King, Jr., with this creative collection of activities.

by Mary Lou Schlosser and Peggy W. Hambright

Happy Birthday To You!

Celebrate the birthday of Dr. Martin Luther King, Jr., with a unique critical-thinking activity. First separately wrap the lid and bottom of a box with birthday paper. Add a colorful bow to the lid. Next read aloud one of the following books:

Happy Birthday, Martin Luther King by Jean Marzollo (Scholastic Inc., 1993)

Martin Luther King by Rosemary L. Bray (Greenwillow Books, 1995)

Martin Luther King, Jr. by Kathie B. Smith (Silver Burdett Press, 1987)

With the wrapped box on display, ask each class member to think of a gift he would like to have given Dr. King. Ask the student to describe his gift idea in a paragraph; then—as he comes to place it inside the gift box—have him share with the class why his gift is an appropriate one for Dr. King.

Peace By Piece

Reconstruct the life of Dr. Martin Luther King, Jr., through a class quilt-making project. Duplicate page 120; then cut apart the pieces on the grid. Give one piece to each student. Have him use encyclopedias, library books, or computer-generated information to research the facts that will answer his square's question. After researching, have the student write a summary—including an illustration—on a white paper square. Ask the student to glue his white square to a larger square of colored tagboard. Help students arrange all of the individual squares into one large square or rectangle, ordering the squares sequentially so that they retell Dr. King's life story. After the squares have been arranged, have students hole-punch the sides of the squares. Then give students yarn for "stitching" the squares together to create a class quilt. Display the completed quilt on a wall for all to enjoy.

Young Crusaders

Instill in children that they—like Dr. Martin Luther King, Jr.—can impact our world. Share ways that young people have made a difference by reading excerpts from *Witnesses To Freedom: Young People Who Fought For Civil Rights* by Belinda Rochelle (Dutton Children's Books, 1993). Ask students to bring in newspaper or magazine articles (or summarized television accounts) of instances when children have brought about positive changes. Then have each student write a news article that tells about herself one year from now. What is she doing that's making a difference? Is she helping a particular group? Why? Will she be honored for her involvement or accomplishments? Allow students to share their stories aloud.

THE MARTINSVILLE TIMES

LOCAL GIRL TO SPEAK AT CONGRESSIONAL HEARINGS

I'll Remember You

People of distinction—like Dr. Martin Luther King, Jr.—are remembered for their accomplishments in different ways. Naming cities, buildings, streets, and parks for important people is just one of the ways that our society honors others. Have students collectively list Dr. King's character traits and accomplishments. Then instruct each class member to become a part of this scenario: "A new building [or street or park] in your town is to be named in honor of Dr. King. Lots of important people have been invited to attend its official dedication. You have been asked to make the introductory speech." Have each student study the list that the class compiled to help him decide what to say about Dr. King. Then have the student compose a speech that would be appropriate for the occasion. After the speeches have been written, allow class members to present them to the class.

About Violence

Martin Luther King once spoke of "...the self-defeating effects of physical violence." Explain to students the meaning of Dr. King's quote—that a person who commits violence against others never benefits personally from it. Let students discuss the meanings of the term *violence.* Then ask each student to respond to one of the following questions in his journal:

- Why do you think violence occurs today?
- What thoughts and feelings do you have when you hear or read about a violent act?
- What are your opinions on violence in today's schools?
- What are some positive ways people can stop violence today?

Let volunteers share their writings with the class.

About Peace

Dr. King once said, "Sooner or later all the people of the world will have to discover a way to live together in peace...." Allow students to symbolically represent this concept by making a cooperative display. From tagboard cut 12-inch letters that spell the word PEACE. Divide students into five groups; then give each group one of the letters and several old newspapers, magazines, photos, or printed sheets of computer-generated clip art. Let each group cut out and glue pictures of as many different kinds of people as possible to its letter to make a colorful collage. Display the decorated letters on a bulletin board along with Dr. King's quote.

I Have A Dream

Extend the thought process begun by Dr. King in his famous "I Have A Dream" speech with a creative-writing assignment. Have students express personal dreams about how people can cooperate and get along in the future by completing the form on page 121. Display the completed forms on a bulletin board titled "Like Dr. King—We Have Dreams, Too."

Civil Rights Sites

Track the places that Dr. Martin Luther King, Jr., traveled in his pursuit of civil rights for blacks. Enlarge and mount a blank United States map on a bulletin board along with a sheet of chart paper. Throughout the study of Dr. King's efforts, keep a running list of the cities he visited on the chart paper. Have students locate them daily on the map by marking each one with a large dot or a star—to differentiate between cities and state capitals. Ask students to also add to the list other cities that they discover during independent studies. As the study progresses, lightly shade in the states Dr. King visited. Ask students to look carefully at the map, noting any areas that Dr. King visited more often than others. Have students draw conclusions about the reasons he concentrated his visits in those regions.

Montgomery, AL

Selma, AL

Chicago, IL

St. Augustine, FL

Washington, DC

Atlanta, GA

Detroit, MI

5. When and where did Dr. King receive his Ph.D. degree? Explain the difference between the doctoral degree he received and the one received by a medical doctor.

10. Tell how Dr. King became involved in working for civil rights while in Montgomery, Alabama.

15. What was the main purpose of Dr. King's famous "I Have A Dream" speech?

20. Explain the nonviolent strategies Dr. King encouraged people to use in getting the attention of government leaders.

25. Dr. King's birthday is now celebrated every year as a federal holiday. How did it become a national holiday?

4. What did Dr. King study in college? What did he do just before he graduated?

9. Why did Dr. King move his family to Montgomery, Alabama?

14. Describe the March on Washington led by Dr. King and others. Tell why it was planned.

19. What did Dr. King think of the "Black Power" movement?

24. Explain the Civil Rights Act of 1968, which was passed after Dr. King's death.

3. Which college did Dr. King attend? How old was he when he enrolled? What was college life like for him?

8. What was Dr. King's profession? Describe some of his duties.

13. What were some of the ways people tried to discourage Dr. King and other protestors from working for civil rights?

18. What were some of the conditions that Dr. King worked to improve in Chicago, Illinois?

23. Explain how Dr. King died.

2. Find out all you can about the kind of student Dr. King was.

7. How many children did Dr. King and his wife have? What were his children's names?

12. Describe Dr. King's speaking ability.

17. Find out why Dr. King organized protests and marches in and near Selma, Alabama. Were they successful?

22. What honor did Dr. King receive in 1964 and why?

1. When and where was Martin Luther King, Jr., born? Describe his family.

6. Who was Dr. King's wife? Where did they meet? What did she study?

11. Find out why Dr. King moved from Montgomery, Alabama, to Atlanta, Georgia.

16. Explain the Civil Rights Act of 1964.

21. On what did Dr. King base his program of nonviolence?

Note To The Teacher: Make one copy of this reproducible to use with "Peace By Piece" on page 116. Cut apart the pieces. Then give one or more pieces to each student to research.

I Have A Dream

Fill in the blanks. Then color the border.

I dream that one day I will _____

I'll help this dream come true by _____

I dream that one day my family will _____

I'll help this dream come true by _____

I dream that one day all the people in my neighborhood will _____

I'll help this dream come true by _____

I dream that one day all the people in my country will _____

I'll help this dream come true by _____

I dream that one day all the people in the world will _____

I'll help this dream come true by _____

Name _____

A Very Busy Man

Dr. Martin Luther King, Jr., lived in Montgomery, Alabama. While he was working there as a church pastor, Rosa Parks was arrested for refusing to give her bus seat to a white man. Dr. King formed a nonviolent plan that asked all black citizens to stay off the buses until unfair laws were changed. Throughout the 381 days of this bus boycott, Dr. King was a very busy man. Below is an imaginary schedule for a typical day in Dr. King's life during this historic time. Use the clues on the bus tickets to list the events in the order they occurred on his schedule.

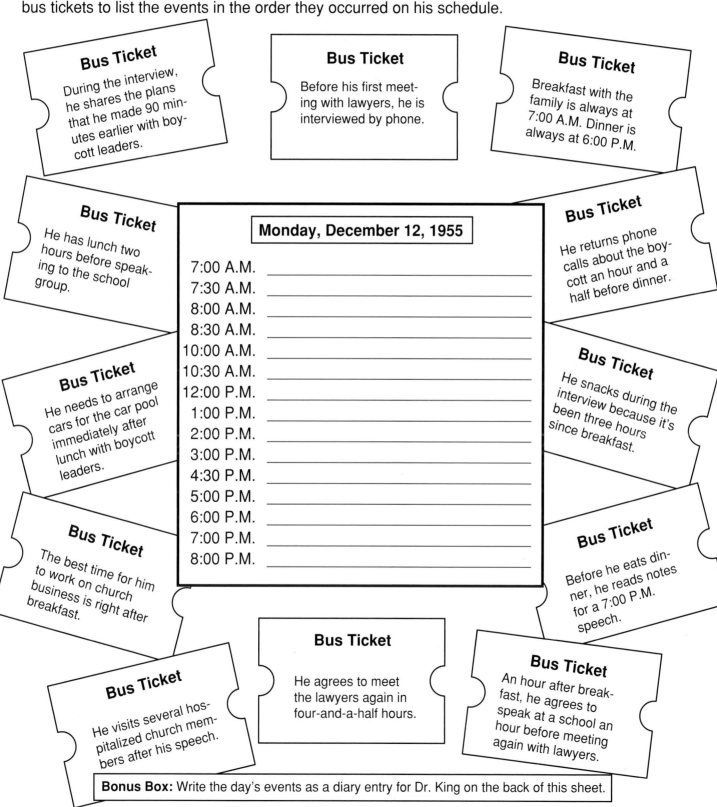

Bus Ticket
During the interview, he shares the plans that he made 90 minutes earlier with boycott leaders.

Bus Ticket
Before his first meeting with lawyers, he is interviewed by phone.

Bus Ticket
Breakfast with the family is always at 7:00 A.M. Dinner is always at 6:00 P.M.

Bus Ticket
He has lunch two hours before speaking to the school group.

Monday, December 12, 1955

7:00 A.M. _____
7:30 A.M. _____
8:00 A.M. _____
8:30 A.M. _____
10:00 A.M. _____
10:30 A.M. _____
12:00 P.M. _____
1:00 P.M. _____
2:00 P.M. _____
3:00 P.M. _____
4:30 P.M. _____
5:00 P.M. _____
6:00 P.M. _____
7:00 P.M. _____
8:00 P.M. _____

Bus Ticket
He returns phone calls about the boycott an hour and a half before dinner.

Bus Ticket
He needs to arrange cars for the car pool immediately after lunch with boycott leaders.

Bus Ticket
He snacks during the interview because it's been three hours since breakfast.

Bus Ticket
The best time for him to work on church business is right after breakfast.

Bus Ticket
Before he eats dinner, he reads notes for a 7:00 P.M. speech.

Bus Ticket
He visits several hospitalized church members after his speech.

Bus Ticket
He agrees to meet the lawyers again in four-and-a-half hours.

Bus Ticket
An hour after breakfast, he agrees to speak at a school an hour before meeting again with lawyers.

Bonus Box: Write the day's events as a diary entry for Dr. King on the back of this sheet.

What Would Dr. King Do?

Read the paragraphs about Dr. Martin Luther King, Jr., below. Then read the ten situations at the bottom of the page. What do you think Dr. King would have done in each situation? Write answers for five of the situations on the back of this paper. Support each answer with one or more facts from the paragraphs.

Dr. Martin Luther King, Jr., had an older sister and a younger brother. He was a good student. He was so smart that he skipped the 9th and 12th grades in school. He started college when he was 15 years old. Martin later received a doctorate of theology degree and became a Baptist minister.

Dr. King was an excellent speaker. He became the main leader of the civil rights movement in the United States during the 1950s and 1960s. Even after his home was bombed, he still believed that nonviolence was the way to get freedom and end discrimination. He led more than 200,000 Americans in the March on Washington. It was during this march that Dr. King made his famous "I Have A Dream" speech.

Dr. King worked to get the Voting Rights Act of 1965 passed. He also worked to increase employment opportunities, and improve bad housing and poor schools. Many times he was arrested and jailed for protesting against unfairness and discrimination. It worried him that the "Black Power" movement did not support his nonviolent ways of solving problems.

In 1964 Dr. Martin Luther King, Jr., won the Nobel Peace Prize for leading nonviolent civil rights demonstrations. Sadly, he was assassinated at the age of 39. After his death Congress passed the Civil Rights Act of 1968. This act prevented racial discrimination when persons were buying and renting most homes. Dr. King's birthday is now a federal holiday celebrated on the third Monday in January.

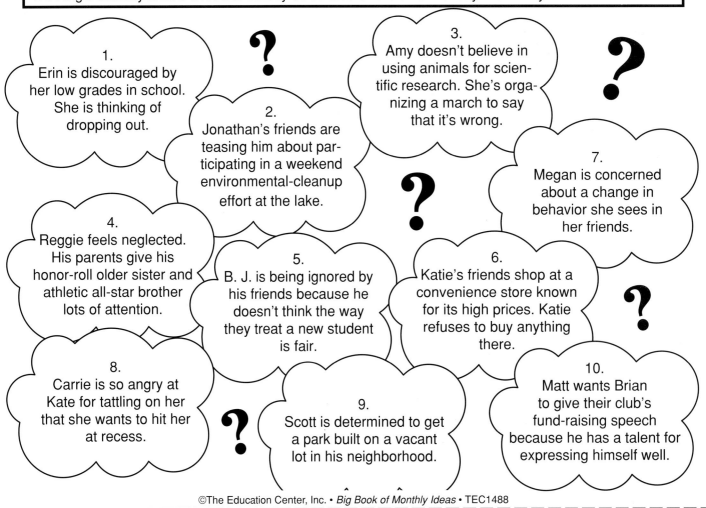

1. Erin is discouraged by her low grades in school. She is thinking of dropping out.

2. Jonathan's friends are teasing him about participating in a weekend environmental-cleanup effort at the lake.

3. Amy doesn't believe in using animals for scientific research. She's organizing a march to say that it's wrong.

7. Megan is concerned about a change in behavior she sees in her friends.

4. Reggie feels neglected. His parents give his honor-roll older sister and athletic all-star brother lots of attention.

5. B. J. is being ignored by his friends because he doesn't think the way they treat a new student is fair.

6. Katie's friends shop at a convenience store known for its high prices. Katie refuses to buy anything there.

8. Carrie is so angry at Kate for tattling on her that she wants to hit her at recess.

9. Scott is determined to get a park built on a vacant lot in his neighborhood.

10. Matt wants Brian to give their club's fund-raising speech because he has a talent for expressing himself well.

Note To The Teacher: Duplicate one copy of this sheet for each student or group. As a variation, ask each student or group to give a lengthier and more-detailed explanation of only one or two situations.

Searching The Friendly Skies

Out-Of-This-World Activities For Studying Space

Three...two...one...blast off into a new year with some truly far-out space activities! The month of January has a payload of space history milestones (see the chart below). What better time than now to propel your students into a thematic study of space, the final frontier?

by Patricia Twohey

Extraterrestrial Terminology

Help your students latch on to space vocabulary with easy-to-make flash cards. Duplicate the vocabulary list on page 128. Cut out each word/definition strip and wrap it around a 4" x 6" index card as shown. Use the resulting flash cards in the following ways:

- Place the cards at a learning center for students to use when quizzing each other.
- Shuffle the cards and give one to each student. Instruct each student to act out the term without speaking. Have other class members try to guess the word.
- Divide the class into two teams. In turn, have a member from each team come to the board. Call out a definition. Have each student write the correct term on the board. Award teams a point for the correct answer and an extra point for correct spelling.
- Duplicate page 128 for each student to use for making his own card set.

Space Milestones In January

Date	Milestone
Jan. 31, 1958	*Explorer I,* the first successful U.S. satellite, was launched. It transmitted signals until May 23, 1958, and discovered the Van Allen Belt.
Jan. 2, 1959	*Luna 1* (USSR) became the first spacecraft from Earth to orbit the sun.
Jan. 31, 1961	A Mercury capsule was launched carrying Ham, the chimpanzee. Ham successfully transmitted signals and was returned safely to Earth.
Jan. 31, 1966	*Luna 9* (USSR) was launched and later conducted the first soft landing on the moon. The unmanned ship sent photos back to Earth.
Jan. 27, 1967	Fire broke out on *Apollo I* (USA) during a launching simulation test, killing three astronauts.
Jan. 14, 1969	*Soyuz 4* (USSR) launches and docks with another manned spacecraft and conducts the first interchange of spaceship personnel in orbit.
Jan. 31, 1971	*Apollo 14* (USA) was launched and later landed on the moon.
Jan. 16, 1973	*Luna 21* (USSR), an unmanned vehicle, landed on the moon carrying a radio-controlled vehicle that explored its surface.
Jan. 10, 1975	*Soyuz 17* (USSR) was launched carrying two cosmonauts who spent 28 of their 30 days in the space station *Salyut 4.*
Jan. 10, 1978	*Soyuz 27* (USSR), carrying two cosmonauts, was launched and linked with the *Salyut 6* space station.
Jan. 24–27, 1985	The space shuttle *Discovery* (USA) conducted a secret, all-military mission to deploy an eavesdropping satellite.
Jan. 28, 1986	The space shuttle *Challenger* (USA) exploded shortly after takeoff, killing seven crew members, including schoolteacher Christa McAuliffe.

All In One Year

Many characteristics of the Earth can be explained using a model. Place a brightly colored Post-it® Brand note on a globe to mark your state's location. Point out that the Earth tilts about 23.5° on its axis. Have a student stand in the center of the class holding a lit flashlight to represent the sun. Have another child hold the globe tilted at an angle. Instruct the Earth student to walk in a counterclockwise orbit around the sun, turning the globe in a counterclockwise direction as he walks (to represent the passing of days). Instruct the sun to shine its light on the globe as the Earth student circles her. Point out that it takes 365 days (one year) to complete this orbit. Discuss the effect this movement has on the length of the Earth's seasons.

Next ask students, "Would you be the same age if you lived on another planet in our solar system?" Help students find the answer by having them complete copies of page 130.

Seeing Is Believing

Help students visualize the huge orbits of the planets around the sun with the following model. Duplicate page 129 for each student. After completing the chart on the page, assign each of nine groups a planet. Give each group a pair of scissors, a 9" x 12" sheet of colored paper, a ruler, and a colored marker. In addition you will need a supply of yarn. Instruct each group to label its paper with the name of the group's planet. Then have the group cut a length of yarn equal to the measurement figured on the fourth column of the chart on page 129.

Next have each group carry its yarn and label out to the playground or to the gym. Place a large yellow circle in the center of the area and have a volunteer stand on it to represent the sun. Beginning with Mercury, have a member from each planet's group hold an end of the yarn length in one hand and the planet label in the other hand; then have him give the other end of the yarn to the sun to hold. Because the planets Mercury, Venus, and Earth are relatively close together, the students representing these planets will have to stand close together. Once the student-sun is holding the end of each planet's yarn, instruct all of the planets to move slowly in a counterclockwise circle around the sun. Direct each planet to move carefully—using the yarn length as a guide—in order to maintain the correct distance from the sun. As each student-planet moves around the sun, explain that the actual orbit of each planet is elliptical, not circular, in shape. Point out that this model simply shows students the relative distance and size of each planet's orbit.

Postcards From Space

Here's a far-out way to share space research with fellow classmates! Have each student imagine that she is on vacation in space (for instance, soaking up solar rays on Venus, roping a rocky ride on an asteroid, or spelunking on a cavernous moon). Have her research the location and imagine what it would be like to vacation there. Then have her write a postcard to a friend expressing her feelings and insights about this particular vacation. Give each student a 9" x 6" sheet of heavy white paper on which to write her message and the address of the recipient. Instruct her to add a stamp and a postmark for an authentic look. Then have her flip over the card and add an illustration of her intergalactic destination.

Dear Mike,
This planet is really great! Jupiter is so big that I won't have time to see the other side. Our hotel is a giant, floating space station. Yesterday we parachuted through the clouds. It was spooky not seeing where we were landing. Later we took a shuttle ride over the Great Red Spot—awesome! See you soon with more news!

Pat

Mike Joseph
320 Appletree Lane
Ciderville, RI 02020
U.S.A.
Earth

Space Pioneers

Introduce your students to the first men and women of space by copying the names of space pioneers below on slips of paper. Have each student draw one name to determine the space pioneer he will research. Duplicate the astronaut pattern on page 132 for each student. Instruct each student to use the *who, what, when, where,* and *why* categories on his pattern to guide his research. After completing the information on the pattern, have each student attach it to a bulletin board. Cut out a simple spaceship outline and label it "Space Pioneers"; then color the spaceship and mount it on the bulletin board. Attach each of the completed astronauts to the spaceship with a tether of colorful yarn.

Nicolaus Copernicus
Isaac Newton
Konstantin Tsiolkovsky
Clyde Tombaugh
Alan B. Shepard, Jr.
Alexei Leonov
Edwin E. Aldrin, Jr.
Sally K. Ride
Bruce McCandless
Christa McAuliffe
Eileen M. Collins

Johannes Kepler
Edmond Halley
Edwin P. Hubble
Wernher von Braun
John H. Glenn, Jr.
Edward H. White II
Michael Collins
Guion S. Bluford
Marc Garneau
Norman Thagard
Galileo Galilei

William Herschel
Robert H. Goddard
Yuri A. Gagarin
Valentina Tereshkova
Neil A. Armstrong
James A. Lovell, Jr.
Svetlana Savitskaya
Kathryn D. Sullivan
Mae C. Jemison
Shannon W. Lucid

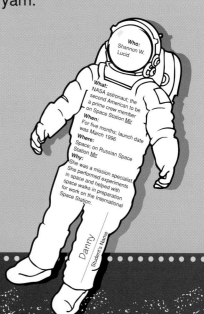

Who:
Shannon W. Lucid

What:
NASA astronaut; the second American to be a prime crew member on Space Station Mir

When:
For five months; launch date was March 1996

Where:
Space: on Russian Space Station Mir

Why:
She was a mission specialist. She performed experiments in space and helped with space walks in preparation for work on the International Space Station.

Danny
Student's Name

Satellite Savvy

Take a closer look at the members of our solar system with this investigative activity. Divide the class into nine groups. Randomly assign one planet to each group to research. Duplicate two copies of page 131 for each group. Give the group one copy to use as a guide during its research. Have the group complete another copy to display. After each group has cut out the three pieces on its completed sheet and glued them together as shown below, post the resulting satellites on a bulletin board titled "Satellite Savvy." Then give each group five index cards. Instruct each group to use its research to devise five riddles—writing the riddle on one side of each card and the name of the planet on the opposite side. Gather the cards from each group, shuffle them, and store them in a pocket on the bulletin board. Invite students to quiz each other during free time.

Moonstruck

Scientists have identified over 60 moons in our galaxy. Listed to the right are the names of the larger, better-known moons (excluding ours). Duplicate 28 copies of the moon pattern on page 132. Copy the name of each moon onto a separate pattern. Pin these on a bulletin board titled "Moonstruck." Challenge each student to research one or more moons. Then have him write a short fact on the front or back of the corresponding pattern along with his initials. Reward each student with one point for each fact.

As an alternative, pass the completed moon patterns to the nine groups used in the "Satellite Savvy" idea above. Have each group write one or more riddles for the moons on index cards. Then add the moon patterns and riddles to the "Satellite Savvy" board.

Moons

Ananke	Leda
Ariel	Lysithea
Callisto	Mimas
Carme	Miranda
Charon	Nereid
Deimos	Oberon
Dione	Pasiphae
Elara	Phobos
Enceladus	Phoebe
Europa	Rhea
Ganymede	Sinope
Himalia	Tethys
Hyperion	Titan
Io	Triton

Vocabulary Strips

Use with "Extraterrestrial Terminology" on page 124.

air pressure	Force of the atmosphere pushing on the Earth
asteroids	Rocky bodies that orbit the sun mainly between Mars and Jupiter
astronaut	Person from the United States who travels outside the Earth's atmosphere
atmosphere	Layer of gases around a planet, star, or moon
axis	Imaginary line through the middle of a planet
chromosphere	Middle layer of the sun's atmosphere
colonization	Establishing a new community of inhabitants where they had not lived before
convection zone	Layer of sun just below the surface that carries energy to the surface
corona	Outermost layer of the sun's atmosphere
cosmonaut	Person from the former Soviet Union who travels outside the Earth's atmosphere
craters	Holes on a planet's or moon's surface, made by meteorites or volcanoes
force	A cause that changes an object's shape or motion
gravity	Force that pulls objects toward the Earth
habitat	Place where one lives; environment
lift	The force created by high and low air pressures, which get a plane off the ground
light speed	The speed at which light travels (186,000 miles per second)
lunar	Having to do with the moon
meteor	Tiny meteoroid or asteroid that has entered the Earth's atmosphere
meteorite	Meteoroid that has hit a planet's surface
meteoroid	Metallic or rocky matter drifting in space
Milky Way galaxy	The spiral group of stars, dust, and gas that contains our sun and planets of the solar system
NASA	National Aeronautics & Space Administration
nova & supernova	Exploding stars that become dim again
orbit	In space, the path one body takes around another
photosphere	The surface of the sun
pioneer	Person who explores the new/unknown
planetarium	A model of the solar system
radiative zone	Middle layer of the sun; draws heat from the center out to the convection zone
revolution	One full trip on an orbit
rotation	One full turn on an axis
satellite	A smaller body that orbits a larger body
science fiction	Imaginative stories about science
simulator	Device that creates conditions almost exactly like those one expects in an actual situation; usually used for testing and training
solar system	The sun and all of the planets and other bodies that orbit it
space shuttle	A reusable spacecraft controlled or piloted by astronauts
spicules	Streams of gas that shoot up from the chromosphere
sunspots	Dark patches on the sun's surface
telescope	Tool used to see the stars in our galaxy and beyond
terraforming	Altering a planet's atmosphere so that it can be inhabited by people from Earth
thrust	Forward-directed force
universe	Everything that we know exists and believe may exist
weight	Force of gravity placed on an object

My Very Educated Mother Just Served Us Nine Pizzas

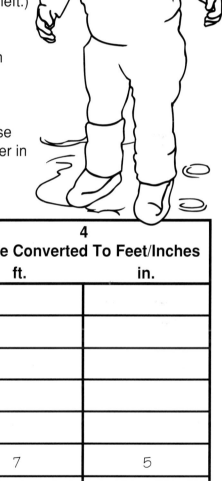

Did somebody say pizza?

Does the title above make any sense? It does if you're trying to memorize the order of the nine planets from the sun. The first letter of each word stands for a different planet. These planets travel in the same direction around the sun. Their *orbits,* or paths, lie in a flat plane except for Pluto's orbit, which is tilted. Each orbit is shaped like an elongated circle, or *ellipse.*

The chart below will help you make a model of the planets' orbits. Follow these steps to complete the chart (Saturn has been done as an example):

1. First divide Saturn's distance from the sun by 10 million. (Dividing by 10 million is the same as moving the decimal seven places to the left.) This will convert the distance to a more manageable scale *(88.82000000).*
2. Round this number to the nearest whole; then write this number in column 3 *(88.82000000 = 89).*
3. Pretend that each number represents inches. For instance, the distance from Saturn to the sun is now 89 inches.
4. Convert Saturn's inches in column 3 to feet and inches. Write these new numbers in column 4 *(89 ÷ 12 = 7 feet 5 inches).* If the number in column 3 is less than 12, just write it as inches in column 4.
5. Repeat steps 1 through 4 for the other eight planets.

1 Planet	2 Distance From The Sun (In Miles)	3 New Scale	4 Scale Converted To Feet/Inches	
			ft.	in.
Mercury	35,980,000.0			
Venus	67,230,000.0			
Earth	92,960,000.0			
Mars	141,000,000.0			
Jupiter	483,600,000.0			
Saturn	888,200,000.0	89	7	5
Uranus	1,786,400,000.0			
Neptune	2,798,800,000.0			
Pluto	3,666,200,000.0			

Bonus Box: The title above is called a *mnemonic phrase.* Think of another mnemonic phrase that will help you memorize the order of the nine planets. Write it on the back of this page.

Note To The Teacher: Use this page with "Seeing Is Believing" on page 125. Be sure that students understand that because a planet's orbit is elliptical—not circular—the numbers in the "Distance From The Sun" column vary. The numbers given are the mean distances from the sun.

You Look Young For Your Age!

If you like getting lots of birthday presents, you should consider living on Mercury! On Earth you celebrate a birthday every 365 days—the same length of time it takes our planet to make one revolution around the sun. But if you lived on Mercury you'd celebrate a birthday every 88 days. Why? Because it takes Mercury only 88 days to revolve once around the sun.

Complete the information on the cake below. First figure out your age in Earth-days. To do this, multiply your age by 365; then write that number on the top of the cake in the blank. Next figure out your age on the other planets. To do this, use a calculator to divide your age in Earth-days by the number of days in one revolution for each planet (see the chart). Round each number to the nearest whole number, tenth, or hundredth.

EXAMPLE: If you are 6 years old, you have lived 6 x 365 days, or 2,190 days. Divide 2,190 days by 88 days (length of one year on Mercury). The rounded answer is 25 years.

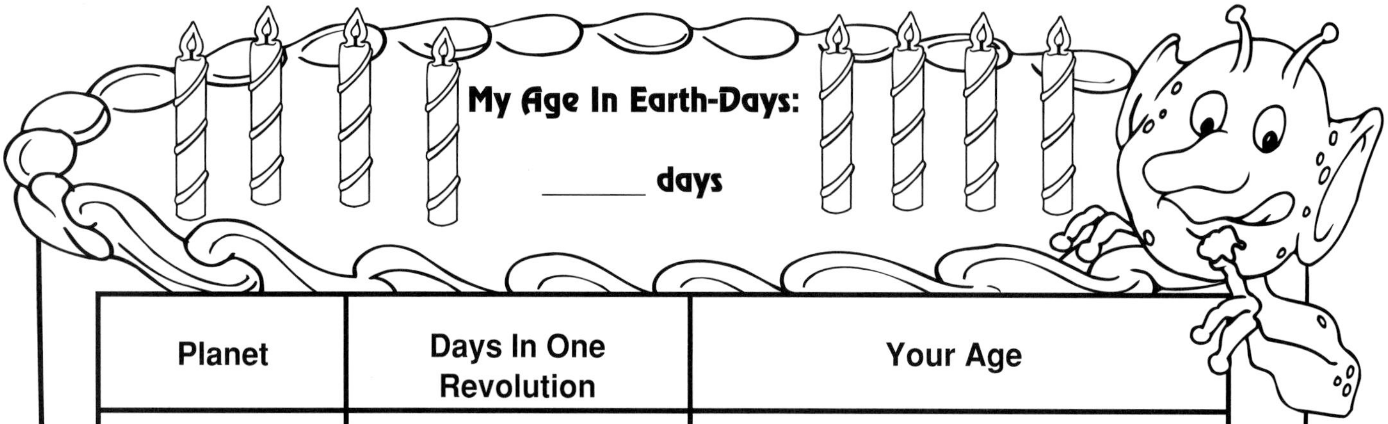

My Age In Earth-Days:

_____ days

Planet	Days In One Revolution	Your Age
Mercury	88	year(s)
Venus	225	year(s)
Earth	365	year(s)
Mars	687	year(s)
Jupiter	4,333	year(s)
Saturn	10,759	year(s)
Uranus	30,685	year(s)
Neptune	60,188	year(s)
Pluto	90,700	year(s)

Note To The Teacher: Use this page with "All In One Year" on page 125. Provide students with calculators.

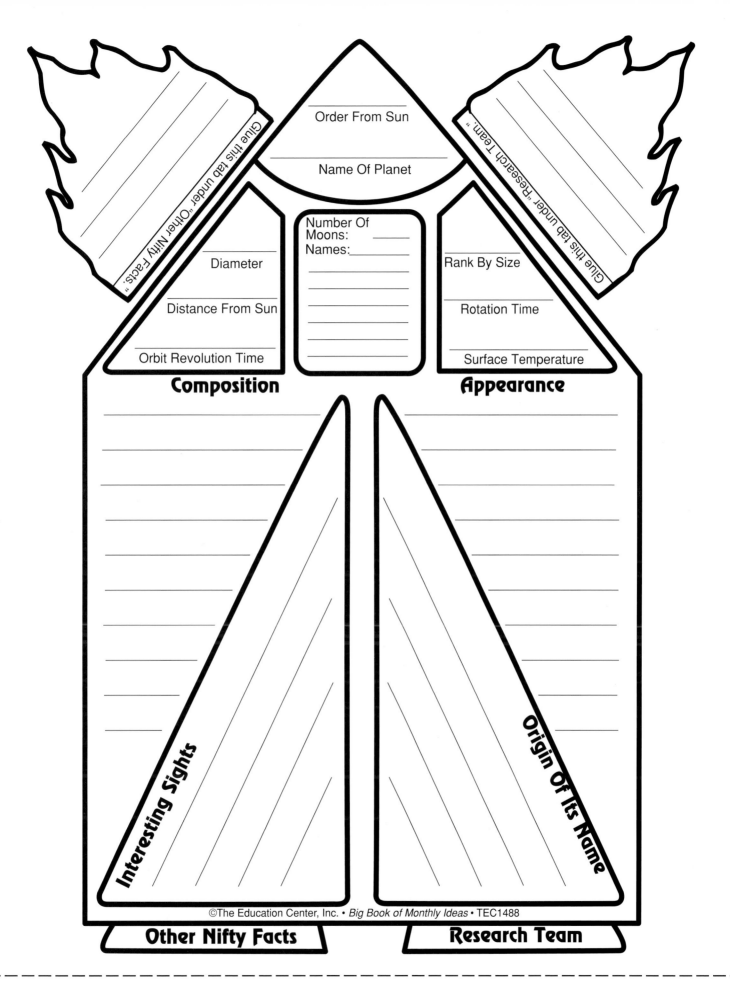

Order From Sun

Name Of Planet

Glue this tab under "Other Nifty Facts."

Glue this tab under "Research Team."

Number Of Moons: _____
Names:_____
_____
_____
_____
_____
_____

Diameter

Distance From Sun

Orbit Revolution Time

Composition

Rank By Size

Rotation Time

Surface Temperature

Appearance

Interesting Sights

Origin Of Its Name

©The Education Center, Inc. • *Big Book of Monthly Ideas* • TEC1488

Other Nifty Facts

Research Team

Note To The Teacher: Use with "Satellite Savvy" on page 127. Students will need access to reference materials. They will also need scissors and glue.

Patterns
Use with "Space Pioneers" on page 126.

Who:

What:

When:

Where:

Why:

©The Education Center, Inc.

Student's Name

Name Of Moon:

Parent Planet:

Moon Facts:

©The Education Center, Inc.

Use with "Moonstruck" on page 127.

FEBRUARY

A HONEY OF A HOLIDAY

Easy And Educational Activities For Valentine's Day

Hearts, hugs, happy smiles, heavenly tasting candy—put them all together and you've got everyone's favorite February holiday! Welcome Valentine's Day with open arms and the following curriculum-friendly activities and reproducibles!

by Chris Christensen and Ann Fisher

A Dilution Solution

Add a sip of science to your Valentine's Day activities with this hands-on demonstration. First show students a half-filled cup of clear soda pop (such as 7-Up® or Sprite®). Add two drops of red food coloring to the cup. After students have noted the change in the color of the liquid, pour it into a large clear bowl. Next add one can of the clear soda pop to the bowl at a time until the red color disappears. Ask students, "Where did the red coloring go?" Have each student answer this question in his science journal. Then explain that the red was visible in the cup of tinted soda because there was a close ratio between the food coloring molecules and the soda molecules. As you began to add additional soda to the mixture, the presence of more soda molecules increased the ratio. The red molecules had to spread out. Finally, because the red molecules were so small and spread so far apart, they became invisible. After discussing this demonstration with the class, distribute paper cups and let students enjoy a sip of their science!

Valentine Symmetry

Sneak a little math into your Valentine's Day party without anyone noticing! Have parent volunteers bring in undecorated heart-shaped cookies (one per student) and tubes of pink, red, and white squeezable frosting or decorating gel. Review the concept of *symmetry* with your class; then challenge each student to use the frosting to decorate her cookie with a symmetrical design. After having a partner or the teacher check her cookie's design, direct each child to snack on her symmetrical sweet!

Love Patches Things Up!

Writing and art go hand in hand in this eye-catching Valentine's Day display! Cut a giant red heart from bulletin-board paper. Draw several lines on the heart to make it appear as if it's been broken; then cut on the lines. Reassemble the heart on a bulletin board or wall as shown. Add the title "Love Patches Things Up!"

Next lead a class discussion about the different forms love can take: a kind deed, the sacrifice of your wishes for those of a loved one, a word of encouragement when a friend is sad, etc. Talk about how love can mend broken friendships and patch up misunderstandings. Then have each student cut a 4" x 4" square of notebook paper. On the square, have the student write about a time when he experienced, initiated, or witnessed a loving act. Next have the student cut a 5" x 5" piece of construction paper and trim its edges with pinking shears. Have the student decorate the resulting patch; then have him tape it to the top of his written square. Staple each finished patch (at the top only) to the bulletin board as shown. Each morning during February, read aloud one or two of the paragraphs from the display. Discuss how love patched up the particular problem or helped those involved.

Holiday Writing Center

Looking for a writing center that your students are sure to be sweet on this February? The pattern on page 139, the list of terrific writing assignments below, and the following directions make this center a sweet—and simple—success!

Preparing the center: Duplicate ten copies of the task card pattern on page 139 onto pink, red, or lavender paper. Label each card with one of the tasks below. At your center, hang red and pink crepe-paper streamers from the ceiling or wall. Display the task cards (laminated if desired) in a basket decorated with a red bow, an empty Valentine's Day candy box, or an inverted red umbrella.

Making writing booklets: Have each student cut out two identical large hearts from red construction paper. Then have him trace one of the hearts on several sheets of notebook paper, cut out the tracings, and staple them between his two heart covers. Encourage each student to personalize the cover of his booklet and complete the center's writing assignments inside it.

Tasks

- Create a sentence with each word beginning with a letter in the word *valentine.* For example: <u>V</u>an and <u>L</u>il <u>e</u>at <u>n</u>ine <u>t</u>omatoes <u>i</u>nside <u>N</u>ana's <u>e</u>levator.

- Research the human heart. Inside your booklet, list ten new facts you learned from your research.

- Invent a new Valentine's Day candy! Write a description of your creation's ingredients. Then write a commercial message describing your scrumptious treat.

- In your booklet, write a thank-you note to someone at school who has helped you in some way. Then make a Valentine's Day card in which you can copy the note. Deliver the card to your friend.

- Someone has sent you a very special Valentine's Day gift. There was no name on the card. Write your strategy for finding out the identity of your secret admirer.

- Pretend that you are a delicious, cherry-flavored Valentine's Day lollipop. Write a journal entry describing your life from the factory to a tummy.

- Valentine's Day is a holiday that focuses on feelings from the heart. What do you wish for most—from the bottom of your heart? Describe your wish in a paragraph.

- How is the emotion of *love* like the emotion of *hate?* How are they different? Write a paragraph that compares and contrasts these two emotions.

- In a paragraph, describe a food that you just *love.* But in your description, do not name the food. Give the description to a classmate. Can he or she guess the identity of the food?

- What famous person would you just *love* to get a valentine from? Write a paragraph that explains why you would like to hear from this person on Valentine's Day.

Candy Heart Graphing

Make math a treat with this oh-so-sweet graphing activity. Purchase a supply of candy hearts so that each child has enough to fill a small plastic bag. Also tape together eight to ten sheets of one-inch graph paper as shown. Along the left side of the far left sheet of paper, color in one square for each color of hearts; then draw a dividing line to separate these squares from the rest of the display as shown. Post the display (soon to be a giant bar graph) on a bulletin board or wall.

Distribute the bags of candy to the class. Direct each child to predict the most frequent color found in his bag of hearts without closely examining its contents. Record these predictions on the chalkboard. Next have each child count each color of hearts in his bag, keeping a tally on a sheet of paper. Instruct the student to bring his completed tally sheet to the graph and color in one square for each heart of each color in his bag. After each student has had an opportunity to add his tallies to the graph, check to see whether the students' earlier predictions were accurate. As a follow-up, have students challenge each other with original word problems based on the graph's information.

Seeing Red!

Haven't got the heart to make students endure boring vocabulary drills? Then introduce them instead to the very vivid vocabulary of Valentine's Day! Begin by having students brainstorm a list of words or phrases that include the word *heart* (*heartburn, heart-to-heart, hearty,* etc.). List their responses on a sheet of chart paper. Have dictionaries handy so students can read aloud the definitions of unknown words or expressions. Post the list so that students can use the words in their Valentine's Day writing activities (see "Holiday Writing Center" on page 136).

Follow up this brainstorming session by having students investigate expressions containing the word *red* with the reproducible activity on page 141.

Have A Heart!

Sharpen multiplication and thinking skills with this exciting game! Have each pair of students cut out nine small hearts from red paper; then have the pair label each heart with a numeral from 1–6, 8–9, and 0. Provide a zippered plastic bag in which the pair can store its hearts, a pair of dice, a small copy of a multiplication table, and a copy of these game instructions:

How To Play:

1. Place the hearts, numeral-side-up, on the desk.
2. Player One rolls the dice, multiplies the two numbers showing, and announces the answer.
3. Player Two checks Player One's answer with the multiplication table. If incorrect, Player Two takes a turn. If correct, Player One removes the cut-out hearts that match the answer's digits. (For example, if a 4 and an 8 are rolled, the player announces that the product is 32. He then removes the 3 heart and the 2 heart from the desk.)
4. Player One continues until he either gives an incorrect answer or cannot remove any hearts from the desk. To determine his score for this round, Player One adds the numerals on the hearts that remain on the desk.
5. Return all of the hearts, numeral-side-up, to the desk. Player Two then takes a turn, following steps 2–4.
6. At the end of ten rounds, the player with the *lowest* score wins.

A Heartfelt Greeting

Here's an easy project that makes a great Valentine's Day gift for your students. (Or have each student make one to give to her parents.) Duplicate one copy of the heart pattern on page 139 on white construction paper for each child. Then follow these simple instructions to make one greeting:

Materials: 16-inch length of gathered white lace, 1 inch wide; 5-inch length of red or pink ribbon, 1/4 inch wide; glue; Valentine's Day lollipop or pencil; scissors; a pencil; markers or crayons

Steps:
1. Cut out the heart shape. Use markers or crayons to add color to it.
2. Glue the lace around the edge of the heart.
3. After the lace has dried, tie a small bow with the red or pink ribbon; then glue it to the bottom point of the heart as shown.
4. Sign your name to the greeting.
5. Gently poke a pencil through the two hole markers on the heart. Insert the Valentine's Day lollipop or pencil through the holes.

This little card
Is meant to say
That you are thought of
In a special way!

Happy Valentine's Day!

Love,
Eva

This little card
Is meant to say
That you are thought of
In a special way!

Happy Valentine's Day!

Love,

Name _____ *Reading and interpreting a pie graph, fractions*

Simply Sweethearts

Mel and Millie had a terrific idea. They decided to open up a new store called "Simply Sweethearts." It sells items for people to give to their sweeties on Valentine's Day and other special occasions. Before Mel and Millie opened their store, they surveyed a group of people to find out the kinds of valentine gifts they gave last year. Mel and Millie made a pie graph to show the data they collected. Look at it carefully as you answer the questions below. **Hint:** It may help to first convert all the fractions to ones with a common denominator.

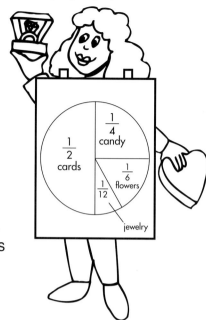

A. Mel and Millie surveyed 120 people.
   1. What number of people gave Valentine's Day cards? _____
   2. What number gave flowers? _____
   3. How many more people gave candy than jewelry? _____

B. Suppose that Mel and Millie surveyed only 60 people.
   4. How many people gave candy? _____
   5. How many people gave their sweethearts jewelry? _____
   6. What total number of people gave cards, flowers, and jewelry? _____

C. Suppose that Mel and Millie really got cracking and surveyed 360 people.
   7. How many people gave flowers? _____
   8. How many more people gave cards than candy? _____
   9. How many fewer people gave jewelry than flowers? _____

D. Now pretend that Mel and Millie were able to survey only 48 people.
   10. How many people did not give candy? _____
   11. How many people did not give jewelry? _____
   12. How many did not give cards or flowers? _____

E. Finally, determine how many people were surveyed if:
   13. 30 people gave candy: _____   16. 120 gave cards: _____
   14. 100 gave flowers: _____   17. 100 gave jewelry: _____
   15. 40 gave flowers: _____   18. 150 gave candy: _____

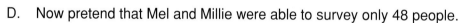

Bonus Box: Out of 90 people surveyed about the gifts they received last Valentine's Day, 10 received perfume, 10 received concert tickets, 10 received CDs, 15 received flowers, 15 received cards, and 30 received candy. On the back of this paper, draw a pie graph with fractions like the one shown above for these statistics.

Seeing Red!

Valentine's Day is the one day of the year on which you're guaranteed to see red! Many expressions found in our language include the word *red*. Some of their meanings may surprise you! Read each sentence below. Use a dictionary to help you find the meaning of each boldfaced word or phrase. After you have located the meaning, color the heart and write your answer in the blank.

1. Would an office worker likely think that lots of **red tape** was pretty? _____

2. If you received a **redingote** as a gift, would you eat it, wear it, or read it? _____

3. Is a **redbreast** a type of flower, food, or bird? _____

4. Was last Valentine's Day a **red-letter** day for you? _____ Explain your answer. _____
   _____
   _____

5. Does news that is **red-hot** mean that it is up-to-the-minute news that everyone would want to know? Or is it news that will probably interest only a few people? _____

6. Describe a time when you were caught **red-handed:**
   _____

7. In what war did the **redcoats** fight? _____

8. Would a **red cap** work at a grocery store, mall, or railroad station? _____

9. Where is the **Red Sea** located? _____

10. Would you give the president the **red-carpet** treatment if he visited your school? _____

11. If the captain of your army unit put you on **red alert,** would you be nervous or joyful? _____

12. Does a **red giant** have something to do with the land, sky, or oceans? _____

13. What flavor is usually associated with a **red-hot** candy? _____

14. If your business were in the **red,** would you be happy or worried? _____

15. If someone is boring or dull, would he or she be described as **red-blooded?** _____

Bonus Box: What color would you use to describe yourself? Write a paragraph on the back of this page explaining why you chose your color and how it best describes you.

Note To The Teacher: Use with "Seeing Red!" on page 137.

A Heroic Heritage

Activities To Celebrate The History And The Accomplishments Of African-Americans

Unlike other immigrants who journeyed to the United States, most African-Americans arrived as captives and were sold into slavery. Use the following activities to help your students understand the inspiring and courageous history of African-Americans.

by Beth Gress and Thad H. McLaurin

Triangular Trade

What do ships, rum, Africa, molasses, the West Indies, slaves, and America have in common? Each was a major factor in the *triangle trade route.* The triangle trade route was a three-stage trading system responsible for bringing 8 to 15 million captive Africans to the New World between the 16th and the 19th centuries. First British ships loaded with rum, iron goods, and guns sailed from America to the West African coast, where they traded their cargo for captured Africans. Next the captive Africans endured a grueling journey known as the "middle passage" to the West Indies, where they were traded for molasses. Finally the slave ships traveled to New England, where the remaining Africans were sold into slavery and the molasses was made into rum. Use one or more of the activities below to help students gain a better understanding of the triangle trade route.

- Have students research why rum, iron goods, and guns were so important to the African slave traders.
- Read the following passage written by Olaudah Equiano—an 11-year-old African boy who survived the grueling "middle passage":
  "The closeness of the place and the number of us crowded so closely together almost suffocated us. The horrible smells made the air unfit to breathe. This brought on sickness that killed many of us."
- Ask students to name the feelings and emotions conveyed in the passage. Then have each student write a journal entry answering such questions as "What would you do if you were suddenly kidnapped and taken from your family?" and "How would you feel if you did not know whether you would ever see your family again?" Have volunteers share their entries.
- Read aloud one of the books listed below. Each tells a unique story of the trials Africans endured when captured and transported to America. As students listen to the story, have them record reflections in their journals.
  — *The Slave Ship* by Emma Gelders Sterne (Scholastic Inc., 1988)
  — *The Slave Dancer* by Paula Fox (Dell Publishing Company, Inc.; 1991)
  — *Ajeemah And His Son* by James Berry (HarperCollins Children's Books, 1994)

Black History Contracts

What is *ethnic pride?* Who were the important leaders of the civil rights movement? Help your students find the answers to these and other questions related to African-American history by completing the following independent activities: Duplicate a class set of "On The Road To Freedom" (page 146), the "Black American Achievers Contract" (page 147), and the "Gallery Of Black American Achievers" (page 148). Direct each student to select a Black American achiever from page 148 to use with the activities on page 147. Provide a variety of resources and literature books for students to use. After each student has completed pages 146 and 147, check the answers for page 146 and have each student share two of his "Black American Achievers Contract" activities with the class. Display the completed contract projects around the classroom.

Here are some suggested books to include:
- *One More River To Cross: The Story Of Twelve Black Americans* by Jim Haskins (Scholastic Inc., 1994)
- *Afro-Bets® Book Of Black Heroes From A To Z: An Introduction To Important Black Achievers* by Wade Hudson and Valerie W. Wesley (Just Us Books, 1988)
- *Now Is Your Time! The African-American Struggle For Freedom* by Walter Dean Myers (HarperCollins Children's Books, 1991)
- *Many Thousand Gone: African-Americans From Slavery To Freedom* by Leo Dillon and Diane Dillon (Knopf Books For Young Readers, 1992)

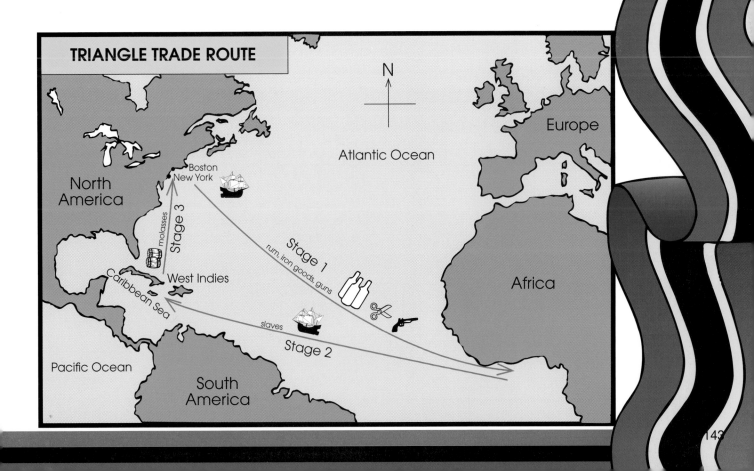

TRIANGLE TRADE ROUTE

N

Atlantic Ocean

Europe

North America

Boston
New York

molasses
Stage 3

Stage 1
rum, iron goods, guns

West Indies

Caribbean Sea

Africa

slaves
Stage 2

Pacific Ocean

South America

Black Author "Quadramas"

Expose your students to the wide variety of African-American books by creating an African-American authors center. Stock the center with books that students can read in the center or check out for several days. Below is a list of children's authors who would be appropriate for the center. After a student reads a book, instruct him to construct a *"quadrama"* (see the instructions below). Display the "quadramas" around the classroom to inspire students to read more books by African-American authors.

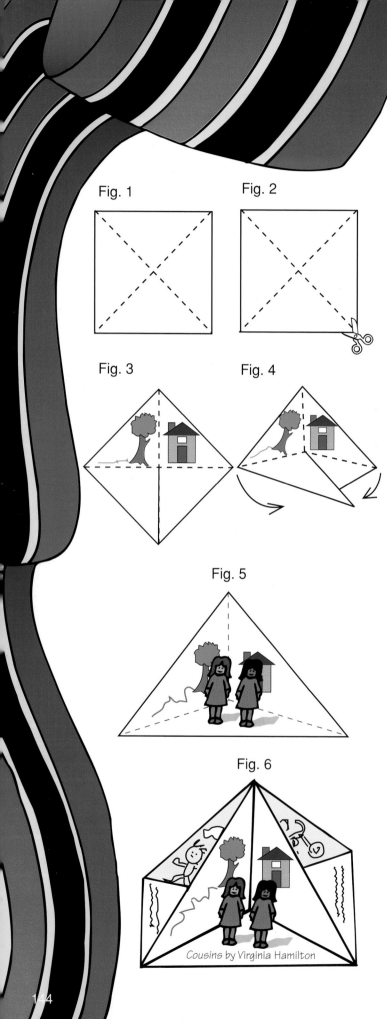

Fig. 1

Fig. 2

Fig. 3

Fig. 4

Fig. 5

Fig. 6

Cousins by Virginia Hamilton

James Berry	Joyce Hansen
Candy Dawson Boyd	Jim Haskins
Deborah M. Newton Chocolate	Elizabeth Fitzgerald Howard
Lucille Clifton	Langston Hughes
Ossie Davis	Fredrick McKissack
Tom Feelings	Patricia C. McKissack
Nikki Giovanni	Walter Dean Myers
Eloise Greenfield	John Steptoe
Virginia Hamilton	Mildred D. Taylor

Materials For Each Student: four 9" x 9" pieces of white paper, two 8 1/2" x 11" sheets of white construction paper, scissors, glue, markers, tape

Directions:
1. Fold a 9" x 9" piece of paper diagonally as shown (see Figure 1).
2. Open and cut along one fold line, stopping at the center (see Figure 2).
3. Repeat Steps 1 and 2 with the other three sheets.
4. Illustrate one scene from the novel on each 9" x 9" square (see Figure 3).
5. Overlap the two bottom triangles of each square and secure them with glue or tape (see Figure 4).
6. Add stand-up characters or scenery to make each scene three-dimensional (see Figure 5).
7. Write a brief description of each scene (see Figure 6).
8. Include the title and author of the book on one of the scenes.
9. Glue the backs of each scene together, creating a pyramid as shown.

Dahomey Appliqués

The Dahomey people of West Africa passed on their cultural heritage through colorful appliqués. Have each student tell about his family by creating his own Dahomey appliqué (see the directions below). Then inspire each student to explain the symbols on his completed wall hanging.

Materials For Each Student: one 12" x 18" piece of black paper, five or six 9" x 12" assorted colored pieces of paper, assorted colored markers or crayons, scissors, glue, one black marker or crayon

Directions:
1. Draw symbols that represent your family on the assorted colors of paper. Then cut out the symbolic shapes.
2. Glue the symbols onto the 12" x 18" piece of black paper.
3. Use a black marker or crayon to make stitch marks around each symbol as shown.

Pride And Prejudice

Black Americans have faced prejudice since the first Africans reached America in the early 1600s. Help students understand that prejudices can be overcome. Read aloud the story "The Sneetches" from *The Sneetches And Other Stories* by Dr. Seuss (Random House Books For Young Readers, 1961). Then have students discuss how the views of the two groups of Sneetches change after the stars keep getting mixed up and McBean leaves with his peculiar machine.

Create a bulletin board that celebrates diversity. Give each student a 4" x 6" index card and these instructions for writing an eight-line Bio Poem.

Line 1: Write your first name.
Line 2: Write three adjectives that describe you.
Line 3: Write three things that you like.
Line 4: Write three things that you fear or dislike.
Line 5: Write the names of your siblings (or of your pets or friends if you have no siblings).
Line 6: Write the names of your parents.
Line 7: Write the name of the town in which you were born.
Line 8: Write your last name.

Photograph each student as she writes her poem. Then post each Bio Poem with the appropriate photograph on a board under the title "Celebrate Diversity."

Bio Poem

Mitzi
Creative, Fun, Kind
Loves chocolate, movies, and reading
Fears mean dogs, storms, and collard greens
Siblings: Doug, Vickie, and Darla
Parents: Evelyn and Douglas
Born in Durham, North Carolina
Knight

On The Road
To Freedom

Increase your vocabulary and Black history knowledge. Use the vocabulary words in the box to complete five of the ten activities described below. Put a check in the box beside each activity you complete.

race	civil rights
ethnic pride	abolitionist
culture	prejudice
segregation	oppression
integration	brotherhood
minority	self-determination
unity	nonviolence
discrimination	Underground Railroad

Vocabulary Activities

☐ 1. Write a definition for each vocabulary word. Do not use a form of the word in the definition.

☐ 2. Draw a picture to illustrate each word. Then write a sentence explaining each illustration.

☐ 3. Use each word in a sentence that also includes the name of a famous Black American.

☐ 4. Use as many of the words as you can in a paragraph about an important event in Black history. Underline the vocabulary words used in the paragraph.

☐ 5. Develop ten questions related to Black history using a vocabulary word in each question. Also provide the answers to the questions.

☐ 6. Make up ten questions for each of which a vocabulary word is the answer.

☐ 7. Write a Black history rap or poem using as many of the vocabulary words as possible.

☐ 8. Create a crossword puzzle on graph paper using all the vocabulary words. Include the answer key on the back.

☐ 9. Construct a rebus puzzle (using letters and pictures) for each vocabulary word.

☐ 10. Make a Concentration game by writing each vocabulary word on an index card and each definition on an index card. Play with a partner to see who can find the most matches when the cards are placed facedown.

Black American Achievers Contract

Select one person from the "Gallery Of Black American Achievers" handout (page 148). Then find out more about that person by completing five of the ten activities described below. Check the box next to each activity that you complete. Be prepared to share two of your five completed activities with the class.

☐ 1. Develop ten questions you would ask if you could meet and interview your subject. Avoid yes/no questions.

☐ 2. Make a timeline of your subject's life. Include at least ten events on the timeline.

☐ 3. Select someone that you think your subject would consider a hero. Explain why.

☐ 4. Create a poster about your subject. Include biographical information, accomplishments, and pictures.

☐ 5. Create an acrostic poem about your subject. Write his or her full name vertically in all uppercase letters. Then think of an adjective or phrase that describes your subject and begins with each letter in his or her name. Write each adjective or phrase horizontally beside the appropriate letter.

Example: **H**elped runaway slaves
                   A woman called Moses
                   Railroad
                   Risked her life
                   Inspirational
                   Escaped to freedom
                   Triumphant

☐ 6. Design a special award honoring your subject for an important achievement or accomplishment. Describe the award; then create a certificate, medal, or trophy labeled with the appropriate information.

☐ 7. If your subject had a motto, what would it be? Explain your reasons.

☐ 8. Create a political cartoon showing one of your subject's accomplishments. Write a brief explanation of the cartoon underneath your illustration.

☐ 9. Make a word find using ten adjectives that describe your subject. Underneath your puzzle, use each of the hidden adjectives in a sentence describing your subject.

☐ 10. If your subject is a historical figure, describe how you think he or she would react to the changes of modern society. If your subject is a modern figure, describe what you think his or her contributions to society may have been had he or she lived 100 years ago.

Gallery Of Black American Achievers

The following list represents just a few of the many Black Americans who have made accomplishments in the fields and professions listed below.

Singers
- Marian Anderson
- Leontyne Price
- Ella Fitzgerald
- Lena Horne
- Sarah Vaughan
- Nat "King" Cole

Educators
- Mary McLeod Bethune
- Booker T. Washington
- Benjamin E. Mays
- E. Franklin Frazier

Film/T.V. Personalities
- Sidney Poitier
- Bill Cosby
- Oprah Winfrey
- Lou Gossett, Jr.
- Spike Lee
- James Earl Jones

Athletes
- Jesse Owens
- Jackie Robinson
- Arthur Ashe
- Wilma Rudolph
- Althea Gibson
- Jackie Joyner-Kersee

Government Officials
- Shirley Chisholm
- Ralph Bunche
- Barbara C. Jordan
- Thurgood Marshall
- Thomas Bradley
- Andrew Jackson Young, Jr.

Musicians
- Louis Armstrong
- Count Basie
- Dean Dixon
- Duke Ellington
- Dizzy Gillespie
- Charlie Parker

Civil Rights Leaders
- Rosa Lee Parks
- Fannie Lou Hamer
- Coretta Scott King
- Dr. Martin Luther King, Jr.
- Jesse Jackson
- W. E. B. Du Bois

Poets/Playwrights
- Phillis Wheatley
- Maya Angelou
- Gwendolyn Brooks
- Paul Laurence Dunbar
- Lorraine Hansberry

Doctors/Nurses
- Charles Richard Drew
- Daniel Hale Williams
- Susie King Taylor
- Mary Elizabeth Mahoney

Astronauts/Explorers
- Ronald McNair
- Guion Bluford
- Mae Carol Jemison
- Frederick Drew Gregory
- Matthew Henson
- James Pierson Beckwourth

Writers
- Virginia Hamilton
- Alice Walker
- Toni Morrison
- Alex Haley
- Julius Lester
- Langston Hughes

Scientists/Inventors
- Ernest Everett Just
- Benjamin Banneker
- George W. Carver
- Garrett Morgan
- Jan Ernst Matzeliger
- Lewis Howard Latimer

Name _____

©The Education Center, Inc. • *Big Book of Monthly Ideas* • TEC1488

Note To The Teacher: Use with "Black History Contracts" on page 143.

Causes & Effects In Black History

Match each cause to its effect by writing the letter of each effect in the box by its cause.

Causes

☐ Rosa Parks refuses to give up her seat to a white person.

☐ Public city school districts are ordered to desegregate schools.

☐ Jackie Robinson joins the Brooklyn Dodgers baseball team.

☐ The 13th Amendment to the Constitution is passed in 1865.

☐ Harriet Beecher Stowe's book *Uncle Tom's Cabin* is published.

☐ Abraham Lincoln signs the Emancipation Proclamation in 1863.

☐ Three police officers are found *not guilty* of all charges pertaining to the Rodney King beating.

☐ The Underground Railroad is organized.

☐ George Washington Carver writes and teaches about soil conservation and how to improve crop production.

☐ The triangle trade route is established.

Effects

A. Riots break out in Los Angeles.

B. Thousands of southern slaves escape slavery and gain freedom.

C. The Montgomery bus boycott begins.

D. Thousands of Africans are brought to North America.

E. Southern farmers learn how to be more productive.

F. Major-league professional sports become integrated.

G. Slavery is constitutionally abolished in the United States.

H. Slavery is made illegal in the Confederate States.

I. The argument over slavery becomes more intense.

J. Both black and white students are bused to schools outside their neighborhoods.

Bonus Box: On the back of this paper, write down two positive things you've done this year and their effects.

Hail To The Chief!

Thematic Activities For Learning About The Presidents

Step into the Oval Office for an inside look at the presidency. As you celebrate the births of Lincoln and Washington, use the following activities to enrich your students' knowledge of the more than 40 men who have been called "Mr. President."

by Thad H. McLaurin and Elizabeth Lindsay

Executive States

Can your state boast as the birthplace of a president? Help students find out by dividing the class into ten groups. Assign each group four or five different presidents. Instruct each group to research the birthplaces of its presidents and share its findings. Tally the results on the board as each group presents its data. Then have students help you compile the data into a class graph. List the states on the vertical axis and the number of presidents on the horizontal axis.

Arkansas—William J. Clinton
California—Richard M. Nixon
Georgia—James E. Carter
Illinois—Ronald Reagan
Iowa—Herbert Hoover
Kentucky—Abraham Lincoln
Massachusetts—John Adams, John Quincy Adams, John F. Kennedy, George Bush
Missouri—Harry S. Truman
Nebraska—Gerald Ford

New Hampshire—Franklin Pierce
New Jersey—Grover Cleveland
New York—Martin Van Buren, Millard Fillmore, Theodore Roosevelt, Franklin D. Roosevelt
North Carolina—James K. Polk, Andrew Johnson
Ohio—Ulysses S. Grant, Rutherford B. Hayes, James Garfield, Benjamin Harrison, William McKinley, William H. Taft, Warren G. Harding

Pennsylvania—James Buchanan
South Carolina—Andrew Jackson
Texas—Dwight D. Eisenhower, Lyndon Johnson
Vermont—Chester A. Arthur, Calvin Coolidge
Virginia—George Washington, Thomas Jefferson, James Madison, James Monroe, William Henry Harrison, John Tyler, Zachary Taylor, Woodrow Wilson

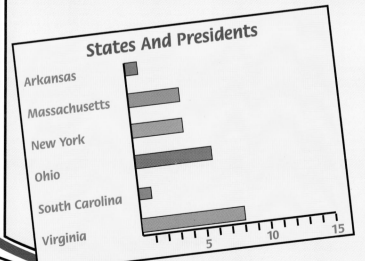

"Presidential Rap"

Help students learn some simple facts about the presidents by introducing the "Presidential Rap" on page 155. Make one copy of the rap for each student. Rehearse the rap a few minutes each day during the week before Presidents' Day. Then, on Presidents' Day invite other classes and parents to a special performance of the Presidential Rap. If a new president has been recently elected, have your students create a new verse to add to the end of the rap.

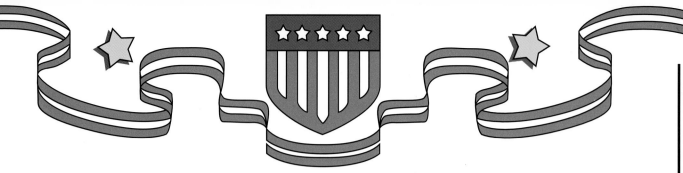

Virginia's Pride

What do Presidents Washington, Jefferson, Madison, Monroe, W. H. Harrison, Tyler, Taylor, and Wilson have in common? They were all born in Virginia, of course. Map out the presidential birthplaces using the data collected in the "Executive States" activity on page 150. Cover a bulletin board with a large U.S. map. Give each student the names of one or two presidents and a slip of 2" x 3" red paper for each one. Instruct the student to write the name of a president on each slip. Then have him staple each slip to the board near that president's birth state. Direct each student to use string and map pins to connect each slip to its corresponding state. When students have completed this display, have them discuss answers to questions such as: Why do some states, such as Virginia, have more presidents than others? Why do many states have no presidents? Why do you think our state does/doesn't have a president?

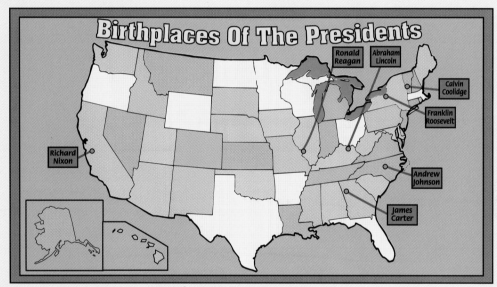

Thomas Jefferson: Jack Of All Trades

Thomas Jefferson did more than write the Declaration of Independence. He studied many different subjects such as mathematics, law, botany, music, architecture, farming, and archaeology. Jefferson also enjoyed inventing gadgets to help improve everyday life. His creations included a quartet book stand, a more efficient plow, and a polygraph machine. Some of Jefferson's gadgets were improvements on existing items, such as his swivel chair.

Let Thomas Jefferson inspire your students to create new or improved gadgets. Divide students into pairs. Direct each pair to think up and illustrate an invented or improved gadget. Then instruct each pair to write a paragraph explaining how its creation will improve everyday life. Have each pair tell the class about its gadget. Then display the illustrations and paragraphs around the classroom.

The First Ladies

From the 1700s to the present, America's first ladies have played a variety of roles as partners to the presidents. Help students understand how the first lady's role has changed over the past 200 years. Assign each student one first lady to research. (Make sure that a student researches the current first lady.) Have the student find information about the first lady's social and political duties, attitudes, and roles. Draw a Venn diagram on the board. In the left circle, list the duties, attitudes, and roles common only to early first ladies (see the diagram). In the right circle, list those items common only to the most recent first lady. Finally list those items that are common to all first ladies in the intersecting section of the circle. Remind students of how changes in transportation and communication have affected the first lady's position and influence. Have students discuss why they think certain duties and responsibilities have not changed over the years. Finally present these questions to the class: "What qualities would the first female president's *husband* need to have?" and "What would his title be?"

First Ladies Of The 18th And 19th Centuries

The Current First Lady

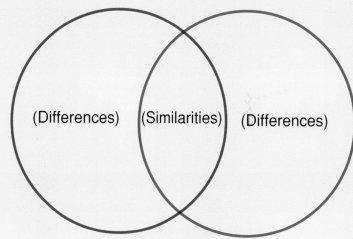

(Differences) (Similarities) (Differences)

Talking Tales

Pair public speaking with basic biography to create a presidential Book Talk—a short, five-minute oral presentation with visuals. Instruct each student to read a presidential biography. Duplicate page 154 for each student. Instruct each student to gather information about the birthdate, birthplace, childhood, family, education, and accomplishments of his president using the "Book Talk Map." Allow the student to use his completed map as a cue card during his presentation. In addition instruct each student to create a visual display to accompany his presentation. The visual may be a poster, model, *realia* box (a box of collected items), video, or diorama. Or suggest that the student present his Book Talk as if he were that president talking about his own life. If desired, videotape each Book Talk presentation and play it back so that the student can critique himself.

Scavenger Hunt Scrapbook

Capture the essence of each president by creating a Scavenger Hunt Scrapbook. Stock the following items at a center in your classroom: 9" x 12" colored paper, glue, scissors, crayons, markers, and old magazines. Assign each student a different president. Instruct her to research that president's characteristics and accomplishments. Then have her use that information to create a one-page collage (front and back) for the scrapbook. Tell her to scavenge through the magazines for items that represent characteristics and accomplishments of her president. Encourage each student to add photocopies from other sources as well as original artwork. Instruct her to mount the collected items and original artwork on a sheet of paper. Enlist a group of students to create a cover and a back for the scrapbook. Punch holes in the left margin of each page using a three-hole punch. Then use yarn or brads to bind the scrapbook. Display the book in the classroom or library. Or send it home each night with a different student to share with his parents.

Scrapbook Of The Presidents

Televised Debates

The 1960 presidential campaign was the first in which the two candidates debated on national television and could be seen by millions of viewers at once. Have students explain how this televised debate made the 1960 presidential campaign different from campaigns of the past. Then ask students what effect this may have had on the outcome of the election. Finally have students share other methods that modern presidential candidates use to spread their values and beliefs all over the country.

Picturing The Perfect President

According to the Constitution, the requirements for the United States presidency are as follows: (1) you must be a natural-born citizen of the United States; (2) you must be at least 35 years old; and (3) you must have been a U.S. resident for at least 14 years. Seems rather easy, right? Well, whoever is elected president will have many national and international issues to face. Have students brainstorm a list of issues, such as crime and drug abuse, that face the president. Have students list other requirements they think a candidate should have to equip him or her to face these issues (examples include knowledge, experience, communication skills, and integrity). Divide the students into small groups. Have each group choose a different issue from the first list. Then have the group select from the second list the presidential characteristics most likely to help a president deal with this issue. Finally have each group share its findings with the rest of the class.

Book Talk Map

Use this Book Talk Map to organize your ideas and thoughts. Use it as a reference during your oral presentation.

Title: _____

Author: _____

Trivia

Major Accomplishments During His Presidency

Education

Birthdate

Birthplace

Childhood And Family

Note To The Teacher: Use with "Talking Tales" on page 152.

Music: rap song

Presidential Rap

U.S. presidents have a tough job, you see;
They've faced many challenges, more than you and me.
So who are these men that have shaped our nation?
Here's 40 or so of whom we'll make a mention!

George Washington, you know he's always number one;
John Adams, number two, moved on to Washington.
Number three, Jefferson, was an inventor and musician;
Number four, Madison, helped write the Constitution.

Monroe and J. Q. Adams were numbers five and six;
Seven, Andrew Jackson, was tough as hickory sticks.
Eight, Van Buren, was a leader during tough times;
Tyler and Will Harrison were presidents ten and nine.

James Polk, number 11, helped acquire more land;
Number 12, Zach Taylor, worked to protect the Union.
Thirteen, Millard Fillmore, helped us all to "compromise";
Fourteen, Franklin Pierce, had nonslave states choose sides.

Fifteen, Buchanan, tried to prevent the Civil War;
Sixteen, Honest Abe, said, "Slavery no more!"
Seventeen, Andrew Johnson, tried to help the South;
Eighteen, Grant's a general not to be left out.

Nineteen, Hayes, thought the telephone truly unique;
Twenty, James Garfield, wrote in both Latin and Greek.
Twenty-one, Chester Arthur, helped the navy even more;
Twenty-two, Grover Cleveland, was also 24!

Twenty-three, Harrison, was called Little Ben;
McKinley, 25, wanted the U.S. great again.
Twenty-six, Roosevelt, was a true "teddy bear";
Taft, 27, on the lawn had cows there.

Twenty-eight, Woodrow Wilson, tried hard to keep from war;
Harding, 29, wanted world peace once more.
Thirty, Calvin Coolidge, was known as Silent Cal;
Thirty-one, Hoover's "depression" is still remembered now.

F.D.R., 32, by the fire liked to chat;
Thirty-three, Harry Truman, World War II he was at.
Thirty-four, Eisenhower, was a general, you bet;
Kennedy, 35, was the youngest yet.

Thirty-six, Johnson, gave a vote that was the right move;
Thirty-seven, Nixon, made foreign relations improve.
Gerald Ford, 38, and 39 was Carter;
Forty, Ronald Reagan, was a great communicator.

George Bush, 41, with Desert Storm to fight;
Forty-two, Bill Clinton, made history all right.
Now you know these great men, the "Famous 42";
Who else will hold the office? Perhaps it could be you!

Note To The Teacher: Use with "Presidential Rap" on page 150.

Presidential Nicknames

Did you know that almost every president has had a nickname? Some presidents received their nicknames as children, whereas others received their nicknames while serving in office. Use reference books to help you match each nickname below with the correct president. Can you find all 20?

Presidents

1. _____ Bill Clinton
2. _____ Richard Nixon
3. _____ William Howard Taft
4. _____ Dwight D. Eisenhower
5. _____ Andrew Jackson
6. _____ Zachary Taylor
7. _____ Grover Cleveland
8. _____ Franklin Pierce
9. _____ Ulysses S. Grant
10. _____ Benjamin Harrison
11. _____ Abraham Lincoln
12. _____ Ronald Reagan
13. _____ Woodrow Wilson
14. _____ Herbert Hoover
15. _____ James Knox Polk
16. _____ George Bush
17. _____ Thomas Jefferson
18. _____ James Buchanan
19. _____ Rutherford B. Hayes
20. _____ William McKinley

Nicknames

A. Old Rough And Ready
B. Handsome Frank
C. Ten-Cent Jimmy
D. Honest Abe
E. Uncle Sam
F. His Fraudulency
G. Little Ben
H. Uncle Jumbo
I. Wobbly Willie
J. Red Fox
K. Old Hickory
L. Young Hickory
M. Big Bill
N. Chief
O. Ike
P. Tricky Dick
Q. Dutch
R. Poppy
S. Bubba
T. Professor

Nicknames often reflect an individual's personality, appearance, career, title, or good deeds. Look at the people listed below. Create a nickname for each person using the positive qualities of their personalities, appearances, careers, titles, or good deeds. Compare your nicknames with those created by your classmates. Are they similar or different?

Your teacher: _____

The principal of your school: _____

Your parent or guardian: _____

Bonus Box: Do you have a nickname? If so, explain how and why you received it. If you do not have a nickname, create one for yourself; then explain why you chose this particular nickname.

Note To The Teacher: Divide students into pairs. Make one copy of this page for each pair. Provide a variety of reference materials.

Saluting The Ladies!

Star-Spangled Suggestions For Teaching About Famous American Women

March is National Women's History Month. Participate with these star-studded activities honoring the women who have inspired our country from sea to shining sea.

by Patricia Twohey

Women Worth Remembering

Part One: Ignite interest about famous American women with this simple investigation. Ask each student to write the names of five famous American women who have contributed to our society. Then instruct the student to write a sentence next to each name that tells why he selected that woman. Collect the students' papers, keeping them until the end of the unit.

Part Two: To culminate the unit, return the papers collected in Part One. Have students discuss whether they would change any of their choices and why. Then give each student a 12" x 18" sheet of white paper. Instruct the student to divide the sheet into six 6-inch squares using a marker. Direct the student to choose five women whom he has learned about in the unit and write the name of each woman in a different square. In the sixth and remaining square, have him write the name of a woman he knows personally who has been important to him. Distribute crayons so that the student can illustrate each square, with an event from each woman's life as shown. Assess each student's learning by having him explain his artwork to the class.

Famous First Ladies

Many outstanding women have served as first ladies of our country while their husbands were president. Challenge your students to a scavenger hunt to acquaint them with some of the women who have worked alongside their husbands to make our country great. Give each team of two or three students a copy of the reproducible on page 162 and ample resources for conducting the search. After the hunt take time to discuss each first lady's contribution.

To obtain resources and additional information, contact the National Women's History Project (an educational nonprofit organization), 7738 Bell Road, Dept. P, Windsor, CA 95492; (707) 838-6000; www.nwhp.org.

Martha Washington

Notable Singers

Create a melodious bulletin board from notes that feature American female singers. On light-colored paper, duplicate two copies of the musical-note pattern on page 163 for each student. Next print each name from the list below on the stem of a different music note. Give each student a programmed note plus a blank note pattern. Instruct the student to use reference materials to find and fill in the information about the singer on the programmed note. Then direct the student to repeat the assignment using the blank note pattern to feature his favorite contemporary female singer.

Meanwhile cut one treble clef symbol and one bass clef symbol from black paper. Staple the clefs to the left edge of the bulletin board as shown. Then make a musical staff by stapling five horizontal rows of black yarn from each clef to the right edge of the board as shown. Pin the students' completed notes to the bulletin board. If desired, encourage students to bring in cassette tapes or compact discs of these recording artists to share with the class!

Extend the life of the board by updating it as each new category of women is studied. Just change the title and duplicate additional music-note patterns after whiting-out and reprogramming the original one.

American Female Singers

Marian Anderson	Carole King
Joan Baez	Barbara Mandrell
Maria Callas	Reba McEntire
Mariah Carey	Bette Midler
Judy Collins	Rosa Ponselle
Ella Fitzgerald	Leontyne Price
Aretha Franklin	Beverly Sills
Billie Holiday	Bessie Smith
Lena Horne	Barbra Streisand
Whitney Houston	Tina Turner
Mahalia Jackson	

Marian Anderson

You've Come A Long Way, Ladies!

Honor the women who have blazed the trail to women's rights by creating a class timeline. Gather encyclopedias, biographies, and other resources related to women's rights. Duplicate a supply of the timeline form on page 163 for each student. Write each name listed below on a separate slip of paper. Have each student draw one name. Direct the student to research and complete a timeline form about that woman. If a student finishes early, have him complete a timeline form for one or more of the dates listed on the historical background chart below. Stretch a string from one corner of the classroom to another. Attach the completed forms to the string in chronological order. Have students examine the completed timeline, noting any patterns or trends in this visual history of women's rights.

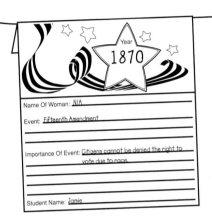

Year 1870

Name Of Woman: *N/A*

Event: *Fifteenth Amendment*

Importance Of Event: *Citizens cannot be denied the right to vote due to race.*

Student Name: *Jamie*

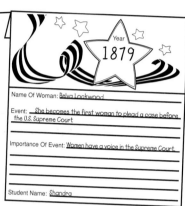

Year 1879

Name Of Woman: *Belva Lockwood*

Event: *She becomes the first woman to plead a case before the U.S. Supreme Court.*

Importance Of Event: *Women have a voice in the Supreme Court.*

Student Name: *Shandra*

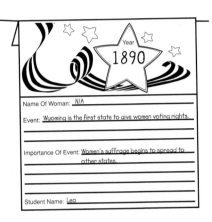

Year 1890

Name Of Woman: *N/A*

Event: *Wyoming is the first state to give women voting rights.*

Importance Of Event: *Women's suffrage begins to spread to other states.*

Student Name: *Leo*

Women Who Worked For Women's Rights

Bella Abzug
Mary Anderson
Susan B. Anthony
Amelia Jenks Bloomer
Hattie Wyatt Caraway
Carrie Chapman Catt

Shirley Chisholm
Geraldine Ferraro
Betty Friedan
Ruth Bader Ginsburg
Belva Lockwood
Clare Boothe Luce

Patsy Mink
Carol Moseley-Braun
Lucretia Mott
Sandra Day O'Connor
Frances Perkins
Jeannette Rankin

Janet Reno
Margaret Chase Smith
Elizabeth Cady Stanton
Gloria Steinem
Lucy Stone
Naomi Wolf

Historical Background

1830 All white males can vote.

1870 Citizens cannot be denied the right to vote due to race (Fifteenth Amendment).

1890 Wyoming is the first state to give women voting rights.

1920 All citizens can vote regardless of sex (Nineteenth Amendment).

1923 The Equal Rights Amendment is presented to Congress for the first time.

1964 The Civil Rights Act is extended to include women.

1972 Congress passes an Equal Rights Amendment and sends it to the states to be ratified.

1982 The Equal Rights Amendment fails (only 35 of the needed 38 states ratify it).

Sandra Day O'Connor

Concentrating On Achievements

Celebrate National Women's History Month with a game that combines history and graphing skills. Duplicate and cut apart the 42 game cards on page 164. Cut 21 index cards in half; then paste a different game card onto each index-card half. Laminate the cards if desired. Next pin colored yarn to a bulletin board to form a 6 x 7 grid as shown. Staple cut-out letters that spell the words WOMEN IN and HISTORY along the *x* and *y* axes as pictured. Shuffle the game cards and pin one card facedown to each of the grid's points.

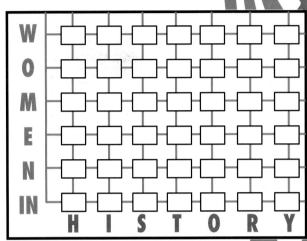

To play the game, divide students into two teams. Have a Team A member call out two coordinate pairs of letters from the board, such as (W, R) and (IN, H). Instruct a Team B member to turn over the cards located at those intersecting points. Have this player also read the cards aloud and check to see if the letters in the corners of the cards match. If they do match, direct the student to remove the cards and give them to the player from Team A. Then award Team A two points and give Team B a turn at play. If the cards do not match, have the student turn the cards back over and proceed to give a Team B member a turn. End the game when all the cards have been matched. The team with the most points wins.

The "Write" Stuff!

Add a cooperative twist to your usual book-reporting format while studying American women. Divide students into teams of four. Display the list of American women authors below; then have each team select a different author. Give each team two to four weeks to read as many different books by this author as possible, with each team member reading a different book. At the end of the reading period, give each team a copy of the reproducible on page 165. Instruct each team to complete the activities on the reproducible and share its findings with the class. Repeat the activity as often as you like by having each team choose a different author each time.

American Women Authors For Children

Louisa May Alcott	Marguerite Henry
Judy Blume	Madeleine L'Engle
Frances Burnett	Lois Lenski
Betsy Byars	Lois Lowry
Ann Nolan Clark	Patricia MacLachlan
Beverly Cleary	Phyllis Reynolds Naylor
Elizabeth Coatsworth	Emily Neville
Marguerite de Angeli	Katherine Paterson
Elizabeth Enright	Cynthia Rylant
Eleanor Estes	Kate Seredy
Rachel Field	Elizabeth George Speare
Esther Forbes	Mildred D. Taylor
Paula Fox	Cynthia Voigt
Jean Craighead George	Laura Ingalls Wilder
Virginia Hamilton	Elizabeth Yates

Betsy Byars

Name(s) _____

162

Famous First Ladies Scavenger Hunt

The wife of our country's president serves as first lady while her husband is in office. Every first lady works in her own way to serve our country. Help your group research the first ladies listed below. Then match each first lady with her accomplishment(s) by writing her initials inside the square of a clue box.

1.	2.	3.	4.
She was America's first first lady.	She redecorated the White House and made the mansion a historic tourist attraction.	She fought for equal rights for minority groups and worked with young people and the underprivileged.	She chaired the United Nation's Human Rights Commission and headed the Commission on the Status of Women.
5.	**6.**	**7.**	**8.**
She was a great-great-niece of Franklin Pierce, the 14th president of the United States.	She saved George Washington's portrait and many important government papers when the city of Washington was invaded by the British in 1814.	She supported women's rights and urged her husband to "remember the ladies" as new laws were proposed.	She was so popular that many women copied her hairstyle and fashions.
9.	**10.**	**11.**	**12.**
She wrote a daily newspaper column, many magazine articles, and several books.	She started the Foundation for Family Literacy and supported reading programs throughout the United States.	She was a distinguished lawyer and speaker who actively participated in her husband's presidency.	She was the first first lady to address the United Nations.
13.	**14.**	**15.**	**16.**
She shared her husband's battlefield hardships and even organized a sewing circle to mend soldiers' uniforms.	She wrote two books from her dogs' points of view and gave the money earned from them to charities.	She was the wife of the second president and the mother of the sixth president.	She helped write a low-cost health-care plan for her husband's administration on which Congress chose not to act.

Abigail Adams   Barbara Bush

Hillary Rodham Clinton   Jacqueline Kennedy (Onassis)

Dolley Madison   Nancy Reagan

Eleanor Roosevelt   Martha Washington

Note To The Teacher: Use with "Famous First Ladies" on page 158. Duplicate one copy for each group. Supply reference materials such as encyclopedias, almanacs, and biographies. *America's Most Influential First Ladies* by Carl S. Anthony (Oliver Press, Inc.) and *The Smithsonian Book Of The First Ladies* (Henry Holt & Company, Inc.) are recommended as resources.

Pattern

Use with "Notable Singers" on page 159.

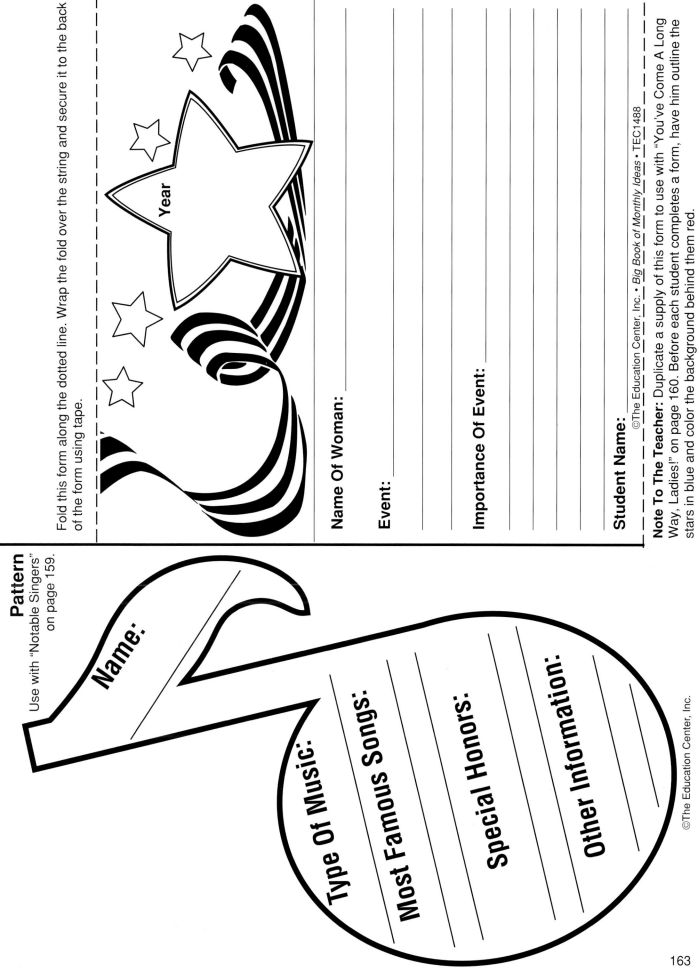

Fold this form along the dotted line. Wrap the fold over the string and secure it to the back of the form using tape.

Year

Name Of Woman: _____

Event: _____

Importance Of Event: _____
_____
_____
_____

Student Name: _____

©The Education Center, Inc. • *Big Book of Monthly Ideas* • TEC1488

Note To The Teacher: Duplicate a supply of this form to use with "You've Come A Long Way, Ladies!" on page 160. Before each student completes a form, have him outline the stars in blue and color the background behind them red.

Name: _____

Type Of Music: _____

Most Famous Songs: _____

Special Honors: _____

Other Information: _____

©The Education Center, Inc.

A Margaret Corbin	**A** This woman took her husband's place at his gun post after he was killed in a Revolutionary War battle in 1776.	**B** Rosa Parks	**B** This African-American woman's refusal to give up her bus seat to a white passenger led to the desegregation of the bus system in Montgomery, Alabama, in 1956.
C Pocahontas	**C** According to legend this Native American saved Captain John Smith from death in 1608.	**D** Betsy Ross	**D** This seamstress is believed to have sewn the first American flag in 1776.
E Harriet Tubman	**E** This former slave led about 300 slaves to freedom in Canada along the Underground Railroad.	**F** Lydia Darragh	**F** This woman saved American troops from disaster by warning General Washington about British battle plans.
G Esther Morris	**G** In 1870 this woman became the first woman justice of the peace in the United States.	**H** Sybil Ludington	**H** In 1777 this 16-year-old gathered together her father's regiment to fight the British at Danbury, Connecticut.
I Anne Hutchinson	**I** This religious reformer moved to Rhode Island after being banished from the Massachusetts Bay Colony in 1637.	**J** Clara Barton	**J** This woman gave supplies to wounded soldiers during the Civil War and later founded the American Red Cross.
K Dorothea Dix	**K** Through her activities hospitals for the insane and homeless were founded throughout the United States and Canada during the 1800s.	**L** Kateri Tekakwitha	**L** This seventeenth-century Native American was the first layperson to be recommended for sainthood in the Roman Catholic Church.
M Juliette Gordon Low	**M** This woman started the Girl Scouts of the United States of America in 1915.	**N** Sacagawea	**N** This Native American was the interpreter and guide for the Lewis and Clark expedition in 1805 and 1806.
O Sojourner Truth	**O** This former slave preached against slavery and for women's rights during the 1800s.	**P** Narcissa Whitman	**P** In 1836 she became the first white woman to cross the Rocky Mountains.
Q Jane Addams	**Q** This woman established the first settlement house, Hull House, in 1889 in Chicago. She won the Nobel Peace Prize in 1931.	**R** Julia Lathrop	**R** In 1899 this social worker set up the first juvenile court in the world. In 1912 she became the first chief of the U.S. Department of Labor's Children's Bureau.
S Molly Pitcher	**S** This woman carried water to thirsty soldiers during a Revolutionary War battle.	**T** Annie Oakley	**T** This famous markswoman performed with Buffalo Bill's Wild West Show from 1885 to 1902.
U Helen Keller	**U** Blind and deaf from the age of two, this woman became a famous speaker and writer during the early twentieth century.		

Note To The Teacher: Duplicate one copy of these game cards to use with "Concentrating On Achievements" on page 161.

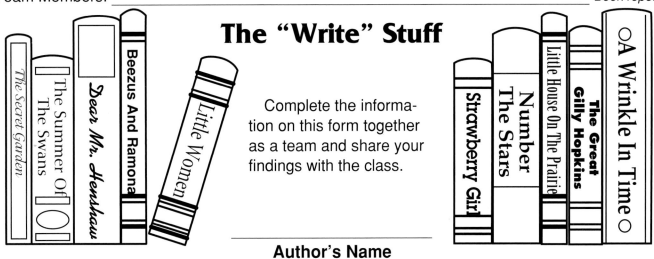

The "Write" Stuff

Complete the information on this form together as a team and share your findings with the class.

_____
Author's Name

A. Interesting Facts About The Author's Life:	B. Titles Of The Books We Read:
_____ _____ _____ _____ _____ _____ _____	_____ _____ _____ _____ _____ _____ _____
C. How The Books Were Alike: (Type of literature, characters, setting, plot, theme, style) _____ _____ _____ _____ _____ _____	**D. How The Books Were Different:** (Type of literature, characters, setting, plot, theme, style) _____ _____ _____ _____ _____ _____
E. What We Liked About The Books: _____ _____ _____ _____ _____ _____	**F. Why Others Should Read The Books:** _____ _____ _____ _____ _____ _____

Note To The Teacher: Duplicate one copy of this page for each group to use with "The 'Write' Stuff!" on page 161.

Top O' The Mornin' To Ye!

Activities To Explore Ireland—
The Land Of Mist, Magic, And Mystique

Journey with your students to the Emerald Isle. Use the following activities to introduce your students to the people, land, and culture of Ireland.

by Caroline Chapman, Kelly Gooden, Thad McLaurin, Karen Richmond, and Irene Taylor

Over The Rainbow

Legend says that if you are clever enough to catch a leprechaun, he might share his pot of gold. Have students fill their own pots of gold with facts about Ireland. Divide students into small groups. Give each group one 8" x 18" sheet of black paper, one 1" x 18" strip of black paper, one 9" x 12" sheet of green paper, scissors, a stapler, and tape. Have each group follow these directions to construct its pot of gold:

1. Make a series of two-inch cuts along one of the long sides of the large piece of black paper. Space the cuts 1 1/2 inches apart to resemble flaps as shown.
2. Form a cylinder by overlapping the two short ends of the paper. Secure the ends with tape.
3. Fold the flaps inward to form the bottom of the pot. Secure the flaps with tape.
4. Staple each end of the 1" x 18" strip to the inside of the pot to create a handle.
5. Decorate the outside of the pot with shamrocks cut from the green paper.

Direct each group to research five topics related to the culture of Ireland, such as family life, celebrations, folklore, foods, and crafts. Have each group create an artifact or information pamphlet to illustrate each topic. After each group presents its information to the class, place the group's items in its pot. Staple the pots to a bulletin board as shown.

Lucky, Lucky, Lucky Charms

One American cereal company has capitalized on the Irish legend of leprechauns to create Lucky Charms® cereal. The ads for this product encourage consumers to eat such marshmallow shapes as hearts, moons, and clover. Use this familiar cereal to review and improve each student's predicting, averaging, and graphing skills. Divide the class into groups of three. Give each group a plastic bowl filled with one cup of Lucky Charms®, a calculator, and one copy of page 169. Have each group follow the directions on page 169 to record a predicted and actual number of each marshmallow shape. Next write the actual totals from each group on the board (see the illustration). Direct the students to find the sum (the class total) of each shape and divide that number by the number of groups to get an average number of shapes in the box of cereal.

In the next chart, have each group graph the totals for each marshmallow shape. Finally, guide each group to find the cost per ounce of the cereal. To do this, have each group divide the total cost of the cereal by the total number of ounces.

Marshmallow Shapes	Group Totals								Class Totals
	1	2	3	4	5	6	7	8	
Heart	10	3	12	6	5	14	9	18	77
Moon	6	8	2	5	9	6	6	7	49
Rainbow	11	10	6	14	8	2	8	9	68
Clover									
Pot Of Gold									
Balloon									
Horseshoe									
Star									

A Taste Of Ireland

Mmm! Can you smell it? Nearly every block in Belfast—Northern Ireland's capital city—has a bakery. And nearly every bakery features Soda Farls (small, triangular cakes). They are quick and easy to make. So use the recipe below and treat your class to some Soda Farls and cups of hot tea during your study of Ireland.

Ingredients:
1 cup all-purpose flour
1 cup cake flour
2 teaspoons baking soda
1 teaspoon salt
1 cup buttermilk

Directions:
Mix the dry ingredients together. Add buttermilk and stir to form a dough. Place the dough onto a floured board and knead gently. Divide the dough in half. Form each half into a circle about 10–12 inches in diameter; then cut each circle into quarters to form *farls*. In a skillet fry each farl in a "wee" bit of butter or margarine until browned (about 5–7 minutes on each side). You may need to set each farl on end to help cook the sides. This recipe makes eight farls. To conserve your ingredients, split one farl between two students or cut each farl into bite-size pieces.

'Tis A Soft Day

The climate in Ireland is surprisingly mild given its northern latitude. To help students compare temperature variations around Ireland, have them prepare temperature bar graphs for the cities of Dublin, Cork, and Belfast by using the information below. Also have students graph and compare the high, low, or average temperatures for each city.

After they complete their graphs, have students discuss the ranges between the months with the highest and lowest temperatures. Based on their graphs, have students describe the climate for Ireland.

	Dublin		Cork		Belfast	
	High	Low	High	Low	High	Low
Jan.	47°F	34°F	49°F	36°F	43°F	36°F
Feb.	47°F	36°F	49°F	38°F	45°F	36°F
Mar.	50°F	38°F	52°F	40°F	49°F	38°F
Apr.	56°F	40°F	56°F	41°F	54°F	50°F
May	59°F	43°F	61°F	45°F	59°F	43°F
June	65°F	49°F	67°F	50°F	65°F	49°F
July	68°F	52°F	68°F	54°F	65°F	52°F
Aug.	67°F	52°F	68°F	54°F	65°F	52°F
Sept.	63°F	49°F	65°F	50°F	61°F	49°F
Oct.	58°F	43°F	58°F	45°F	56°F	45°F
Nov.	50°F	40°F	52°F	40°F	49°F	40°F
Dec.	47°F	38°F	49°F	38°F	45°F	38°F

Two Faces Of Ireland

The island of Ireland has two different and distinct faces. The Republic of Ireland, an independent nation, shares the Emerald Isle with Northern Ireland, a province of the United Kingdom. Duplicate page 170 for each group of three students. Instruct each group to research the differences and similarities between these two countries and record its findings on page 170. Then have each group use the information to write two paragraphs—one describing the similarities between The Republic of Ireland and Northern Ireland, and one describing the differences. Enlarge and copy the map of Ireland (page 170) onto green bulletin-board paper. Instruct each group to write a final draft of its paragraphs on a green shamrock cutout. Post these cutouts around the map of Ireland for an attractive display.

Northern Ireland

The Republic Of Ireland

Names _____ *Math: predicting, graphing, and averaging skills*

Lucky Hearts, Moons, And Stars

Add a little luck to your math and observation skills to get a handle on these lucky charms!

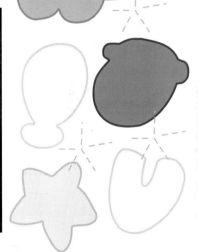

Part A:

1. Look at the bowl of cereal your teacher has given you. Without touching the cereal, predict how many of each marshmallow shape are in the bowl. Record your predictions in column A on the chart below.
2. Pour out the cereal and count each shape. Record those totals in column B.
3. Give the teacher the totals from column B to record on the board.
4. Using the information from the board, add up each group's totals for each shape. Record each class total in column C.
5. Divide each class total by the number of groups to get an average for each shape. Record that number in column D.

Marshmallow Shapes	A Prediction	B Actual Amount	C Class Total	D Average
Heart				
Moon				
Rainbow				
Clover				
Pot Of Gold				
Balloon				
Horseshoe				
Star				

Part B: Use the information in the chart above to graph the total number of each type of marshmallow in one box of cereal.

Class Total Of Marshmallows

Marshmallow Shapes (y-axis): Heart, Moon, Rainbow, Clover, Pot Of Gold, Balloon, Horseshoe, Star

x-axis: 0 5 10 15 20 25 30 35 40 45 50 55 60 65 70 75 80 85 90 95 100

Total Number Of Marshmallows

Part C:

Total Cost Of Cereal $ [ ] ÷ Total Ounces [ ] oz. = Cost Per Ounce $ [ ]

©The Education Center, Inc. • *Big Book of Monthly Ideas* • TEC1488

Note To The Teacher: Use with "Lucky, Lucky, Lucky Charms" on page 167. Provide each student group with one cup of cereal in a bowl and a calculator.

169

Two Faces Of Ireland

The Republic of Ireland, an independent nation, shares the Emerald Isle with Northern Ireland, a province of the United Kingdom. As a group, research the two lands and use the space below to record the similarities and differences between them in such areas as government, economy, culture, and climate. Next use this information to write two paragraphs—one describing the similarities between The Republic of Ireland and Northern Ireland, and one describing the differences.

Northern Ireland: _____

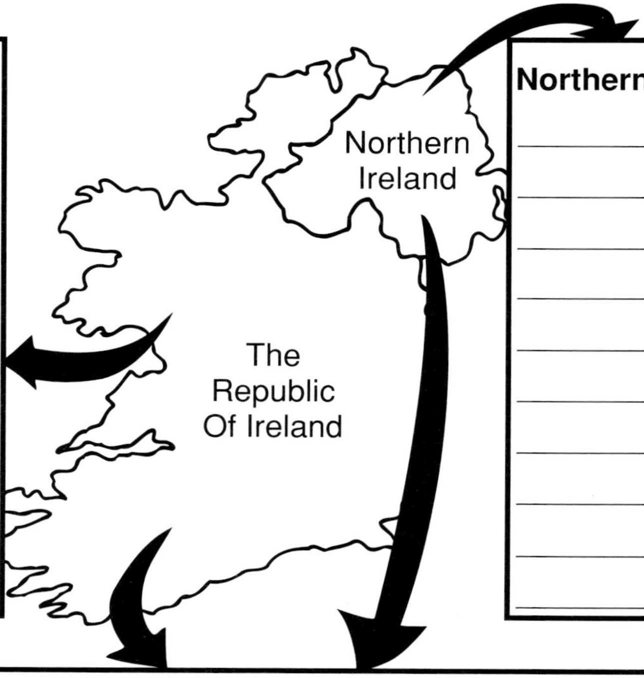

Northern Ireland

The Republic Of Ireland

The Republic Of Ireland: _____

Both Countries: _____

Note To The Teacher: Duplicate this page for each group and use it with "Two Faces Of Ireland" on page 168.

Four Of A Kind

Tom, Patrick, Stephen, and Sean are very close friends who live in four different cities and come from four different families. They share many hobbies and interests. Use the clues below to match each boy's first name with his last name and hometown. Use an *X* to eliminate options, and use an *O* to indicate a match. After completing the chart, fill in the map below by writing the first and last name of each boy by his hometown.

	Dublin	Limerick	Kilkenny	Tipperary	McMurphy	McNamara	O'Leary	O'Mally
Tom								
Patrick								
Stephen								
Sean								
McMurphy								
McNamara								
O'Leary								
O'Mally								

Ireland

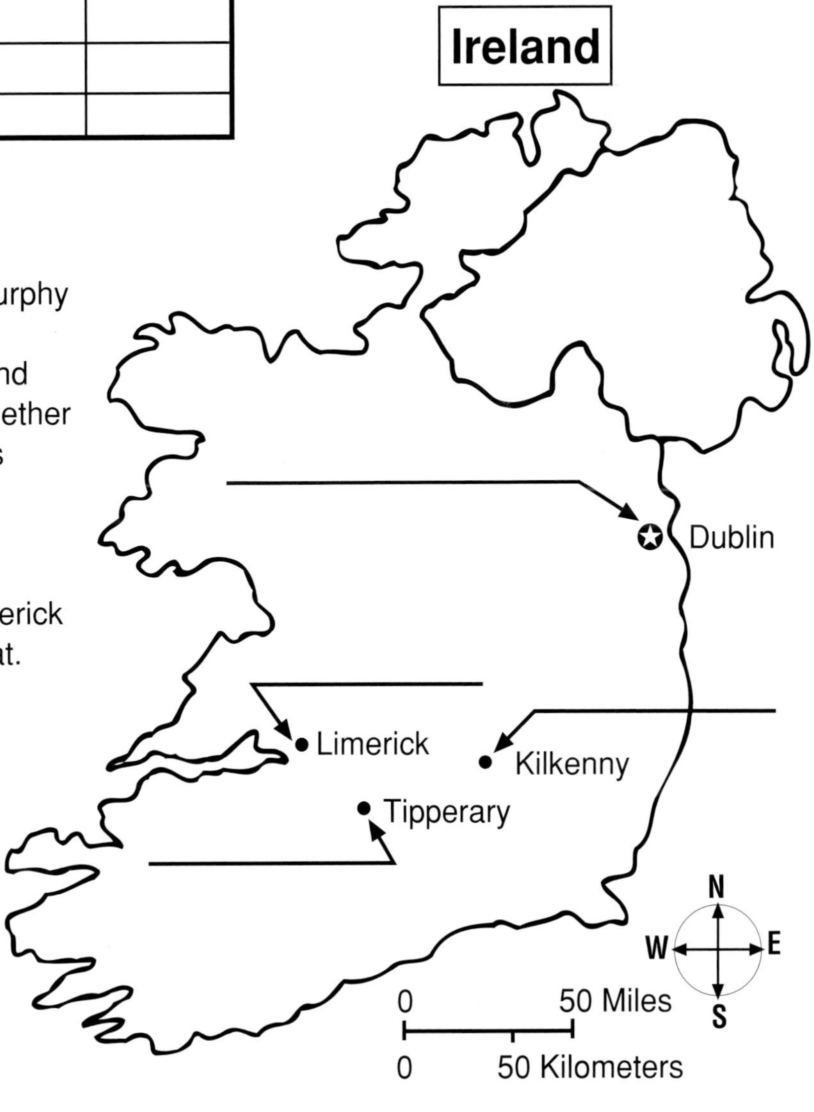

Clues:

1. Tom and O'Mally like to visit McMurphy in Tipperary.
2. Stephen, the boy from Limerick, and O'Leary all play Gaelic football together while the boy from Tipperary takes pictures.
3. Neither Sean nor O'Leary lives in Kilkenny.
4. Both Patrick and the boy from Limerick enjoy fishing on the Dubliner's boat.
5. McNamara lives in Kilkenny.
6. Sean's name is not McMurphy.
7. Tom has lived in Dublin all his life.

Dublin

Limerick

Kilkenny

Tipperary

N
W — E
S

0   50 Miles

0   50 Kilometers

Bonus Box: Use the map of Ireland to calculate the distance that each boy lives from Ireland's capital city.

Strengthening Measurement Skills

Do measurement skills weigh your students down? Then lighten their loads with the following exercises guaranteed to pump them up during National Weights And Measures Week (the first week in March) or any time of the year!

by Geri Harris, Judy Henline, and Marsha Schmus

Handy Hints And Useful Units

A centimeter is about the width of an index finger. An inch is about the length of a standard paper clip. Share additional measurement-training tips like these with students for times when rulers cannot be found. Next challenge each child to find and list several objects that are approximately the same length as a foot, a yard, a meter, and a millimeter. Then have each student share his list of nonstandard units with other class members to make measurement easier for them, too! See the reproducible activity "How Do You Measure Up?" on page 176 for a great follow-up.

Walk A Mile In My Shoes

The ancient Romans—who used the word *mille* to mean 1,000—decided that it took 1,000 paces to equal a mile. But not everyone's *stride,* or long step, was the same length, so problems arose with this standard. Demonstrate this dilemma by having each student measure his stride.

First use a 100-foot measuring tape to mark off a 66-foot length on the playground. Instruct each student to walk from one end of the length to the other end using a comfortable stride. Make sure he counts the number of strides it takes to walk one length. After repeating this process two more times, have him find the average of his three walks. Finally have him multiply that average by 80 to determine the number of strides it would take for him to walk a mile. Is the number close to 1,000?

Hey! Wait up!

Goofy Portraits

Listen for giggles as students complete this zany metric activity! Label eight containers as follows: Head Length, Head Width, Hair Length, Ear Length, Ear Width, Eye Width, Nose Length, and Mouth Width. Instruct each student to write these labels down the left side of a sheet of notepaper. Fill each container with a class set of paper strips on which you have written a different metric length such as 7 cm, 50 mm, 25 cm, or 1 dm. Have every student pull one strip from each container and write that dimension next to the appropriate label on her notepaper. Next instruct the student to use colored paper, scissors, glue, markers, and metric rulers to construct a cut-paper portrait of an alien or monster. Stress that each student use the metric ruler to accurately measure her creature's features. Have each student label the creature's dimensions, then name and frame her goofy creation before displaying it on a bulletin board. If desired, have each student write a paragraph describing her metric monster.

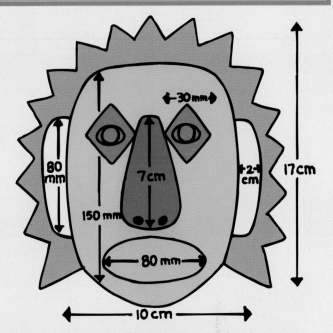

Suggested Widths And Lengths

2 dm	25 cm	10 mm	6 cm
18 cm	3 dm	1 dm	60 mm
150 mm	2.5 dm	90 mm	7 cm
15 cm	24 cm	2 cm	70 mm
200 mm	270 mm	20 mm	8 cm
16 cm	22 cm	3 cm	1.5 cm
1.5 dm	26 cm	30 mm	15 mm
110 mm	19 cm	4 cm	45 mm
120 mm	210 mm	5 cm	75 mm
13 cm	1 cm	50 mm	65 mm

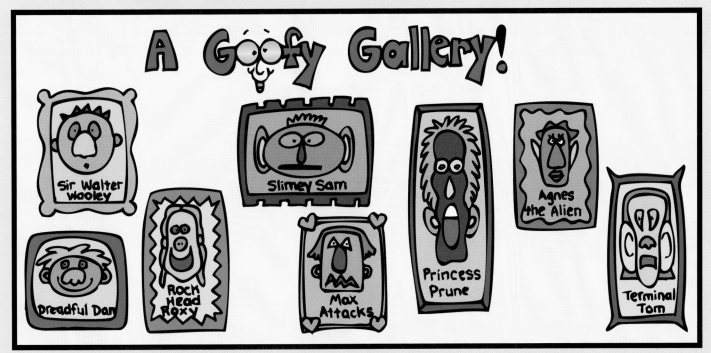

A Goofy Gallery!

Sir Walter Wooley

Slimey Sam

Agnes the Alien

Dreadful Dan

Rock Head Roxy

Max Attacks

Princess Prune

Terminal Tom

Measurement Scavenger Hunt

Strengthen your weight lifters' skills with a most-unusual scavenger hunt. First provide the following measuring tools in a central location in your class: rulers, yardsticks, a bathroom scale, a food scale (standard measurement), a two-cup measuring cup, and empty gallon jugs and quart containers. Next duplicate the scavenger-hunt form on page 178, one copy for each student in a pair. After discussing the directions on the sheet, encourage your hunting pairs to complete as many of the tasks on the form as possible within a 15-minute time period. Encourage students to find unusual objects to measure by informing them that teams win points only when the objects they measure differ from every other team's objects. When time expires, have student teams share their findings with the class, and then award points. The team with the most points wins.

Circles Of Fun

Are you going around in circles trying to help students understand circumference? If so, try this simple hands-on activity. Have each student bring in the plastic lids from a variety of containers such as coffee cans, potato-chip canisters, and margarine tubs. Pair students and give each pair a 24-inch length of string, a ruler, a lid, and a marker. Instruct the pair to wrap the string around the perimeter of the lid and mark the spot on the string where the two ends meet. Next direct the pair to measure the distance between the two ends using a ruler. Provide additional practice by having the pairs exchange lids. Point out that the string method of finding circumference works well if the object is small. However, finding the circumference of a large object—such as a planet—requires the use of a special formula. Introduce students to the formula for finding circumference: diameter x π (π = 3.14). Have each pair figure the circumference of a lid using the string method and the formula. Compare the results to check for accuracy.

174

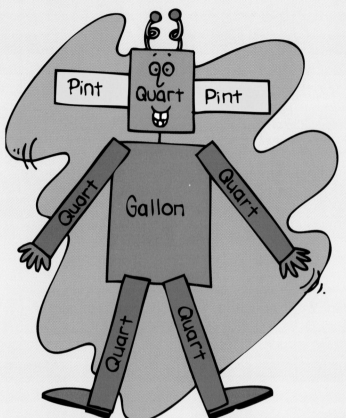

Measurement Models

Improve your students' measurement fitness with an exercise that becomes a fun visual activity. Have each student choose a category: length, capacity, or weight measurement. Then challenge each child to select two units from that category that have some proportional relationship to one another. For instance, two *cups* make one *pint,* or 12 *inches* make one *foot,* or 16 *ounces* make one *pound.* Next have each student cut shapes from colorful paper that match the proportions of the units selected. Instruct the student to label each cutout as shown. After making a few sets of these relational cutouts, have the student combine them to construct a measurement character (see illustration). Display these colorful measurement models on a bulletin board to help the whole class review.

Measurement Bingo

What better way to keep students' measurement skills fit than playing a fun game? Duplicate a copy of the bingo gameboard on page 177 for each student. Also duplicate and cut apart one copy of the 24 measurement cards on the same page. Have each student write each of the following measurements in a separate box on his board (some of the measurements will be repeated): 1 ft., 1 yd., 1 mi., 2 ft., 2 yd., 1 cm, 1 dm, 1 m, 1 km, 2 dm, 2 m, 2 km, 5 dm, 5 m, 5 km, 1 yd., 1 mi., 2 yd., 1 dm, 1 m, 2 dm, 2 m, 5 dm, and 5 m. Distribute dried beans to students for covering the boxes during the game. To play, call out the measurement on one of the cards. Direct students to find the box containing an equivalent measurement on their gameboards and cover that box with a bean. The first student to cover five boxes in a row vertically, horizontally, or diagonally wins the round.

B	I	N	G	O
	5 dm	1 ft.	2 ft.	5 m
5 dm	2 yd.	1 mi.		1 dm
1 yd.		FREE SPACE	2 dm	5 km
2 yd.	1 cm	1 dm		1 km
	2 m	1 m	5 m	1yd

5,280 feet

200 centimeters

2,000 meters

200 millimeters

100 centimeters

How Do You Measure Up?

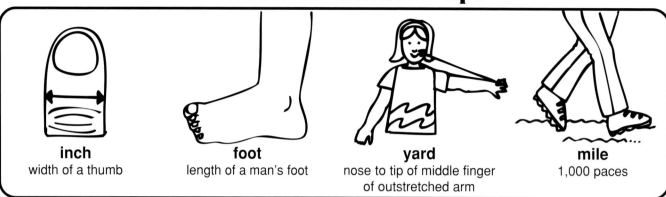

inch	**foot**	**yard**	**mile**
width of a thumb	length of a man's foot	nose to tip of middle finger of outstretched arm	1,000 paces

In earlier times people used different parts of their bodies to measure length. Do the activities in Parts A and B below to help your measurement skills grow.

Part A: Work with four of your classmates. Use a tape measure to measure the width of the thumb and the lengths of or distances between the other body parts listed below. To measure a *stride* (long step), place the tape measure at the back of the heel of one foot. Then measure to the heel of the other foot. Record your measurements in the chart below.

What To Measure	Student 1	Student 2	Student 3	Student 4	Student 5
Thumb					
Foot					
Outstretched Arm From Nose To Fingertips					
Stride From Heel To Heel					

What observations can you make about the accuracy of your measurements? _____

_____

_____

Part B: Invent your own measuring device. Without using standard measuring tools, find the heights of yourself and your classmates from Part A above.

	Student 1	Student 2	Student 3	Student 4	Student 5
Height in _____ (nonstandard unit)					

Bonus Box: Each of the following terms relates to some form of measurement. Use a dictionary to tell what each one measures: knot, fathom, watt, speedometer, odometer.

Note To The Teacher: Use this reproducible to follow up "Handy Hints And Useful Units" on page 172. Duplicate one copy for each student.

24 inches	2,000 meters	36 inches
3 feet	12 inches	5,280 feet
1,760 yards	10 centimeters	100 millimeters
20 decimeters	200 centimeters	50 decimeters
500 centimeters	10 decimeters	100 centimeters
200 millimeters	20 centimeters	6 feet
72 inches	10 millimeters	5,000 meters
50 centimeters	500 millimeters	1,000 meters

B	I	N	G	O
		FREE SPACE		

Note To The Teacher: Use the bingo gameboard and measurement cards with "Measurement Bingo" on page 175. Duplicate one gameboard for each student. Duplicate one copy of the cards—laminating them if desired—before cutting them apart.

©The Education Center, Inc. • *Big Book of Monthly Ideas* • TEC1488 • Key p. 232

Name _____

Measurement

Measurement Scavenger Hunt

You are about to embark on a very interesting search. Read through the list below. Then search the classroom for one unusual object to match each given measurement.

Find an item that:

Remember:
You earn a point for each object only if your answer is correct *and* is not mentioned by someone else!

1. Is less than 8 inches long:

2. Is more than 1 foot long:

3. Is less than 3/4 of an inch long:

4. Is about 1 yard long:

5. Weighs more than 1 pound:

6. Weighs about an ounce:

7. Weighs about the same amount as you:

8. Holds about 1 gallon of liquid:

9. Holds about 1 quart of liquid:

10. Holds about 1 pint of liquid:

©The Education Center, Inc. • *Big Book of Monthly Ideas* • TEC1488

Note To The Teacher: Duplicate one copy of this page for each student to use with "Measurement Scavenger Hunt" on page 174.

178

Deep-Sea Measuring

Do you enjoy riddles? Study the information in the chart. Then read each of the clues below. Use the data in the chart to help you identify the deep-sea dwellers described below.

Dolphin	Length	Shark	Length	Whale	Length
Bottle-nosed Dolphin	12 ft.	Bull Shark	11 ft.	Blue Whale	98 ft.
Spinner Dolphin	7 ft.	Scalloped Hammerhead Shark	13 ft. 9 in.	Humpback Whale	53 ft.
Striped Dolphin	9 ft.	Tiger Shark	18 ft.	Killer Whale	31 ft.
		White Shark	21 ft.		

1. I am 12 inches shorter than the bottle-nosed dolphin. Who am I? _____

2. I am 540 inches shorter than the blue whale. Who am I? _____

3. I am 4 yards 1 foot longer than the tiger shark. Who am I? _____

4. I am 2 yards longer than the bottle-nosed dolphin. Who am I? _____

5. I am 165 inches long. Who am I? _____

6. I am 48 inches shorter than the bull shark. Who am I? _____

7. I am 1 yard longer than the striped dolphin. Who am I? _____

8. I am 24 inches longer than the spinner dolphin. Who am I? _____

9. I am 1,176 inches long. Who am I? _____

10. I am 7 feet 3 inches longer than the scalloped hammerhead shark. Who am I? _____

11. I am half as long as a tiger shark. Who am I? _____

12. I am about eight times longer than the bottle-nosed dolphin. Who am I? _____

13. We are the closest in length. Who are we? _____ and _____

14. Our combined lengths equal the length of a tiger shark. Who are we?

_____ and _____

15. It would take about nine of me to equal the length of a blue whale. Who am I? _____

Bonus Box: If all of the animals above were lined up end-to-end, how long would the line be?

Name _____   *Exact measurement, fractions*

Cracking The Ruler Code

Bruno and his friend want to meet at the roller rink for some exercise. To keep Bruno's pesky little brother from finding out, they made the plans using a "Ruler Code." Study the rulers below and decode the boys' messages.

1. I will meet you at ___ ___ ___   ___ ___ ___ ___ ___   ___ ___ ___.
$1\frac{1}{2}$ $2\frac{3}{4}$ 1 $\frac{3}{8}$ $3\frac{1}{2}$ $4\frac{7}{8}$ 6 $1\frac{3}{4}$ 4 $4\frac{7}{8}$ $\frac{1}{8}$

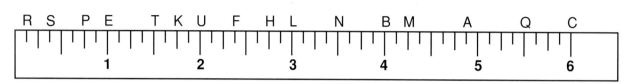

2. Don't forget to bring your ___ ___ ___ ___ ___   ___ ___ ___ ___.
$1\frac{3}{8}$ $3\frac{3}{8}$ $2\frac{5}{8}$ 5 6 $5\frac{3}{4}$ $1\frac{7}{8}$ $3\frac{1}{4}$ $2\frac{3}{4}$

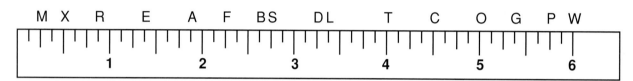

3. Bring some money to ___ ___ ___   ___ ___ ___ ___   ___ ___ ___ ___ ___.
$3\frac{1}{2}$ $2\frac{1}{4}$ $\frac{4}{8}$ $5\frac{1}{4}$ 4 $2\frac{3}{4}$ $2\frac{1}{4}$ 1 $5\frac{1}{2}$ $1\frac{2}{8}$ $1\frac{2}{8}$ $1\frac{3}{4}$

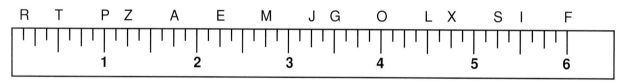

4. I might bring ___ ___   ___ ___ ___ ___ ___ ___   ___ ___ ___ ___ ___.
$1\frac{1}{2}$ $\frac{3}{4}$ 5 $2\frac{1}{4}$ $3\frac{3}{8}$ 4 $4\frac{1}{2}$ $\frac{2}{8}$ $2\frac{1}{2}$ 6 $3\frac{1}{8}$ $3\frac{1}{8}$ $\frac{3}{4}$

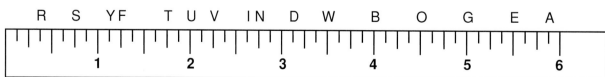

5. I need to be home ___ ___   ___ ___ ___ ___.
4 $1\frac{1}{8}$ $1\frac{1}{4}$ $2\frac{5}{8}$ $2\frac{1}{4}$ $5\frac{1}{2}$

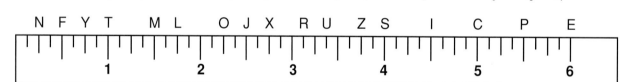

Bonus Box: Choose one of the rulers above and use its letters to write a ruler-code message to a friend. Then give the message to the friend to solve.

We've Got The Whole Earth In Our Hands

First celebrated on April 22, 1970, Earth Day continues to remind us to "Give Earth A Chance." Use the following activities to help students understand and appreciate the importance of protecting our earth and all of its wonderful resources.

by Cindy Mondello and Thad McLaurin

The Global Gazette

During your Earth Day unit, have each student keep a journal of his thoughts and feelings about various environmental topics. Duplicate the journal cover on page 186 for each student. Have each student create his journal by stapling the cover to 20 sheets of notebook paper. Provide each student with markers or crayons to decorate his cover

Suggested journal topics to get your students started:

- Is your town or city experiencing pollution problems? What are they? Make a list of possible solutions to the problems.
- Close your eyes and picture yourself in a special place surrounded by nature. Where are you? What sounds do you hear? What do you see? How does this place make you feel?
- You are an alien from a distant planet, and you have just landed on the earth. Describe the things you like best about this planet.
- Pretend you are Mother Earth. Write a letter urging humans to protect the environment. Suggest ways that humans can help preserve the earth.
- Why is it important to recycle?
- Illustrate a bumper sticker with a catchy, but meaningful, environmental message.
- We are rapidly running out of landfill space. What are some ways people can decrease the amount of garbage they produce each day?
- Oil spills have caused much destruction along our shores. How can future oil spills be prevented?
- Your best friend just threw his soda can out the car window. How do you handle this situation?

Acid Rain—Silent But Deadly

Cars and coal-burning electric-power plants spew pollutants into the atmosphere where they are chemically changed into *acid rain*. Acid rain erodes buildings and destroys plants and animals. Demonstrate the effects of acid rain by placing a piece of chalk in a glass jar containing vinegar. Tell students that the acidic vinegar eating away at the chalk is similar to acid rain slowly eroding buildings. Next recruit student volunteers to help test the effects of acid rain on plants.

Materials: two small plants, water, vinegar, two plastic containers

Directions:
Step 1: Mix three cups of water and one cup of vinegar in a plastic container. Label this container "Acid Rain."
Step 2: Fill the other container with four cups of water. Label this container "Water."
Step 3: Label one plant "Acid Rain" and one plant "Water."
Step 4: Water each plant every three days for two weeks, using equal amounts of liquid from the appropriate containers.
Step 5: At the end of two weeks, have the students describe the two plants. Then ask the students, "What do you think happens to an entire forest when acid rain falls on it week after week?"

The plant watered with the acid rain mixture will be limp and the leaves will turn brown. The plant receiving only water will be healthy and strong.

Trash Troopers

One of the biggest ways people pollute the environment is by dropping "stuff" on the ground that does not belong there. It's called littering. Help your students learn more about litter and clean up your school's campus at the same time with the following activity: Divide students into teams of three or four. Supply each team with one copy of the reproducible on page 187, a trash bag, rubber gloves, a marker, and several sheets of newspaper. Review the directions and rules for trash collecting on page 187. Then assign each team a specific area of the school grounds. Tell each team to spend 15 minutes collecting trash in its assigned area, then meet back at a designated location to complete the rest of the activity. Have each team follow the directions on page 187 for sorting and graphing its trash. Conclude the activity by having each team present its litter graph to the rest of the class.

A Rotten Recipe

Teach your students how to reduce, reuse, and recycle all at the same time by making *compost*—an organic fertilizer. Recruit a parent volunteer to construct a 4' x 4' wooden bin with a removable top. Set the box on a level area of your schoolyard. Place fresh straw in the bottom. Have students save salad, fruit, vegetable, and bread scraps from their lunches. Also ask the cafeteria staff to save eggshells for the compost. Do not add dairy products, meats, or fats to the bin. Cover the scraps with a thin layer of soil and a layer of grass or weed clippings. Continue the process of building layer upon layer. *Aerate,* or get air circulating through the compost, by turning the scraps and soil over with a shovel or pitchfork each week. If desired, add earthworms to the compost to speed up the breakdown of the materials. Keep the compost moist, but cover it if heavy rain is forecast. In four to six weeks, the compost will be ready to spread around trees and shrubbery. Also mix with the soil in any planting beds on the school grounds. Keep up the rotten work!

Trash Town, USA

Tell your students they have just become citizens of Trash Town, USA. Some very serious pollution problems are threatening the town. Divide the students into four "Pollution Preventing Teams." Duplicate the reproducible on page 188. Cut along the dotted lines and give each team a different "Pollution Problem Card." Have each team research the questions on its problem card. Then instruct each group to develop a plan to solve or correct the pollution problem. Have each group present its problem, its research, and its plan of action to the rest of the class. Encourage the class to suggest other actions to help solve the pollution problems.

Earth-Smart Cleaners

Television commercials have familiarized students with the latest bathroom/kitchen cleaners and furniture polishes. But most students aren't aware that many cleaning products are harmful to the environment. Send home the following environmentally safe cleaner recipes for your students and their families to make and use:

Earth-Smart Glass Cleaner:
Mix four tablespoons of vinegar with four cups of water in an empty spray bottle. Spray on any type of glass and wipe dry with a clean cloth.
©The Education Center, Inc.

Earth-Smart Bathroom And Kitchen Cleaner:
Use baking soda to clean the kitchen sink and counters as well as the bathroom tub and tile. Rinse well with water and wipe dry with a clean cloth.
©The Education Center, Inc.

Earth-Smart Furniture Cleaner:
Combine one cup of water with one cup of lemon juice in an empty spray bottle. Spray a clean cloth; then wipe the furniture clean. Keep refrigerated when not in use.
©The Education Center, Inc.

What A Waste

Have you ever bought something that had so much packaging you ended up throwing away as much as you kept? Packaging makes a product look more attractive and helps to hold items together, but often a lot of unneeded layers are used. For example, a box of chocolates may have five or six layers of packaging. All this extra packaging creates a lot of unnecessary trash. About one-third of the garbage in a landfill consists of discarded packaging.

Help your students become more informed consumers by asking each student to bring in one packaged product to analyze. Then have the student answer the following questions: Does it contain excess packaging? How can the packaging be improved? Can it be sold without packaging? Then have each student present his product and his suggestions for improving its packaging to the class.

185

_____

(Student's Name)

EARTH DAY JOURNAL

Note To The Teacher: Duplicate this page for each student to use with "The Global Gazette" on page 182.

Trash Troopers To The Rescue!

Many people litter by leaving trash where it doesn't belong. Become a "Trash Trooper" and help clean up your environment. As a team, complete the activity below by following the steps provided, as well as any directions given by your teacher.

Materials:
one trash bag, rubber gloves for each team member, several sheets of newspaper, a marker, and the graph below

Directions:

Step 1: Put on your rubber gloves. Collect litter in the area assigned by your teacher. Do not pick up any glass or other dangerous materials. Return to the area designated by the teacher in 15 minutes.

Step 2: Spread out your litter collection on the newspaper. Sort your collection into the following categories: plastic, cloth, cans, food waste, paper, and other.

Step 3: Count the number of items in each category. Use this information to complete the bar graph below.

Step 4: Present your graph to the other teams. In your presentation recommend two or three ways litter can be decreased at your school or in the community.

Step 5: Place your litter collection back in the plastic trash bag. Dispose of the trash properly. Return any dry sheets of newspaper to your teacher for recycling.

Team Litter Graph

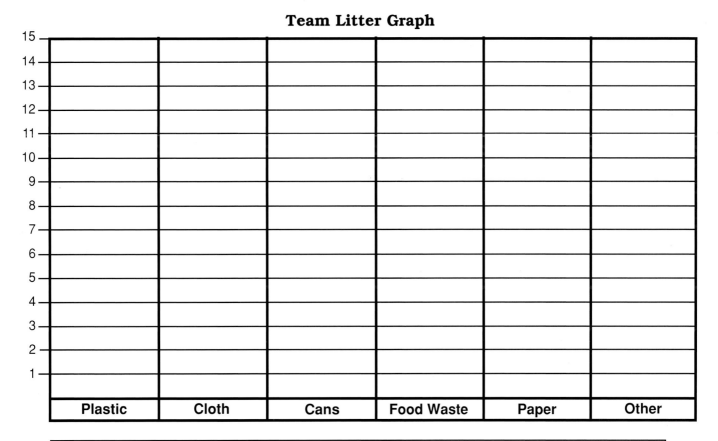

Bonus Box: On the back of this page, list any items in your litter collection that can be recycled or reused.

- -

Note To The Teacher: Duplicate this page for each team to use with "Trash Troopers" on page 183.   187

Pollution Problem Card 2—Recycling

Problem: Trash Town doesn't have a recycling program.

Research Questions:
1. What does it mean to *recycle?*
2. What kinds of materials can be recycled?
3. Does nature recycle?
4. What is composting?

Action: As a team, develop a plan for beginning a recycling program in your town.

©The Education Center, Inc.

Pollution Problem Card 4—Land Pollution

Problem: Trash Town's land has become polluted by garbage, litter, and industrial waste.

Research Questions:
1. What are the major causes of land pollution?
2. How does land pollution contribute to water pollution?
3. How does land pollution affect plant and animal life?
4. Can polluted soil be cleaned and restored?

Action: As a team, develop a plan for cleaning up Trash Town's land and preventing further land pollution.

©The Education Center, Inc.

Pollution Problem Card 1—Air Pollution

Problem: Trash Town's factories and heavy traffic have polluted the air.

Research Questions:
1. What are the main causes of air pollution?
2. What is *smog?*
3. What is currently being done to prevent air pollution in other towns?
4. How does air pollution from one country affect another country?

Action: As a team, develop a plan for decreasing the amount of air pollution in your town.

©The Education Center, Inc.

Pollution Problem Card 3—Water Pollution

Problem: Trash Town's lakes, rivers, and groundwater are polluted.

Research Questions:
1. What are the main causes of water pollution?
2. How does soil contamination or land pollution affect the water supply?
3. How does water pollution affect plants and animals?
4. How have oil spills along our coasts affected the water?

Action: As a team, develop a plan for cleaning up Trash Town's water and preventing further water pollution.

©The Education Center, Inc.

Note To The Teacher: Duplicate this page to use with "Trash Town, USA" on page 184. Cut along the dotted lines and give a different "Pollution Problem Card" to each team.

Camouflaged Contaminant

Industry dumps a lot of undesirable chemicals into our water supply. Although rivers have the ability to naturally clean themselves, many chemicals resist being neutralized. Complete the following activity to understand how pollution doesn't have to be visible to be present.

Materials:

• six clear plastic cups   • water   • red food coloring   • one plastic straw

Procedure:

1. Assign each cup a number from 1 to 6. Fill the first cup with water; then add one drop of red food coloring. Stir the mixture using a plastic straw. This represents a harmful chemical. Observe the color of the water.
2. Pour half of the water from the first cup into the second cup. Add fresh water to the second cup until it is full. Observe the color of the water.
3. Pour half of the water from the second cup into the third cup. Add fresh water to the third cup until it is full. Observe the color of the water.
4. Pour half of the water from the third cup into the fourth cup. Add fresh water to the fourth cup until it is full. Observe the color of the water.
5. Repeat the process until you have filled the sixth cup.

Observations:

1. How did the water in each cup change as you added fresh water to it?_____
_____

2. Even though the sixth cup appears to be colorless, does it contain any food coloring? _____
Explain your answer._____
_____
_____

3. Can a river or lake that looks clean be polluted? _____ Explain your answer. _____
_____
_____

Conclusions: What have you learned about pollution of the earth's water supply?_____
_____
_____

Bonus Box: Can soil that looks clean really be polluted? Explain your answer on the back of this page.

Note To The Teacher: Divide the students into groups of three. Duplicate one copy of this page for each group. Give each group the materials listed. Instruct each group to follow the procedures above to complete the experiment. After completing the experiment, have each group state its observations and conclusions to the rest of the class.

AMAZING OCEANS

Looking down from space, the oceans appear to cover the entire planet—earning Earth its nickname, the "Blue Planet." What kind of environment is this vast expanse of clear blue water? What mysteries lie beneath its surface? Introduce your students to the amazing world of our oceans with the following thematic activities, reproducibles, and literature suggestions.

by Irene Taylor, Pat Wimberley, and Thad McLaurin

BACKGROUND: THE OCEAN—A COMPLEX ECOSYSTEM

The oceans cover 71 percent of the Earth's surface. The Atlantic, Pacific, Indian, and Arctic oceans make up the four large bodies of water separating the continents. The many seas, bays, and gulfs are actually smaller parts of these four oceans.

An ocean is a complex *ecosystem* containing a vast number of unusual creatures and plants that are specially adapted to live in their salty world. Each ocean layer, or *zone,* holds its own unique sea life. From the countless plankton that provide the basis for the food chain, to the luminescent creatures that live in the very deepest, darkest, and coldest regions, all are joined together in a complex web of life. As the modern world impacts the oceans through pollution and misuse, it often threatens the sea life that inhabits each ocean layer.

Many mysterious secrets of the ocean have been unlocked through modern-day exploration. We now know of the ocean's rugged floor, with areas deeper than the highest mountains found on land. We've learned about the amazing creatures that can exist at great depths—withstanding cold, darkness, and great pressures. We've discovered the many riches the ocean provides such as food, minerals, medicines, and energy sources.

Many questions still remain unanswered. Finding the answers to these questions is becoming more and more important as human dependence on the ocean grows.

3-D OCEAN

Breathe life into your ocean studies with the following three-dimensional bulletin board activity. Inform students that ocean life is divided into three groups: *plankton, nekton,* and *benthos.* *Plankton* includes plantlike organisms and animals, such as diatoms and jellyfish, that drift in the upper layers of the ocean. *Nekton* is made up of free-swimming animals, like fish, that live in surface and deep waters. *Benthos* consists of plants and animals, such as kelp and starfish, that live on the ocean floor.

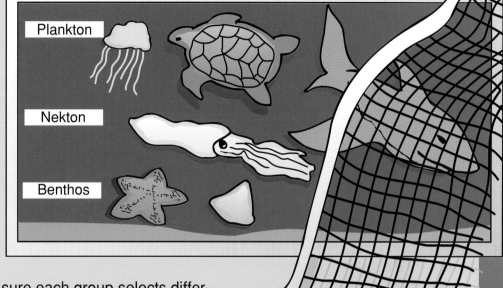

Have students work in six research teams. Assign two teams to research each of the three ocean-life groups. Instruct each team to find information on the feeding habits and the physical traits of two organisms from its group. Make sure each group selects different organisms. Instruct each group to follow the directions below to create a model of each organism.

Cover a large bulletin board with blue paper. Along the bottom of the board, tack a thin strip of brown paper to represent the ocean floor. Label the name of each ocean-life group on a separate 2" x 11" strip of white paper; then post the strips on the board as shown. Hang an old soccer net from the ceiling and drape it across the bulletin board. Attach each model to the board or place it in the net. Add other sea-related items such as a lobster trap, shells, or driftwood. After all the models are displayed, have each team give a short presentation identifying and describing its models.

Materials for each group:
four large sheets of butcher paper, tissue paper, scissors, glue, paint, paintbrushes

Directions:
1. Place two sheets of butcher paper on top of each other. Draw the shape of one organism on the top sheet. Be as accurate as you can with size and shape.
2. Cut out the drawing, making sure to cut through both sheets of paper.
3. Paint both sides of the model as accurately as you can. Add details using markers.
4. Glue the outer edges of the drawing together, leaving an opening at the top.
5. Stuff the model with tissue paper; then glue the opening together.
6. Repeat the first five steps to create the second model.

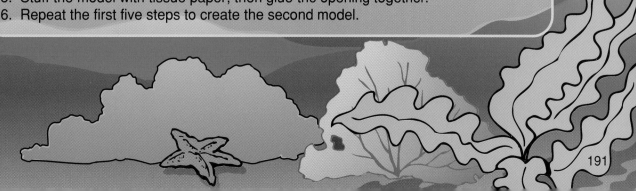

OCEAN LAYER FLIP BOOKS

Descend into the ocean depths and you will pass through four distinct layers on your way to the ocean floor. The deeper you go, the colder and darker the water becomes.

The most productive layer—the *sunlight zone*—lies just beneath the surface of the ocean and extends down to 650 feet. Beneath the sunlight zone, you will find the *twilight zone,* which begins at 650 feet and continues down to 3,250 feet. Leaving the twilight zone, you enter the *bathypelagic zone,* which ends at approximately 19,700 feet below sea level. Anything below 19,700 feet, including the ocean floor, exists in the *hadal zone.*

Take your students on a deep-sea dive through the layers of the ocean. Instruct each student to research the four layers. Then have your junior oceanographers create flip books to record and present their findings. Have each student follow the steps below to create his own "Under The Sea" flip book.

Materials for each student:

Provide each student with markers, crayons, scissors, and one sheet of construction paper in each of the following colors and dimensions:
- white—12" x 5"
- light blue—12" x 7"
- dark blue—12" x 9"
- black—12" x 11"
- brown—12" x 12"

Directions for the student:

Step 1: Carefully trim one 12-inch edge of each sheet of paper (except the brown sheet) in a wavy pattern as shown. No more than one-half inch should be trimmed off. This will form the bottom edge of each page.

Step 2: Stack the colored paper in the following order: white (top sheet), light blue, dark blue, black, and brown (bottom sheet). Be sure that the bottom edge of each sheet is visible as shown.

Step 3: Staple all the sheets together at the top to bind the booklet.

Step 4: The brown, black, dark blue, and light blue pages represent the four layers of the ocean. Label the bottom of each page with the appropriate zone name. On each page, include drawings of plant and animal life found in that zone as well as a brief description of the zone.

Step 5: Decorate the white cover with illustrations and the title "Under The Sea."

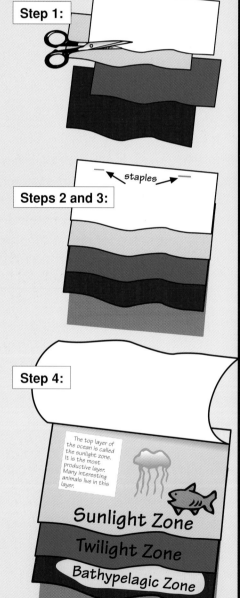

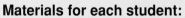

DEEP-SEA STATISTICS

How deep is the ocean? Divers wearing special pressure suits have been able to dive down to about 1,650 feet. But the ocean is much deeper than that! The average depth of the ocean is about 12,500 feet; however, many ocean basins are 18,000 to 20,000 feet deep. The deepest parts of the ocean are found in *trenches*—long, narrow cracks in the ocean floor found near the edges of continents and island chains.

Help your students learn more about the ocean's deepest trenches. Duplicate page 194 for each student. Then discuss the terms *mean* and *range*. Explain that *mean* is the average of a group of numbers, and that *range* is the difference between the greatest and least numbers. Provide students with calculators; then instruct each student to follow the directions on the reproducible. After each student has completed page 194, collect the questions and answers collected from the Bonus Box directions. Use these to help the class discuss the data revealed on the graph.

HIDE AND SEEK

Survival is a daily challenge for creatures of the sea. Many sea animals have developed special characteristics that help protect them from predators. Share with your students the following ways various sea creatures hide in the sea:

- **Camouflage**—Camouflage helps animals blend in with their surroundings. Some, like the octopus, even have the ability to change their skin color or texture to match the background.
- **Counter shading**—Dark backs and white stomachs are common characteristics of sea animals. Predators looking up at the animal's white belly have a hard time seeing it against the sunlight reflecting off the water. From above, the animal's dark back blends in with the dark ocean water.
- **Disruptive Coloration**—Some sea creatures, especially ones that live in coral reefs, make use of brightly colored stripes and spots that break up the body shape. This helps to conceal them against their backgrounds.
- **False Eye Spots**—Other sea creatures make use of unusual patterns and colors to conceal vulnerable body parts. Some fish have spots that look similar to eyes on the opposite ends of their bodies. This will often confuse predators.

Enlist the aid of your librarian in finding various pictures of sea creatures that utilize these protective coloration techniques. Show these to your students; then challenge each student to create his own sea creature that makes use of one or all of the camouflaging methods described above. Duplicate page 195 for each student. Instruct each student to follow the directions on the handout. Then have each student present his sea creature to the rest of the class and explain how it hides itself in the sea. Bind the completed pages into a booklet. Add a cover with the title "Now You See Me, Now You Don't!"

Deep-Sea Statistics

Answer each question below and complete the graph to learn more about the ocean's depths. Use a calculator if needed.

Some Of The Deepest Recorded Depths
Puerto Rico Trench—28,374 ft.
Diamantina Depth—26,400 ft.
Mariana Trench—36,198 ft.
Aleutian Trench—25,194 ft.
Cayman Trench—23,288 ft.

Ocean Depths In Feet

20,000
21,000
22,000
23,000
24,000
25,000
26,000
27,000
28,000
29,000
30,000
31,000
32,000
33,000
34,000
35,000
36,000
37,000
38,000
39,000
40,000
41,000

1. Number the ocean trenches below in order from the shallowest to the deepest.

   _____ Puerto Rico Trench

   _____ Diamantina Depth

   _____ Mariana Trench

   _____ Aleutian Trench

   _____ Cayman Trench

2. Round each depth to the nearest thousand feet.

   23,288 ft. _____

   25,194 ft. _____

   26,400 ft. _____

   28,374 ft. _____

   36,198 ft. _____

3. Write the name of each trench or depth along the bottom of the graph as ordered in Step 1.

4. Plot each depth on the graph. Then connect the points to create a line graph showing the rounded depth of each trench.

5. To find the *range* of these depths, subtract the smallest depth from the largest depth.

   _____

6. To find the *mean*, add each rounded depth together; then divide by the number of addends.

   _____

7. Draw a line across the graph identifying the mean depth. How many of the trenches are above the mean? _____ How many are below the mean? _____

> **Bonus Box:** Create five study questions using the line-graph information. Write all five questions and their answers on a sheet of notepaper.

©The Education Center, Inc. • *Big Book of Monthly Ideas* • TEC1488 • Key p. 234

Hide And Seek

Survival is a daily challenge for creatures of the sea. Many sea animals have adapted special characteristics that help camouflage them from predators. Read the four coloration techniques described below.

- **Camouflage**—Camouflage helps animals blend in with their surroundings. Some, like the octopus, even have the ability to change their skin color or texture to match the background.
- **Counter shading**—Dark backs and white stomachs are common characteristics of sea animals. Predators looking up at the animal's white belly have a hard time seeing it against the sunlight reflecting off the water. From above, the animal's dark back blends in with the dark ocean water.
- **Disruptive Coloration**—Some sea creatures, especially ones that live in coral reefs, make use of brightly colored stripes and spots that break up the body shape. This helps to conceal them against their backgrounds.
- **False Eye Spots**—Other sea creatures make use of unusual patterns and colors to conceal vulnerable body parts. Some fish have spots that look similar to eyes on the opposite ends of their bodies. This will often confuse predators.

Directions:

In the box below, create a sea creature that uses one or more of the coloration techniques described above. Be very detailed and specific in your drawing. Fold a sheet of notepaper in half. On the bottom half of the paper, write a brief description of the sea creature. Include information on where it lives in the ocean and how it makes use of the coloration technique(s). Cut out your illustration and glue it to the top of the notepaper.

Bonus Box: If you had the ability to blend in with the background, which coloration technique would you use and when would you use it? Write your response on the back of this page.

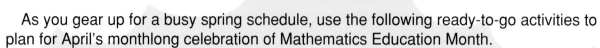

MATH-MONTH MANIA
Activities For Celebrating Mathematics Education Month

As you gear up for a busy spring schedule, use the following ready-to-go activities to plan for April's monthlong celebration of Mathematics Education Month.

by Peggy Hambright

Star Wars

Celebrate Mathematics Education Month with a place-value activity that students will request again and again. Using the digits 1–8 one time each, write any eight-digit number on the board with headings underneath it as shown. Explain to students that the eight digits represent nuclear warheads targeted at our country, and that the warheads must be eliminated one at a time in ascending order. Give each student a calculator; then guide him through the directions below. Record the keystrokes that show how to eliminate each digit on the board, and have students copy them.

1. Clear the display.
2. Enter 38,741,526.
3. Identify the place value represented by the digit *1 (thousands place)*.
4. Think how this digit's value can be changed to zero *(subtract 1,000)*.
5. Press the subtraction key. Enter 1,000. Then press the equal key.
6. Check the display to see if a zero has replaced the 1 and that the number now reads 38,740,526. If not, reenter the previous display and try again.
7. Subtract 20 to get 38,740,506.
8. Subtract 30,000,000 to get 8,740,506.
9. Subtract 40,000 to get 8,700,506.
10. Subtract 500 to get 8,700,006.
11. Subtract 6 to get 8,700,000.
12. Subtract 700,000 to get 8,000,000.
13. Subtract 8,000,000 to get zero.

For independent practice, give students copies of the top half of page 201 and a different eight-digit number. Have them use the form to record the steps needed to eliminate the assigned number's digits.

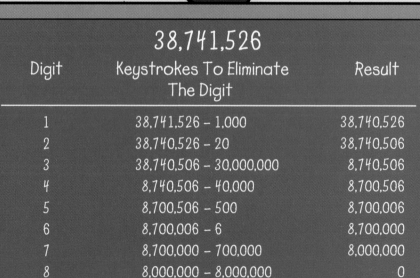

38,741,526

Digit	Keystrokes To Eliminate The Digit	Result
1	38,741,526 – 1,000	38,740,526
2	38,740,526 – 20	38,740,506
3	38,740,506 – 30,000,000	8,740,506
4	8,740,506 – 40,000	8,700,506
5	8,700,506 – 500	8,700,006
6	8,700,006 – 6	8,700,000
7	8,700,000 – 700,000	8,000,000
8	8,000,000 – 8,000,000	0

Curved-Angle Designs

Your students' eyes will be following curves with this math-month activity! Challenge students to create curved-angle designs to showcase on a bulletin board. First help students discover how to construct curved angles. Give each student a copy of the bottom half of page 201 and a ruler. Have students connect the consecutive number pairs in each angle, such as 1 and 2, 3 and 4, and so on.

Next have students practice *sewing* angles. Give each student a six-inch construction paper square, a large-eyed craft needle, a seven-foot length of solid- or multi-colored cotton Knit-Cro-Sheen® thread, transparent tape, and scissors. Instruct students to follow these directions:

1. Place the acute angle on page 201 on top of the construction-paper square. Punch holes with your needle at the numbered marks. Make sure that you make holes in the construction paper.
2. Thread your needle with the seven-foot length of thread. Insert the needle so that it comes up through the paper at 1.
3. Pull the thread through the paper so that just enough of it remains on the back of the paper to tape it down.
4. Continue following the stitching pattern directions on your angle-pattern sheet until all the segments have been sewn.
5. Cut off any extra thread. Tape the end of the thread to the back of the paper.

When students are comfortable with this sewing process, give them larger pieces of construction paper and additional lengths of thread. Ask them to use various sizes of angles to create pictures of sailboats, fishes, or whatever comes to mind! Proudly display the students' creations.

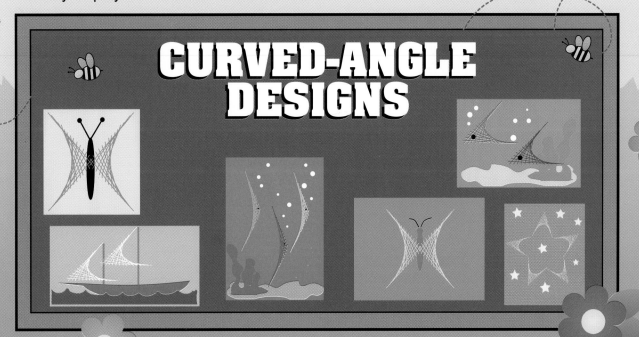

CURVED-ANGLE DESIGNS

Geo-Bingo

Radius…trapezoid…in a bingo game? Provide a relaxed setting and resurrect a fashionably old game to review complex geometric terms. Give each student a copy of the patterns on page 202. Have the student cut apart the symbols and randomly glue any 24 of them to his gameboard's spaces. Prepare the game's calling cards by writing each term below on a different index card—laminating these cards if desired. Give each student a small cup of dried beans to use as game markers. Then shuffle the game cards and call them one at a time. Do not precede each call with a bingo letter. Direct students to cover the spaces that match the called clues with their beans. Play until one student wins by filling a row horizontally, vertically, or diagonally. Allow the winner to call the next game.

perpendicular line segments	parallelogram
right angle	rectangle
equilateral triangle	rhombus
scalene triangle	parallel line segments
vertex	quadrilateral
right triangle	octagon
pentagon	circle
square	trapezoid
intersecting line segments	ray
acute angle	closed curve
chord	isosceles triangle
radius	hexagon
line segment	diameter
line	obtuse angle
point	

"Tangranimals"

Envision a zoo of tangram-shaped animals invading your classroom during Mathematics Education Month. To make this happen, give each student a set of tangram patterns from the top of page 203, an 18" x 24" sheet of colored paper, scissors, glue, and markers. Challenge each student to cut out and then manipulate the tangram's seven pieces to create a real or an imaginary animal on the colored paper. Then have the student glue the tangram pieces on the colored paper. Supply a variety of other art materials so that students can showcase their "tangranimals" in their natural habitats. Display your students' creations on a bulletin board titled "Room [_____]'s Tangram Zoo!" Extend this lesson by having students write adventure stories about their "tangranimals" and share the stories—and their pictures, too—with younger groups of children.

Math For Young Minds

Are your students capable of communicating math concepts to other youngsters via stories? Why not discover the answer? Gather samples of children's books written to help young minds grasp math concepts (see the list below), and use these books as writing models. Share several of these books aloud with your class to stimulate a brainstorming session about topics for other math-related books. List your students' suggestions on the board. Then challenge each student to choose one of the listed topics or an idea of his own to use to write a story that illustrates a math concept. Further challenge students to transform their edited stories into picture books—with hardback covers if desired. Plan times for your students to share their books with classes of younger students during your math-month celebration.

Alexander, Who Used To Be Rich Last Sunday by Judith Viorst (Simon & Schuster Children's Division, 1987)
Anno's Mysterious Multiplying Jar by Mitsumasa Anno (The Putnam Publishing Group, 1983)
Harriet's Halloween Candy by Nancy Carlson (The Lerner Group, 1994)
How Much Is A Million? by David M. Schwartz (William Morrow & Co., Inc.; 1994)
If You Made A Million by David M. Schwartz (William Morrow & Co., Inc.; 1993)
One Hundred Hungry Ants by Elinor J. Pinczes (Houghton Mifflin Company, 1995)
A Remainder Of One by Elinor J. Pinczes (Houghton Mifflin Company, 1993)
The Toothpaste Millionaire by Jean Merrill (Houghton Mifflin Company, 1993)

Measurement Mystery Bags

Arouse students' interest in metric measurement during Mathematics Education Month by preparing mystery bags. Fill each bag with three items of varying lengths. Use things that you have on hand, such as lengths of yarn or ribbon, crayons, strips of paper, plastic (or paper) math manipulatives, index cards, markers, old photographs, etc. Next cut two 10-unit strips of centimeter-grid paper from page 203 to use as measuring tapes. Place the strips in the bag along with the three objects. Then pair students and give each pair a mystery bag. Instruct each pair to open its bag, measure the lengths of the objects inside with the centimeter strips, and list each item and its measurement on paper. Afterward have each pair construct a bar graph that shows the differences in the objects' lengths. Then direct each pair to collaborate with another pair of students to write a paragraph that compares their two graphs.

Perceiving Patterns

How easy is it to perceive a geometric pattern and continue it? Make a transparency of the centimeter grid on the bottom half of page 203. Copy and display the first line of any pattern below with a wipe-off marker—beginning in the top row of the grid. Give students copies of the grid on page 203. Then have them duplicate the displayed pattern in the top rows of their grids—first in pencil. Layer newspapers or paper towels underneath each student's grid to protect his desktop before he colors the pattern with markers. As time permits, challenge students to duplicate and extend as many of the remaining patterns as possible.

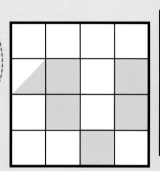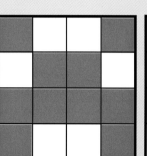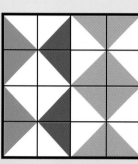

Gridiron Competition

Your math-month celebration has never known team competition like this! Prepare a gameboard by copying the grid below on poster board, laminating it for use with a wipe-off marker. Display the resulting grid with a cutout of an obstacle—such as a hurdle or a bridge—pinned to it at (4, 4).

Next divide your class into two teams. Explain that the object of the game is to be the first team to reach the finish line. Establish that a team can begin anywhere on the grid. But explain further that each team must draw a continuous line stretching from its starting point either across or up the grid to the obstacle, then from there to the finish line opposite its team name. Begin play by having a child from Team A call out a set of coordinates for plotting its starting point. Allow a child from Team B to do the same. Plot these points that identify the starting points for both teams with different-colored wipe-off markers. Before having the second player on each team call out the next coordinate pair, explain that from now on, the lines can advance only one square at a time. Remind players that they should choose their coordinates carefully so that the lines lead first toward the obstacle and then to the finish line.

Increase the difficulty level of subsequent rounds by adding a new obstacle to the gameboard each time—and requiring each one to be reached in sequence!

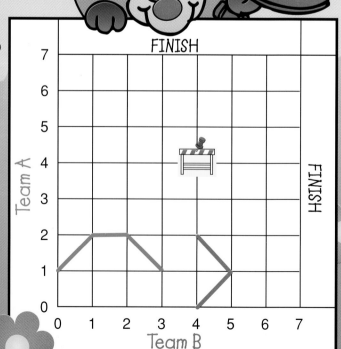

Star Wars

Enter the eight-digit number your teacher gives you in the box below.
Then write the steps to show how to eliminate it.

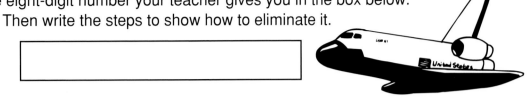

Digit	Keystrokes To Eliminate The Digit	Resulting Number In Display
1	_____	_____
2	_____	_____
3	_____	_____
4	_____	_____
5	_____	_____
6	_____	_____
7	_____	_____
8	_____	_____

©The Education Center, Inc. • *Big Book of Monthly Ideas* • TEC1488

Note To The Teacher: Duplicate one copy of this form for each student to use with "Star Wars" on page 196.

Patterns

Use with "Curved-Angle Designs" on page 197.

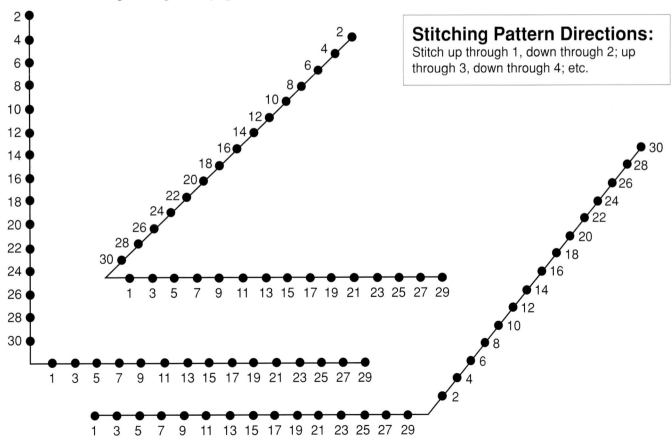

Stitching Pattern Directions:
Stitch up through 1, down through 2; up through 3, down through 4; etc.

Patterns

Use with "Geo-Bingo" on page 198.

Centimeter Grid
Use with "Measurement Mystery Bags" on page 199 and "Perceiving Patterns" on page 200.

What A Workout!

Complete the following workout to keep your problem-solving strategies in good condition! Show your work in the spaces provided.

1. Alan wants to work up to doing 50 sit-ups a day. He plans to start with 20 and add 3 more each day. On which day will Alan do 50 sit-ups? Fill in the chart to show your answer.

Day	1	2	3													
Number Of Sit-Ups	20															

2. Alan went shopping for new workout clothes. He purchased three T-shirts: blue, red, and white. He bought three pairs of mesh shorts: black, gray, and brown. He also got three towels: striped, solid-colored, and checked. How many combinations can Alan make? Extend and label the tree diagram to show all of the possible combinations for Alan on the back of this sheet.

3. Alan's two friends, Jeremy and Trevor, asked to meet him at the Y to work out. One boy had his mother bring him by car, one walked, and the other rode his bicycle. Jeremy did not walk. Alan did not come by car. Trevor rode his bike. How did Alan get to the Y? Complete the chart by marking a √ in a box for a match and an X if no match is possible.

	Alan	Jeremy	Trevor
Traveled By Car			
Walked			
Rode A Bicycle			

4. Alan decided to add bicycling to his workout schedule. The shop he visited carried bicycles and tricycles. If there were 48 wheels and 18 cycles in all, how many bicycles were in the shop? Continue the chart to find out.

Number Of Tricycles	Number Of Tricycle Wheels	Number Of Bicycles	Number Of Bicycle Wheels	Total Number Of Cycles	Total Number Of Wheels
1	3	17	34	18	37
2	6	16	32	18	38
3	9	15	30	18	39

Bon Voyage!

Teacher-Tested Activities For The End Of The Year

Before your students pack up their bags—and their minds—for summer vacationland and camp, grab their attention with these motivating activities.

by Chris Christensen, Beth Gress, and Thad McLaurin

Been There, Done That!

What memories and experiences will your students take with them after this school year? Find out by having each student complete the following activity. Duplicate the suitcase pattern on page 210 for each student. Brainstorm several examples for each topic to get students thinking. Instruct each student to fill in the information on his suitcase, then color and cut it out. Enlarge, color, and laminate the traveler pattern on page 211. Mount all the suitcases and the traveler on a bulletin board as shown. If desired, add photographs of class events that took place throughout the year. Encourage each student to read his fellow classmates' reflections.

Let The Games Begin

Use a life-size version of tic-tac-toe to review concepts at the end of the school year. Give each student three 3" x 5" index cards. On the board list nine major subject areas your class has studied this year, such as Reading, Math, and Punctuation. Instruct each student to select three of the listed subject areas. On each of his cards, have the student write the name of the subject, a related review question, and its correct answer. Collect the cards and group them according to subjects. Add a few challenging, review question cards of your own.

Next create a large tic-tac-toe board on the floor with masking tape. Label each square with a different subject area. Divide your class into two teams: the *X's* and the *O's*. Instruct each student to write his name on a strip of paper. Gather the strips from each team in a separate container. To begin the game, draw a name from one of the containers. Direct the student whose name is drawn to select any square on the gameboard and stand on it. Then ask that student a review question from that subject. If the student answers correctly, he remains on the square. Then draw a name from the other team. When a student does not answer correctly, he must leave the square, and the other team gets to play. The first team to have three students standing in a row vertically, horizontally, or diagonally wins the game.

Science
Q. What is the chemical symbol for water?

A. H_2O

Spanish Science Health
Social Studies Writing Reading
Math Punctuation Spelling

Head Games

Enjoy a little summer fun with this crazy art activity. Have each student provide a head-shot photo of himself. Give each student a sheet of 9" x 12" white construction paper and one 3" x 5" index card. Instruct each student to cut out the head from his photo and glue it to the construction paper, leaving enough space underneath the photo to draw his body. Tell the student to draw his body enjoying a favorite summer activity, such as running, diving, or skateboarding. Once the student has completed drawing and coloring his body, direct him to cut out the completed figure. Then instruct each student to write a short sentence describing his favorite summer activity on the index card. Display the photos/drawings and their index-card captions on a bulletin board titled "Summer Fun, Here We Come!" Enlarge the sun pattern on page 211 and mount it in one of the upper corners of the board. Students will get a kick out of getting into each other's heads!

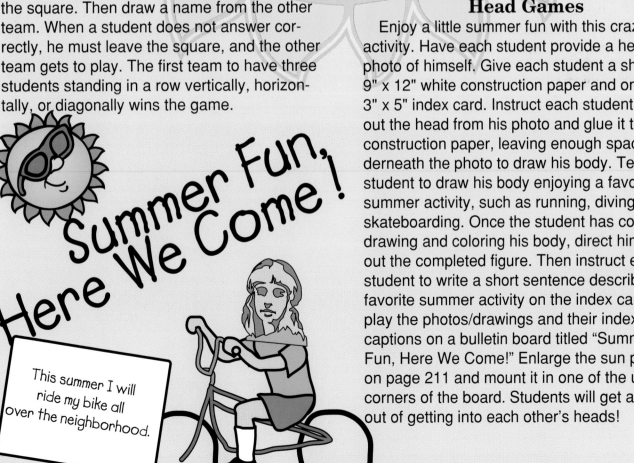

Summer Fun, Here We Come!

This summer I will ride my bike all over the neighborhood.

End-Of-The-Year Mail

Culminate the year's writing skills and stimulate enthusiasm for the new school year with the following letter-writing activities:

- **Dear Future Teacher**—Help prepare your students for the next school year by having each of them write a personal letter of introduction to an upcoming teacher. (The student doesn't need to know the name of the specific teacher.) Encourage the student to include information about her interests, hobbies, and talents. Also have the student include goals she hopes to accomplish during the new school year. Collect these letters and distribute them to the specific teachers once the new class lists are available.

- **Welcome To The New Crew!**—What better way to calm a student's anxiety about a new classroom than by sending a personal letter of encouragement. Encourage your current class to help the upcoming students feel more at ease by having each current student write a personal letter of welcome.

  To get started, first ask each student to recall how he felt on the first day of this school year. Duplicate page 212 for each student. Instruct the student to read the reproducible first, then think carefully about what to write in each blank. As a final touch, direct each student to illustrate a memorable event from the past school year on the back of his letter. Collect these letters and store them in a safe place until you're ready to pull them out and distribute them on the first day of the new school year.

- **Dear Self**—Have each student write a letter to himself about the past school year. Record the following questions on the board to help guide the student:
  —What were your favorite school activities of this year?
  —What was the most important thing you learned this year?
  —What skill, subject, or character trait do you want to work on for next year?
  —In what ways have you changed the most this year?

  After each student has finished writing his letter, give him an envelope and instruct him to address it with his name and home mailing address. Then have the student put his letter in the envelope and seal it. Collect each envelope and inform the student that you will mail the letter to him sometime at the beginning of the next school year. Each student will be amazed at the changes he has already experienced since he wrote the letter.

Trash Or Treasure?

Don't throw away all those dried-up markers, broken crayons, scraps of colored paper, dried-up paints, and unclaimed desk accessories at the end of the year. Have your students turn them into art! Post a large sheet of colored poster board on a wall in your classroom or in the hallway outside your door. Instruct students to search their desks for "junk" to contribute. Pool their collected materials together in a box. Also place a supply of glue and scissors near the box. Then instruct each student to spend a few minutes of her free time during the last week of school arranging and gluing items from the box onto the poster board. When the artwork is complete, have the class vote on a name for this interesting collage of found items.

Summertime...And The Reading Is Easy!

Are you searching for a good list of books that your students can enjoy over the summer vacation? Here's the solution! Duplicate the "Super Summer Reading List" on page 213 for each student. Distribute this list during your last parent-teacher conference, include it with your last classroom newsletter, or simply send it home with students on the last day of school. If desired, duplicate the bookmark below and give it to each student as a summer reading incentive.

Set Sail For Summer Reading!

Realistic Fiction
Adventure
Fantasy
Historical Fiction
Mystery
Humor

Pattern

Use with "Been There; Done That!" on page 206.

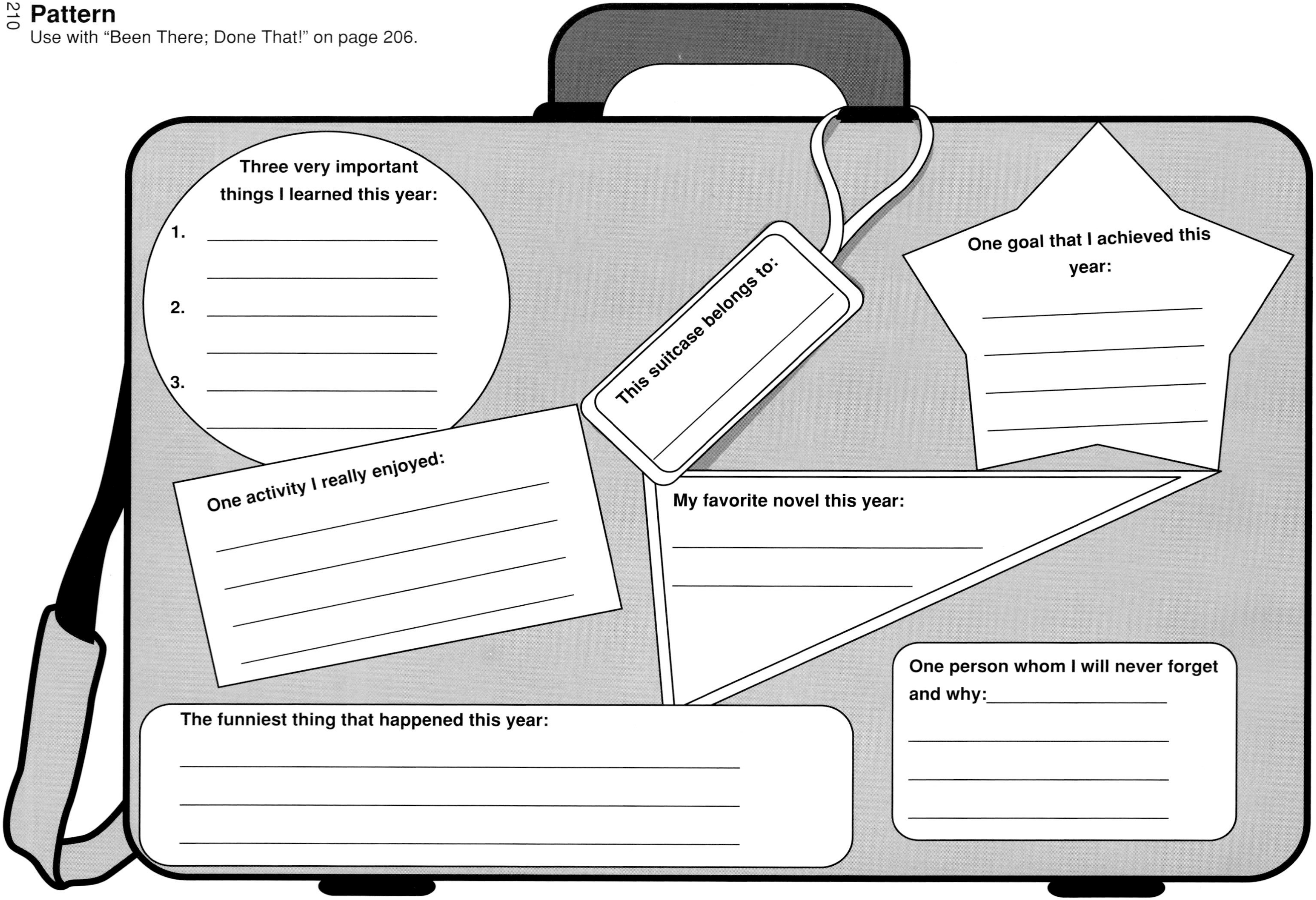
Three very important things I learned this year:
1.
2.
3.
This suitcase belongs to:
One goal that I achieved this year:
One activity I really enjoyed:
My favorite novel this year:
One person whom I will never forget and why:
The funniest thing that happened this year:

Pattern
Use with "Head Games"
on page 207.

Welcome Back To School!

_____ _____, _____
(month)   (date)   (year)

Dear _____ Grader,

Welcome back to school! Congratulations on being placed in _____'s classroom! I was in this class last year and really liked it because _____ _____ _____.

You will really enjoy _____ grade!
I learned a lot while I was in _____'s class. My favorite subject was _____. I liked this subject because _____ _____.

We were involved in a lot of projects. You can look forward to _____ _____ _____.

The unit I enjoyed the most was _____.
I learned a lot during this unit, such as _____ _____.

The best novel I read this year was _____ by _____. I hope you get to read it too. I enjoyed reading it because _____.
You have a lot of neat things to look forward to this year, but I'm not going to tell you everything, because I don't want to spoil them for you.
A couple of hints to help you have a successful school year include _____ _____ and _____ _____. Remember the rules, and things will go smoothly for everyone. Get ready for an awesome year!

Good luck,

_____

Note To The Teacher: Duplicate this page for each student and use with "Welcome To The New Crew!" on page 208.

Super Summer Reading List

Looking for an inexpensive way to travel this summer? Read a book!
A book will transport you to anywhere and any time. Listed below are six
categories of fiction. Challenge yourself to read one book from each section
over the summer. Post this list on your refrigerator and place a check in the box
beside each book that you read. Enjoy your vacation and happy reading!

_____
(Teacher)

Realistic Fiction	Mystery
❑ *Cousins* by Virginia Hamilton	❑ *The Egypt Game* by Zilpha K. Snyder
❑ *Hoops* by Walter Dean Myers	❑ *The Eyes Of The Amaryllis* by Natalie Babbitt
❑ *Maniac Magee* by Jerry Spinelli	❑ *The Kidnapping Of Christina Lattimore* by Joan L. Nixon
❑ *The Pinballs* by Betsy Byars	❑ *The Moonlight Man* by Paula Fox
❑ *The Pushcart War* by Jean Merrill	❑ *The Vandemark Mummy* by Cynthia Voigt
❑ *Shiloh* by Phyllis Reynolds Naylor	❑ *The Westing Game* by Ellen Raskin
❑ *Walk Two Moons* by Sharon Creech	❑ *Who Was That Masked Man, Anyway?* by Avi

Historical Fiction	Adventure
❑ *Blitzcat* by Robert Westall	❑ *Banner In The Sky* by James Ramsey Ullman
❑ *Catherine, Called Birdy* by Karen Cushman	❑ *Beardance* by Will Hobbs
❑ *Roll Of Thunder, Hear My Cry* by Mildred D. Taylor	❑ *The Cay* by Theodore Taylor
❑ *Sing Down The Moon* by Scott O'Dell	❑ *Hatchet* by Gary Paulsen
❑ *The True Confessions Of Charlotte Doyle* by Avi	❑ *Julie Of The Wolves* by Jean Craighead George
❑ *The Upstairs Room* by Johanna Reiss	❑ *My Side Of The Mountain* by Jean Craighead George
❑ *To Walk The Sky Path* by Phyllis Reynolds Naylor	❑ *Stone Fox* by John R. Gardiner

Fantasy	Humor
❑ *The Boggart* by Susan Cooper	❑ *The BFG* by Roald Dahl
❑ *The Giver* by Lois Lowry	❑ *Charlie And The Chocolate Factory* by Roald Dahl
❑ *The House With A Clock In Its Walls* by John Bellairs	❑ *How To Eat Fried Worms* by Thomas Rockwell
❑ *The Lion, The Witch, And The Wardrobe* by C. S. Lewis	❑ *Knights Of The Kitchen Table* by Jon Scieszka
❑ *Redwall* by Brian Jacques	❑ *Skinnybones* by Barbara Park
❑ *Searching For Dragons* by Patricia C. Wrede	❑ *Soup* by Robert Newton Peck
❑ *Tuck Everlasting* by Natalie Babbitt	❑ *The Great Brain Is Back* by John D. Fitzgerald

Note To The Teacher: Duplicate this page for each student and use with "Summertime…And The Reading Is Easy!" on page 209.

HAVING A BALL WITH MATH!

SPORTS-RELATED MATH ACTIVITIES

As the weather begins to warm, your students will be anxious to get outside and play their favorite sports. Use the sports-related math activities in this unit to bring the playing field right into your classroom. Your students are certain to have a ball!

by Marsha Schmus and Stephanie Willett-Smith

GET THE BALL ROLLING

Challenge your students with the following interactive bulletin board. Enlarge several different sports balls using the patterns on page 217. Laminate each ball and staple it to a bulletin board. Use a dry-erase marker to record a different math problem daily on each ball. Have your students complete the problems as morning work or as an enrichment activity. This convenient bulletin board will help keep your students on the ball in math!

BARRY SLATE

BATTER UP!

This hands-on multiplication game is sure to hit a home run with your students! Divide your class into pairs. Give each pair three dice, eight game pieces (four red and four blue), a copy of the gameboard found at the bottom of page 217, and a copy of the directions below. Demonstrate the game to be sure your students understand how to play.

Directions For Each Pair Of Students:
1. Select either the red or blue game pieces to determine your team. The red team player places one game piece on home plate.
2. *Red team player:* Roll the three dice. Mentally calculate the product of the three rolled numbers.
3. *Blue team player:* Use a calculator to check the red player's answer.
4. If the answer given by the red player is *incorrect,* he earns an *out.* Players repeat steps 2 and 3.
5. If the answer given by the red player is *correct,* he looks up the product on the scoring chart located in the middle of the playing field to see which move to make. He then moves his playing piece to the appropriate base, unless he earns an out (a product of 0–40).
6. As in baseball, each game piece advances around the bases. Place a new game piece on home base before rolling the dice.
7. When the red team has earned three outs, the blue team takes its turn at bat.
8. Keep track of each team's runs and outs for each inning using the scoring grids at the bottom of the gameboard.
9. The team with the most runs at the end of seven innings wins the game.

SEARCHING FOR THE STAR

Your students will get a kick out of this soccer graph game. Review cardinal directions and coordinate points with your students. Divide students into pairs and provide each student with a copy of page 218, a red pen, and a blue pen. Explain that each partner has a soccer team with one star player who scores all the goals. The object of this game is to locate the opponent's hidden star player. Instruct partners to sit across from each other, with their gameboards hidden. Direct each student to mark one of the coordinate points with a star to show the location of his star player.

To play, have each student take a turn locating his opponent's star player by calling out a coordinate set. Have his opponent confirm if the guess is correct. If the guess is incorrect, direct the opponent to provide a clue about the location of his star player using cardinal directions. For instance, "You are too far southeast." Direct each player to keep track of his guesses using one color pen, and his opponent's guesses in another color. This helps the player develop a strategy and avoid making the same wrong guess twice. Conclude the game when one of the two players successfully locates the other's star player.

GET BACK TO BASICS

Reach your goals with this football spin-off review game. Divide your class into two teams and have each team come up with a team name. Draw a large football field on the chalkboard. Label the yardage lines as well as each team's name in an end zone. Place two small, football-shaped cutouts—one per team—on the 50-yard line. Gather a set of review flash cards. Begin play by having each team take turns drawing a flash card. For each correct answer a team gives, move that team's football ten yards toward the opponent's goal. Whenever a team answers incorrectly, move its team ball ten yards away from the opponent's goal. The first team whose football crosses its opponent's goal line earns six points. Allow the scoring team to earn an extra point after a touchdown by answering an additional question. Once a team has scored, return both footballs to the 50-yard line and begin play again. Continue playing until all cards have been used or a team reaches a predetermined number of points.

CARD COLLECTING

Explore the world of major-league baseball with your class while reading the book *Teammates* (Harcourt Brace Jovanovich) by Peter Golenbock. Ask students, "What would it be like to have been the first African-American to play on a major-league baseball team?" Then discuss ways that the game of baseball and the fans' loyalty to the game has changed over the years. Tell students that you will be looking at change in one area—baseball cards.

Introduce the mathematical concept of *appreciation*—the increase in value of an item over time. Copy the chart below onto the board, recording only the player names at first. Point out the pictures of the 1940s trading cards found on page 4 of *Teammates*. Ask students to estimate how much each trading card was worth during the 1940s. Then share that each of these cards originally retailed for one cent or less. Record that information in the appropriate squares on the chart. Challenge students to predict the present-day value of the same cards. Record the students' estimations on the chart. Finally fill in the actual values on the chart. Ask students to compare the present value to their estimates. Discuss possible reasons for the difference in value of cards from the same time period. Generate a list of factors that might make one card's value increase more rapidly than another's.

(Note: All values given below are the approximate values of trading cards that are in mint condition. Some values may vary.)

Player's Name	1940s Trading-Card Value	Predicted Present-Day Card Value	Actual Present-Day Card Value
Ewell Blackwell	$0.01		$25.00
Ralph Kiner	$0.01		$125.00
Ted Williams	$0.01		$100.00
Jackie Robinson	$0.01		$150.00 and up
Joe DiMaggio	$0.01		$1,500.00 and up

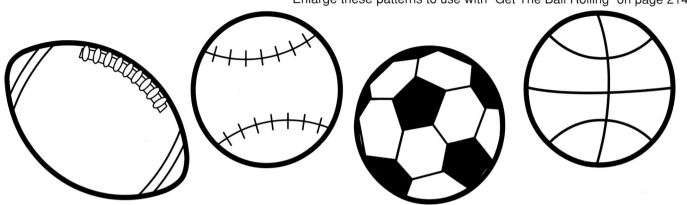

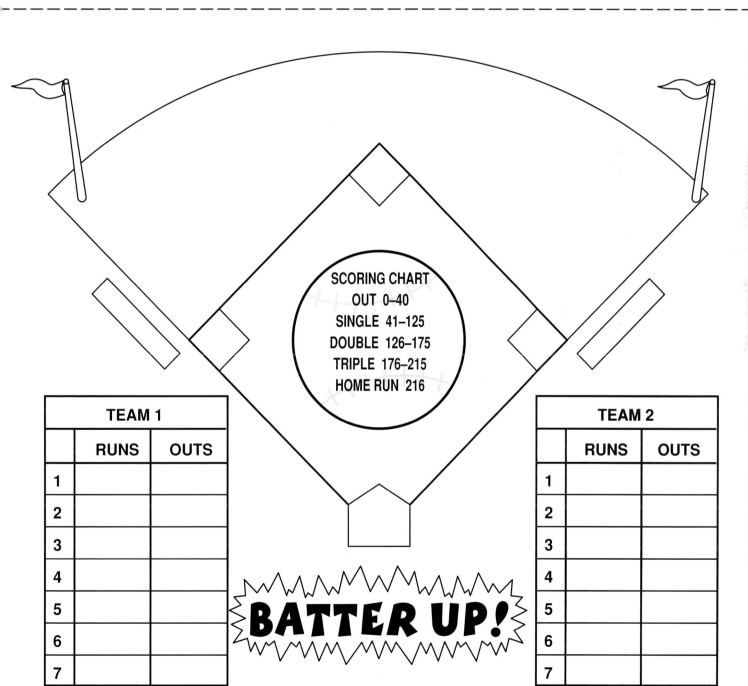

SCORING CHART
OUT 0–40
SINGLE 41–125
DOUBLE 126–175
TRIPLE 176–215
HOME RUN 216

TEAM 1		
	RUNS	OUTS
1		
2		
3		
4		
5		
6		
7		

TEAM 2		
	RUNS	OUTS
1		
2		
3		
4		
5		
6		
7		

BATTER UP!

Note To The Teacher: Use the gameboard above with "Batter Up!" on page 215.

Name _____

SEARCHING FOR THE STAR

Directions:

1. Hide your star player on the grid by placing a star on a coordinate point. Label the point. For instance, (7, E). Do **NOT** show your grid to your opponent.

2. Take turns trying to locate your opponent's star player by guessing a coordinate pair.

3. Mark your incorrect guesses on your grid in one color so you do not guess them again. Mark your opponent's guesses in another color.

4. If your opponent guesses incorrectly, give him a directional clue using cardinal directions.

5. You score a **goal** and win the game when you find the exact coordinate location of your opponent's star player. Happy hunting!

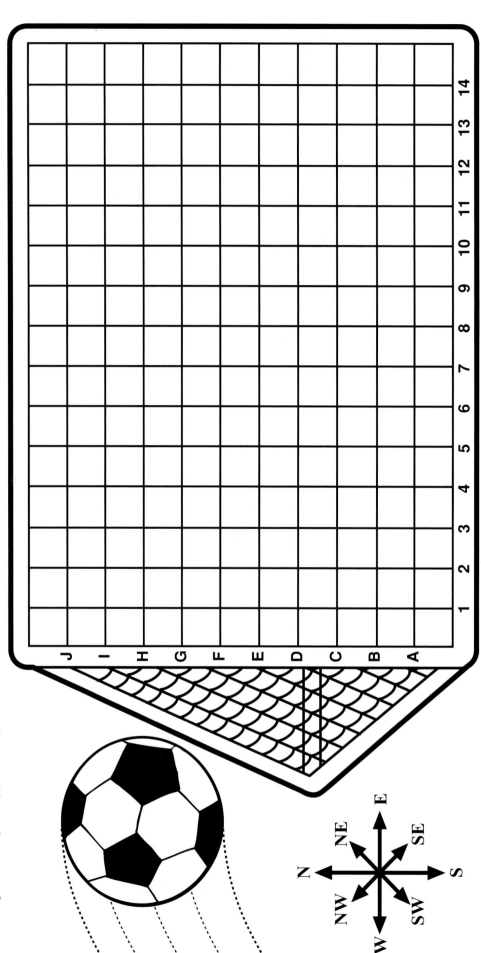

Note To The Teacher: Use with "Searching For The Star" on page 215.

Name_____ *Math: decimals*

DAFFY DECIMALS

Read each problem below. Decide if each number given makes sense in the problem. If it does, write "touchdown" in the space provided. If it does not make sense, move the decimal to correct the number. Then write the new number in the space provided.

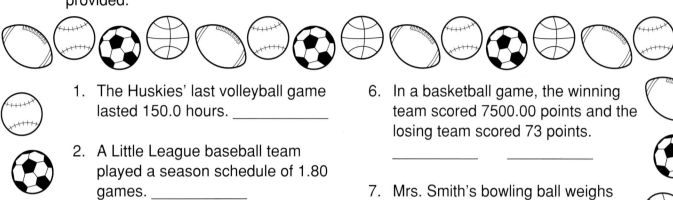

1. The Huskies' last volleyball game lasted 150.0 hours. _____

2. A Little League baseball team played a season schedule of 1.80 games. _____

3. During their last road trip, the Broncos covered 24.0 miles in four hours of driving. _____

4. Mike bought six new baseball bats for his team for $0.08. _____

5. Jeff Larmondra, heavyweight wrestling champion of the world, weighs 3.15 pounds. _____

6. In a basketball game, the winning team scored 7500.00 points and the losing team scored 73 points. _____ _____

7. Mrs. Smith's bowling ball weighs 80.0 pounds. _____

8. An average basketball hoop is positioned 0.10 feet from the ground. _____

9. Mr. Jones bought four hot dogs at a football game for $4.50. _____

10. Mike and Don played 180.0 holes of golf last weekend. _____

Read this article that's about to be printed in *The Sports Gazette*. Find the decimal errors and correct them so that the article makes sense before it goes to print.

In last night's championship game of the season, John Burnor, pride of the Patriot High School football team, scored an impressive 0.420 _____ points during his 40.0 _____ quarters of play. The junior, who weighs in at 1,822.0 _____ pounds and is 63.0 _____ feet tall, has spent his last 0.30 _____ years of high school helping his school win championships. John has been recruited by 1.1 _____ colleges. But after the exciting win last night, John told reporters that he's not sure he wants to leave his 0.05 _____ brothers and move away. We may be lucky enough to keep John right here in Monroe through the 1.998 _____ season.

Bonus Box: On the back of this page, write another nonsense decimal problem for a classmate to solve.

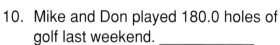
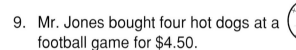

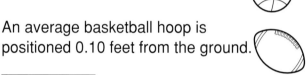

We're Having A Carnival!

A Year-End Celebration Of Books

Looking for a motivating way to end the school year? Or would you simply like to try some fun, literature-related games to liven up those last days before the summer break? Whatever your purpose, this reading carnival will encourage your students to carry those hard-earned reading habits into the summer!

by Simone Lepine

A Reading Carnival

Use the following directions to transform your room into a carnival to celebrate reading. Plan for half the class to run the carnival booths while the other half plays the games; then switch. Or host the carnival for another class on your grade level. If you're not up to organizing a carnival, never fear! Simply use the games on pages 222–226 as centers in your classroom!

Getting Ready

1. Three weeks before Day One, form cooperative groups by having each student sign up for one of the following categories: biography, humor, realistic fiction, poetry, science fiction, historical fiction, folklore, books in a series, books made into movies, or how-to books. Limit each group to two or three members to ensure that each category gets represented at the carnival.
2. Instruct each group to read a total of six different books from its category, with each group member reading a different book. (See pages 213 and 228 for suggested titles.)
3. Solicit for donations of bookmarks to give away on carnival day.
4. Follow the directions for Days One through Five to prepare for and conduct the carnival.

Day One: Make Mini-Review Booklets

Each person who participates in a carnival game will receive a mini-review booklet about one of the novels represented at that booth. To make a supply of these booklets, duplicate six copies of the form on page 227 for each group. Have each group member complete one form for each book he read. Then duplicate copies of the completed forms. (To determine the total number of copies needed of each booklet, divide the number of students in the class [or the invited class] by *six*—the number of books read by each group). Give each group its copies along with instructions to cut off the margins and fold the pages into booklets as shown.

Mini-Review Booklet For...

_____
(Title of book)
By

_____
(Author)

This Mini-Review Booklet Was Made By

_____
(Student name)

©The Education Center, Inc.

Mini-Review Booklet for...

The Cay

by Theodore Taylor

Days Two, Three, And Four: Make The Games And Set Up Booths

Duplicate the appropriate game card for each group from pages 222–226. Direct the group to follow the directions to make six copies of its carnival game. Provide groups with space to set up their booths. Next direct each group to decide who will be the mini-review booklet distributor and the game director.

Day Five: Enjoy The Carnival

Have each group man its carnival booth. When the participants arrive, divide them into ten groups; then assign each group a starting booth. Use a designated signal to let groups know when it's time to switch to the next booth. Each time a participant completes a game, have the mini-review booklet distributor allow the player to choose a review booklet that interests him. At the end of the carnival, present each participant with a bookmark.

Pam Crane

Book-Boosting Balloons

Encourage your students to clown around with a variety of books. Enlarge and color the clown shown. Next cut out ten large, colorful balloons. On each balloon write one of the literature categories used for the carnival. Staple the balloon cutouts to the board in an attractive arrangement; then connect them to the clown's hand with lengths of black yarn. Enlist a student to write in the names and authors of the books that belong to each category. Encourage students to add additional titles to each category. When students are looking for good books to read, point them to the board for some student-tested suggestions.

Game 1—Drop Into The Future

Book Category: Science Fiction

Materials: six shirt boxes, colored markers, scissors, masking tape, six marbles, six small paper cups

How To Make The Game:

1. Turn the top lid of each shirt box upside down. Mark and cut out ten marble-sized holes on the inside of each top lid. Designate one hole as the winning hole by circling it in red.
2. Decorate each top lid so that it advertises one of the books read by the group. Write each book's title and author, along with several adjectives that describe the book, in the spaces between the holes.
3. Cut five slits in the lip of each paper cup to create folding tabs as shown.
4. Attach each cup underneath a winning hole by taping the tabs to the lid.
5. Cut another marble-sized hole in a corner of the lower lid to make an exit hole for any marbles that fall through the nonwinning holes.
6. Tape each upside-down top lid to its matching lower lid as shown. The sides of the top lid form walls to keep the marble from rolling away.

How To Play The Game: Have the player choose a box and place a marble on its playing surface. Then direct him to tilt the box as he tries to get the marble into the winning hole. If he gets the marble in the winning hole, turn the box over to retrieve the marble from the cup. If his marble goes into the wrong hole, tilt the box until the marble exits at the bottom corner. Give each player three tries.

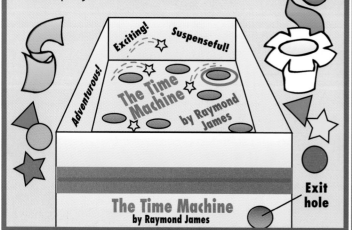

Exciting! Suspenseful! Adventurous!
The Time Machine by Raymond James

The Time Machine
by Raymond James

Exit hole

Game 2—Find The Fake Fact

Book Category: Biography

Materials: 30 unlined index cards, fine-tipped colored markers, six rubber bands

How To Make The Game: Make a set of five cards for each book that was read by your group members. On four of the cards, write a sentence stating a true fact about the story on the front of the card and the word "Fact" on the back. On the fifth card, write a fake fact sentence on the front and the word "Fake" on the back. Place a rubber band around each set of five cards.

How To Play The Game: Instruct the player to choose a set of cards. Shuffle the cards and place them sentence-side up in a row in front of the player. Have the player read each card and point to the fake fact card. Beginning with the first card, turn over the cards one at a time to see if the player is a winner. Let each player try three different card sets.

| Fact | Fact | Fact | Fact | Fake |

Game 3—Putt In A Cup

Book Category: How-To Books

Materials: three golf balls, a putter, three poster-size pieces of stiff cardboard, scissors, a black marker, six large paper cups, six right-angle triangles cut from cardboard, masking tape

How To Make The Game: Divide each piece of cardboard into two halves by drawing a vertical black line. Use a paper cup to trace a circular opening at the bottom of each half as shown; then cut out each circular space. Decorate the front panels above each hole with the title and author of a different how-to book. Use masking tape to attach a cup to the back of the cardboard behind each hole (see Figure 2). Attach two cardboard triangles to the back of each sheet to support it. Line up the gameboards side by side. Place a strip of masking tape about six to eight feet away from each poster.

How To Play The Game: Give the player the putter and a ball and instruct her to stand behind the masking-tape mark. Have the player putt the golf ball through a hole and into a cup to win.

Fig. 2

Fig. 1

Game 4—Coming To A Theater Near You

Book Category: Books That Have Become Movies

Materials: six sheets of poster board, scissors, 60 inches of self-adhesive Velcro®, six Ping-Pong® balls, masking tape, colored markers

How To Make The Game: Press two lengths of loop-sided Velcro® around the middle of each ball to form perpendicular, intersecting lines. Draw a six-inch circle in the center of each poster board sheet. Divide the hook-sided Velcro® into six equal lengths. Cut apart each Velcro® length and press the pieces around the inside of the circle. Write the title of a book and its author on each poster along with comments that tell why reading the book is better than seeing the movie. Thumbtack the posters to a bulletin board or tape them to a wall. On the floor, place a strip of tape eight to ten feet away from each poster.

How To Play The Game: Have each player choose a poster and line up behind the masking-tape line with his Ping-Pong® ball. Give the player three chances to throw the ball and get it to stick to the poster's circle.

Game 5—Wheel Of Historical Fiction

Book Category: Historical Fiction

Materials: a 14-inch cardboard circle (cut from a cardboard box or donated from a pizza restaurant), a 2" x 6" strip of heavy black paper, a ruler, colored markers, one brad fastener, two clothespins, scissors

How To Make The Game: Use the ruler and a marker to divide the cardboard circle into six equal sections as shown. Write the name of a different book in each section. Cut a large cardboard arrow from the black paper. Connect the arrow to the center of the circle with the paper brad so that the arrow spins easily.

How To Play The Game: Have each player choose two books by clipping a clothespin to each of those sections. Allow the player two spins to get the arrow to stop on a section he chose and to win.

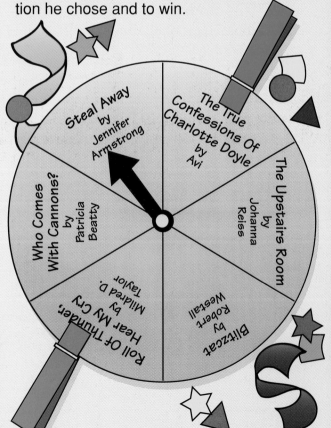

Game 6—Book Bopping

Book Category: Humor

Materials: six clean, half-gallon milk cartons; bulletin board paper; scissors; clear tape; colored markers; fine-tipped markers; six zippered plastic bags, each filled with one cup of flour; two chairs; a six-foot-long wooden board; masking tape; three beanbags

How To Make The Game: Place a bag of flour inside each milk carton to weigh it down. Close and tape the top opening. Cover each milk carton with bulletin board paper, using clear tape to hold the paper in place. On each carton's front, write the title and author of a different book. Decorate at least one side of each carton with an illustration or a written description of a funny scene from the book. Place the backs of the chairs about five feet apart; then balance the wooden board on the backs of the chairs. Arrange the milk cartons in a row on the board as shown. Place a strip of tape on the floor eight to ten feet away from the board. Place the beanbags on the tape.

How To Play The Game: Have each player stand behind the line and throw the beanbags one at a time. Give each player three tries to knock at least one milk carton off the board and win.

Game 7—Ping-Pong® Game

Book Category: Books In A Series

Materials: six medium-sized boxes, three Ping-Pong® balls, bulletin board paper, scissors, clear tape, colored markers, masking tape, a ruler

How To Make The Game: Cover each of the boxes with bulletin board paper, using clear tape to hold the paper in place. On the front of each box, write the name of the series and three to five book titles that represent it. Line up the boxes against a wall in a straight line, spacing them an equal distance apart. Mark a distance six feet away with a strip of masking tape; then place the Ping-Pong® balls on the tape.

How To Play The Game: Have a player stand behind the marked line and bounce the Ping-Pong® balls one at a time toward the boxes. If he lands at least one of the balls in a box, he wins.

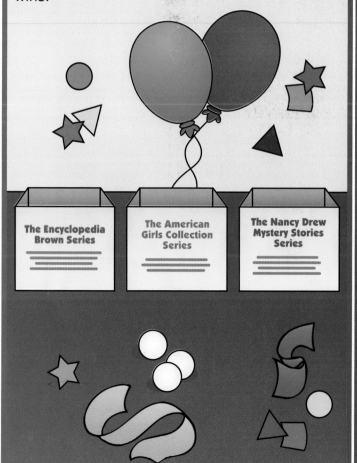

The Encyclopedia Brown Series

The American Girls Collection Series

The Nancy Drew Mystery Stories Series

Game 8—Hide 'N' Seek Poetry

Book Category: Poetry

Materials: six shoeboxes without lids, bulletin-board paper, clear tape, colored markers, fine-tipped markers, two tennis balls

How To Make The Game: Cover each shoebox with bulletin board paper, using tape to hold the paper in place. Turn each box bottom-side up. Write a title and author of a different book on the end of each box. Decorate the sides and bottom of each box with samples of poetry from the book it promotes. Line up the boxes in two groups of three.

How To Play The Game: Have two players stand with their backs to the boxes. Hide a tennis ball under one of the boxes in each set. Ask the players to turn around. Then have each player call out the poet's name from the box he thinks is hiding a tennis ball. Give each player two tries to win.

The Duel

It's Dark In Here

The Vampire

Shel Silverstein

Jack Prelutsky

Eugene Field

Game 9—Book-Character Ring Toss

Book Category: Realistic Fiction

Materials: six playground cones, construction paper of different colors, scissors, glue, clear tape, a black marker, three paper plates, a ruler, masking tape

How To Make The Game: Choose a favorite character from each of the six fiction books read by your group. Create a likeness of each character from construction paper. Write each character's name on the corresponding figure with a black marker; then tape each figure to a different playground cone. Arrange the cones in a triangular pattern. Next make rings by cutting the centers from paper plates—without going through the outside edges. Lay a strip of masking tape on the floor six feet away from the cones.

How To Play The Game: Have the player stand behind the marked line, and toss the three rings one at a time. If he rings one of the characters, he wins.

Salamanca Tree Hiddle

Game 10—Book-Bet Board

Book Category: Folklore

Materials: six sheets of white poster board, colored markers, a die pattern from page 227 duplicated on light-colored construction paper, scissors, clear tape, two game markers (coins or plastic game pieces)

How To Make The Game: Write the title and author of each book read by group members on a different poster. Decorate the posters to advertise the books; then line up the posters side by side on the floor.

To make the die, cut out the die pattern. Write the titles and authors of the six books read by group members on the die's blank faces, one title and author on each face. Fold the tabs and faces along the lines, securing them with clear tape.

How To Play The Game: Have each player in turn place two markers on any two posters of his choice. Give the player three chances to roll the die and get a match to win.

BIG MEN BIG COUNTRY
A Collection Of American Tall Tales
by Paul R. Walker